We Rubies Four

Selected Omega Publications titles

The Art of Being and Becoming
by Hazrat Inayat Khan

Awakening of the Human Spirit
by Hazrat Inayat Khan

The Call of the Dervish
by Pir Vilayat Inayat Khan

The Complete Works of Hazrat Inayat Khan *series*

Introducing Spirituality Into Counseling and Therapy
by Pir Vilayat Inayat Khan

The Message in Our Time
The Life and Teachings of Sufi Master Pir-o-Murshid Inayat Khan
by Pir Vilayat Inayat Khan

The Music of Life; The Inner Nature and Effects of Sound
by Hazrat Inayat Khan

Nature Meditations
by Hazrat Inayat Khan

Song of the Prophets; The Unity of Religious Ideals
by Hazrat Inayat Khan

The Soul's Journey
By Hazrat Inayat Khan

Spy Princess; The Life of Noor Inayat Khan
by Shrabani Basu

That Which Transpires Behind That Which Appears
by Pir Vilayat Inayat Khan

For a complete listing of Omega Publications titles see
www.omegapub.com

We Rubies Four

The Memoirs *of* Claire Ray Harper
(Khair-un-nisa Inayat Khan)

With poems, stories *and* letters *from the* Inayat Khan family

Claire Ray Harper & David Ray Harper

OMEGA Publications
New Lebanon, New York

Published by
OMEGA PUBLICATIONS INC.
New Lebanon, New York
www.omegapub.com

Editing and interior design by Green Lion Press
Cover photo of Vilayat, Noor, Claire and Hidayat Inayat Khan
Cover design by Yasodhara Sandra Lillydahl

This edition is printed on acid-free paper that meets ANSI standard X39-48.
Printed and bound in the United States of America

Library of Congress Cataloging-in-Publication Data

Harper, Claire Ray, 1919–
We rubies four : the memoirs of Claire Ray Harper (Khair-un-nisa Inayat Khan) : with poems, stories and letters from the Inayat Khan family / Claire Ray Harper & David Ray Harper.
p. cm.
Includes bibliographical references and index.
ISBN 978-0-930872-84-7 (alk. paper)
1. Harper, Claire Ray, 1919– 2. Harper, Claire Ray, 1919– —Family. 3. Sufis—Biography. 4. Inayat Khan—Family. I. Harper, David Ray, 1953– II. Title.
BP80.H2845A3 2011
297.4092—dc22
[B]

2011005130

Table of Contents

List of Photographs and Illustrations

FOREWORD

The following offering is a humble attempt at telling the unusual Inayat Khan family story. Some readers may know of the family through one of its members but might not be aware of the stories connected to other family members.

This short and unpretentious family history is built around Claire Harper's (Khair-un-nisa Inayat-Khan's) memoirs which represent the core of the book and which are printed with the shading shown here in order to distinguish easily her contributions from the rest. In addition, the sections written by Claire are labeled with her name.

The remainder of the collection is the result of family research carried out by her son, David, and includes vast input from further contributors. Claire's granddaughter, Tara Dundas-Harper, is the principal author of the section on Noor's heroic war mission as detailed in the chapter "The Secret Agent."

The narration begins with some of Ora Ray Baker's ancestors, as well as a few of Murshid Inayat Khan's forefathers, and ends with their children's generation. Much of the information, as well as poems, letters and photos, were found in boxes that had remained unopened for over sixty years. Among the treasures brought to light for the first time are unpublished poems written by Ameena Begum (née Ora Ray Baker), Noor, and a few by Pir-o-Murshid Inayat Khan.

There are a few numbered notes which can be found in the corresponding section "Notes." The occasional letters A–H following quotes refer to the source material and can be found in the section "Sources." It may also be helpful for readers to refer to the section "Names."

Any incorrect or incomplete information is unintentional. The authors have attempted to relate the stories as accurately as possible and in a spirit of sharing.

May the contents be a tribute to this remarkable family as well as a means of perpetuating the memory of my dear mother Claire who, sadly for us, slipped out of this world on May 31, 2011 to embark on another journey.

David Ray Harper, June 2011

Part One: The Meeting of West and East

THE AMERICAN

Claire Harper: With a smiling sendoff from the heart of the universe, our sweet mother, Ora Ray Baker, was flown by the most elegant queen of the storks from a pink cloud straight down to Albuquerque, New Mexico on May 8th, 1888.[(1)] She was the youngest of three sisters, Allie May, Lula Fay and Lela Murley, and one brother, Earl.[(2)]

Ora Ray was blessed with a large and prosperous family. Though her relatives had settled in several American states, in particular Iowa, Idaho, Kansas, Kentucky and Maryland, Ora Ray's principle homestead was in Wenatchee, Washington.

Among Ora Ray's numerous relatives, one could find doctors, such as her grandfather; lawyers; judges (Judge Benjamin S. Baker served in Albuquerque, New Mexico from 1902 to 1904); and, allegedly, even a senator. One of the wealthiest in the family was George W. Baker. He was born and raised in Iowa, where he became an attorney, but spent some 25 years running a large ranch in New Mexico's Cimarron Valley, where he raised Hereford cattle. Just like his father before him (George C. Baker had owned the Baker Wire Company in Illinois), George W. Baker took an interest in politics and became one of the most well-respected citizens of New Mexico in his day. According to family lore, one of Ora Ray's mother's cousins was Mary Baker Eddy, the founder of the Christian Science movement.

Ora Ray's mother was Alletta (Etta) Margaret Hiatt (born 1859),[(3)] by birth a descendant of a titled family von der Kaempe[(4)] (later changed to Kemp) from St. Gallen, Switzerland, that had immigrated to Pennsylvania in 1733.

Ora Ray's father, Eurastus Warren Baker (born 1845), raised cattle and, later on, became a lawyer, as well as the editor of his own paper. He was also musically inclined and wrote a song entitled "Old Rose."[(5)]

From her father's previous marriage to his distant cousin Catherine Givens, Ora Ray had a half-brother called Pierre Bernard, who became an authority on yoga and Sanskrit, having allegedly studied for years with a teacher from India. Credited with being the first American to introduce the philosophy and practices of yoga and tantra to the American people, Pierre Bernard also owned the largest library of Sanskrit books and manuscripts in the USA. We shall return to Ora Ray's half-brother later.

In a similar way, Pierre Bernard's nephew Theos Bernard, author of *Penthouse of the Gods,* studied the sacred mysteries of yoga and Tibetan Buddhism. He wrote a thesis on Hatha Yoga and traveled extensively throughout India. He was one of the very first Americans to enter Lhasa, Tibet, and was the first American to become initiated into the rites of Tibetan Buddhism. He founded the first Tibetan research institute in the USA and created a Tibetan grammar book for the Western world. He disappeared under mysterious circumstances during one of his expeditions in the Himalayas in 1947—at a time of political unrest—and it is presumed that he was murdered by mountain tribesmen.

Claire Harper: Our mother was deeply attached to her beloved father and, during school holidays when occasion permitted, they traveled in the fashionable American trains of the turn of the century with their exceedingly luxurious and inviting private compartments. To crown all this, the dining cars were decked with white starched tablecloths, flowers and tasty dishes to tempt the palate. This travel highlife was enhanced by the majestic views of America's unspoiled countryside of the early 1900s.

After visiting Boston's Baker Bridge, the next stop brought them to New York. The few skyscrapers, the summits of which seemed to scratch the mirror of the skies, shaped a picture of grandeur. Father and daughter also dared to climb the Statue of Liberty, even mounting into the heroic landmark's head. The view revealed magnificence. They saw other famed sights: the Empire State building, Fifth Avenue, 42nd Street, the East River and, of course, the mighty Hudson. Our mother and grandfather were in Manhattan when Thomas Alva Edison turned on the first lights of the city.

They went on to visit Mother's half-brother, Dr. Pierre Bernard, who had run the New York Sanskrit College, a position that catapulted him into high society and intelligentsia limelight. Pierre would later play a challenging role in his sister's early life, but for the time-being, youth treated our mother with kindness, as the passing of time saw her grow into an enchanting young lady of those grand days of old. One day, in a gesture of love and generosity, our grandfather surprised his daughter with the gift of 25 traveling trunks, each containing a full wardrobe including matching accessories. Occasionally, her father slipped a gold coin or a few dollar bills into her purse.

She was beautiful and frail, yet capable of immense courage. When Mother was a child, she developed a life-threatening case of typhoid, and the doctor expressed little hope of her survival. Over and over, she emphatically repeated that she would survive. And when she did, the doctor was mystified and amazed that her willpower had overcome the all-consuming disease.

It appears that Ora Ray's parents cultivated a somewhat distant relationship in their marriage, because it was decided that Ora Ray would be sent to live under the care of her half-brother, Dr. Pierre Bernard. During the few years when she lived in his home in Manhattan, New York, and later in Leonia, New Jersey, it is interesting to observe that Pierre Bernard renamed his little sister "Ora Marcelle Bernard." A small plaster mold likeness of Ora bears witness to this francophone name.

During his adult life, Pierre Arnold Bernard did not reveal much regarding his origins, but Ora Ray always referred to him as "Pierre, my brother." Mysteriously, he sometimes went under the name "Homer Stansbury Leeds"but intimated to others that he was born as "Peter Coons" to an Iowa barber. Similar to his half-sister in appearance, he had a thin upper lip and piercing blue eyes. In truth, Peter (Perry) Baker was born in Leon, Iowa in 1875. His mother, Catherine Givens, later remarried a John C. Bernard, allegedly related to Claude Bernard, the famous French physiologist who established the use of a scientific approach in medicine. Mr. John Bernard was a barber by trade, a fact which explains why, when asked about his family background, Pierre Bernard rejected connections to his natural father (Erastus Baker) by replying that his father was a barber from Leon, Iowa. He even accentuated the break with Erastus Baker further by taking on his stepfather's last name, Bernard, and emphasizing the connection to France by changing his given name from Peter Baker to Pierre. It is probably for this reason that Pierre gave Ora her new names as well: Ora Marcelle Bernard. As to Pierre's allusion to his being born Peter Coons, this was most likely due to the fact that his maternal aunt married a Mr. Coons.

Pierre Bernard claimed to have traveled to Kashmir and Bengal for several years (sitting at the feet of a great master) before founding the

Tantrik Order of America in 1905, followed by the New York Sanskrit College in 1910. Undoubtedly a pioneer in teaching the benefits of yoga in the United States and considered a mystic by his disciples, he received a substantial donation from a benefactor with which he purchased a seventy-two acre property in Nyack, New York, in 1918. He called it the Clarkstown Country Club (C.C.C.) and advertised it to New York's high society throughout the 1920s and 1930s. In the book he published about the club in 1935, Pierre Bernard claims about his fashionable center: "So, the philosopher has found a place to dance,—and the fool has been provided with a thinking cap!" [H]

The club's main focus was to provide an environment for "yoga education, as applied to the twentieth century and the ways of the western world. It is the philosophy of the Vedas put into practice, and constitutes the source from which the principles of study at the C.C.C. are derived." [H] Among the speakers and members of the club were yogis, scientists, philosophers and business magnates; even two Vanderbilt family members belonged to the C.C.C. The club's members could simply relax at the pools, play tennis or take boat excursions on the nearby Hudson River, and they were encouraged to participate in theater, music and even a circus! Pierre Bernard had a stable full of elephants, seven in all, who would perform alongside juggling, tumbling, clowning and tightrope-walking club members under their own big top, the largest privately-owned tent in the US. Eventually the property spread over one hundred sixty acres and included thirty-four buildings. By 1931, membership passed the four hundred mark.

The leading figure in the yoga, dance and other performing arts activities at the club was Blanche De Vries, Pierre's wife (who continued teaching yoga into her eighties). As for the club's founder, he shifted his attentions to more conventional businesses, including baseball stadiums, dog tracks and an airport, and became president of the State Bank of Pearl River in 1931. Bernard's library was said to have been the best Sanskrit collection in the country and to contain some seven thousand volumes on philosophy, ethics, psychology, education and metaphysics, as well as related material on physiology and medicine.

During the years that Ora Ray spent in Leonia, New Jersey, at her half-brother's home, she traveled considerably. Kansas City (where her grandmother still lived), Seattle and San Francisco were among her regular destinations. It was in San Francisco that she would meet her soul mate.

One evening, Ora Ray had a vision of a sage. The following night, she dreamed of an Eastern mystic, holding her in his arms; both were soaring above the seas, high into the skies.

On another continent, in a distant land, in another time, a man dreamed not of love but of freedom for his people. It was the year 1799, and the Sultan of the vast kingdom of Mysore hoped to break the yoke of colonization with which the British Empire was shackling the Indian nations. Little did Ora Ray know that a tie of blood and destiny would unite her with the sultan's descendants.

THE SULTAN

Born in the Kingdom of Mysore in 1750, Sultan Fateh Ali Khan Shahab was later renamed by his father after a Sufi saint: Tipu Mastan Aulia (with blessings). His mother, Fakhr-un-nissa (also known as Fatima) was a daughter of Moinuddin, the governor of Luddapah Fort. His father, Hyder Fatah Ali Khan Bahadur, was the Noble Ruler of the Kingdom of Mysore, a vast area covering the southwest of India.

Tipu, like his father, was "fair of face, possessed large eyes and was a good man." It is said that when Tipu was a baby, his mother received a message from the great Sufi saint after whom her son was renamed, along with his blessings, that she was to light a candle each day so that her son would grow to be an adept of God. His father saw to it that Tipu received an extensive education, as well as military training. He was well versed in the Kannada, Urdu, Persian, and Arabic languages and received his military education from Ghazi Khan, who was a great warrior and also a military officer in the army of Haider Ali.

At a young age, Tipu already fought at his father's side during two battles against the British, and later proved himself as an excellent general. Striving to uphold high ideals, Tipu achieved great goals for the betterment of his subjects' lives. He helped modernize local industry, schools and public buildings, was solicitous of new inventions, and even founded the Mysore newspaper company. Though Tipu was a Moslem ruling a predominantly Hindu land, he practiced religious tolerance to all Hindus. In a letter to a well-respected Brahmin, a certain "Swamiji," he wrote, "our God and your God is one and unto Him we surrender. We hold this God-given law dear to our heart, based as it is on human dignity; reason and brotherhood of man. With reverence we have also read the Vedas of the Hindus. They proclaim their faith in universal unity and express the belief that God is one although He bears many names."

Tipu's father, Hyder Ali, died of infection from battle wounds, leaving Tipu to rule alone. Unfortunately, the country was in the middle of the Second Mysore War against the English at the time. Undaunted Tipu continued fighting the war and was most successful, emerging as the undisputed victor at the Battle of Pollipur. He was so delighted with this success that he later had the battle scenes painted on the walls of his summer palace.

Tipu renovated forts and palaces, showed skill in architecture and did much for the cleaning up of the towns in his kingdom. One of his goals was to offer his subjects a life of liberty and dignity.

In true Moslem tradition, Tipu Sultan took four wives, by whom he had sixteen sons and at least eight daughters. The fate of his eight daughters remains a mystery. Six years after the victory of the second Mysore War, Charles, 1st Marquis Cornwallis, was given British India to rule. Having realized that Tipu still posed too great a threat to be ignored, Marquis Cornwallis engaged in a third Mysore War in 1790. After three bloody campaigns and with the help of Indian Allies, such as the Nizam of Hyderabad, Marquis Cornwallis finally forced Tipu into submission.

Tipu was obliged to sign a treaty whereby he was to cede half his territories, pay exorbitant sums in indemnities, and until he was able to pay the full sum, his two sons (aged eight and ten) were to be kept as British hostages. It was not until two years later that Tipu was able to pay the sum the British demanded and restore his eldest sons to the family.

"I would not compromise even the smallest piece of my motherland, even in exchange for the supreme ownership of heaven, this earth and hell."

Tipu's passion for reading led him to collect manuscripts and books written in various languages. Interested in Sufism, he treasured the pictures of Sufi saints from India and foreign lands, which he assembled in a large album.

One day, as Tipu hunted with a French guest, he suddenly found himself face-to-face with a tiger. As the tiger pounced upon Tipu, he dropped his gun but, pinned to the ground, managed to retrieve his dagger, with which he slew the tiger. From that time on, Tipu was known as the "Tiger of Mysore." In addition to making the tiger part of in his emblem, Tipu decorated his throne with twelve golden tiger heads and even kept live tigers chained nearby.

Among his deeds in office, he prohibited the sale of children, abolished liquor and was dedicated to preserving not only the status and independence of the Kingdom of Mysore but the sovereignty of India as well. Mysore was profitable and well-organized, with good trade routes and a European-style army—in effect, everything the British feared.

A Jacobin Club of revolutionary ideas of liberty, equality and fraternity was formed at Seringapatam by French soldiers commanded by M. Dompart, a Frenchman who was in Tipu's service. The club counted fifty-nine members, one of whom was Tipu himself. The object of this club was to impart instruction in constitutional principles of a democratic nature, such as those to be adopted in the Republic of France, which had enunciated lofty principles of human rights. This shows to what extent Tipu chose free thinking, breaking away from the orthodox traditions of his forefathers in order to absorb liberal thoughts. A simple "member of the club," Tipu declared when joining: "Behold my acknowledgment of the standard of your country (France), which is dear to me, and to which I am allied; it shall always be supported in my country, as it has been in the Republic, my sister!" He then planted the "tree of liberty" and called himself "Citizen Tipu," a surprising sign that he viewed himself as a servant of the people.

In 1799 British spies reported that Napoleon Bonaparte was arming a huge fleet to sail to India. Napoleon had sought an alliance with Sultan Tipu against the British, but Tipu had stipulated that he would tolerate French soldiers in his kingdom on condition that they drank no alcohol. Nonetheless, Wellesley, the Governor-General of India, knew that this would threaten the British position and so moved to finally destroy the one ally France still had in India, Tipu Sultan.

Tipu was a brave fighter and an excellent military tactician, but in this Fourth Mysore War Tipu was outnumbered, as the forces of the Nizam of Hyderabad had joined hands with the British forces against the "Tiger of Mysore."

In this world, I would rather live two days like a tiger than two hundred years like a sheep. (Tipu Sultan)[E]

One of the regiments was commanded by Richard Wellesley's younger brother, Arthur Wellesley—the future Duke of Wellington—who later was appointed Governor of Mysore. Despite the overwhelming numbers of British and allied assailants, Tipu defended his fort at Seringapatam for weeks at the head of some 20,000 of his soldiers, and by means of an incessant assault of rockets and musket fire on his enemy. Unfortunately for the sultan, a British shot ignited a magazine of rockets in Tipu's fort, causing it to explode and send a towering cloud of black smoke, with cascades of exploding white light, rising up from the battlements. Taking advantage of this enormous explosion and the ensuing confusion, the besiegers swept in; and after hours of hand to hand battle, it was all over for the Sultan.

By nightfall, Tipu's lifeless body was found amongst the dead. He had been shot in the head and stripped of his jewels. His body was discovered where the fighting had been the fiercest. Thus the last hope for India's freedom was extinguished. Upon the news of Tipu's death, Richard Wellesley, the Governor General of India, declared: "Ladies and gentlemen, I drink to the corpse of India." Once Tipu was out of their path, the British dug into the innards of India for a stay that lasted some 150 years, altering the face of India forever. One can consider Sultan Tipu as the first hero of India's freedom movement. Nearly a century and a half later, a descendant of his would also sacrifice her life in the cause of freedom.

Due to the great respect that his subjects developed for him, despite the fact they were Hindus who had been ruled by a Moslem monarch, the people later built palatial homes for those members of Tipu Sultan's family who were not banned by the British Governor. In recent years, the Indian government reinstated princely rank to the descendents of Tipu Sultan.

It is interesting to note that 70 years later, the persona of Tipu Sultan would make its way into Western adventure literature. In 1869 the French novelist Jules Verne created the character Captain Nemo in *Twenty Thousand Leagues under the Sea*. In the bestseller's sequel *The Mysterious Island*, Captain Nemo, on his deathbed, reveals his true identity as the Indian Prince Dakkar, the son of a rajah and a nephew of the Indian hero Tipu Sultan.

THE SAINT

Speaking of the Chishti Sufis, Inayat Khan said: "Music is the source of elevation, by which means they attain to that ecstasy which culminates in the revelation of the truth."[A]

The principal message of the Chishtis, one of India's most important Sufi Orders, is the philosophy of the unity of being. Known for its emphasis on love, tolerance and openness, it was not necessary to convert to Islam in order to be accepted into the Chishti Order. Tuning the heart by means of music is one of the key practices, along with service to humanity.

Originally founded by Khwaja Abu Ishaq around 930 in Chisht, Persia (in present-day Afghanistan), the Order's eighth, in line of succession was Khwaja Moinuddin Chishti, born in Persia around 1135.

The Chishtis maintain that wisdom and inner knowledge are passed on from master to master. They learn their spiritual genealogy and, to them, visiting the shrine of Khwaja Moinuddin Chishti, their greatest saint, is to connect to the very source of that spirituality.

Gharib Nawaz Khwaja Moinuddin Chishti grew up in a well-respected and moneyed family. When he was only in his teens his parents died, and his source of income was the produce of the orchard he inherited. One day when Moinuddin was working in his orchard, a pious dervish, Ebrahim Qandoozi, stopped by and took his seat under the shade of a tree. When the boy saw him, he presented Qandoozi with a bunch of grapes. The visitor ate the grapes and was delighted. He then took something out of his bag, chewed it, and then offered it to his young host. Moinuddin ate it without any hesitation, and at once, the light of wisdom and knowledge dawned upon him. Immediately he disposed of all of his worldly belongings and distributed whatever money he had among the poor.

Having thus broken all ties with worldly affairs, he set off for Samarkand and Bukhara, the great centers of learning for religious education and knowledge. He then went to various places in search of a murshid. Finally he met the Sufi saint Khwaja Uthman Harooni, who admitted Moinuddin as a disciple. Initiated at the age of eighteen, he served for the next 22 years merely as the water boy. Eventually, when he reached the age of forty, Khwaja Uthman Harooni called him to his court, showed him his two fingers, and asked him what he saw between those two fingers. Moinuddin Chishti replied, "I am watching 18 thousand galaxies."

Years later, Moinuddin Chishti received the order from Prophet Muhammad to go to Ajmer. This pleased him greatly, but it worried him as well, since he did not know where Ajmer was in India, and so he asked the Prophet Muhammad. The way to the mountain near Ajmer was clearly shown to him in a vision so that there would be no doubt as to his destination.

On his arrival in India, Khwaja Moinuddin Chishti found the country in a state of depression. Foreign invasions had weakened India and the social conditions were deteriorating. On a divine mission, Khwaja Moinuddin Chishti founded the spiritual movement of the propagation of the Truth. His efforts bore fruit and, within a short period of sixteen years, Ajmer became the source of moral and spiritual leadership in India which leveled the way for a grand religious and social revolution, and provided opportunity to countless people to lead a life of equality and honor.

Khwaja Moinuddin Chishti was kind and forgiving. Once a man came to him with the intention of murdering him, but the master sensed his intentions and spoke to him most kindly, asking him to do what he had intended. The man was ashamed and requested to be punished. Khwaja Moinuddin Chishti replied, "The mendicant's habit is, whoever does evil to them, they treat him well." He forgave the man, who later became his follower.

In spite of his renunciation of worldly things, his monastery was famous for his generosity and magnanimity, which is why he became known as Gharib Nawaz, the "patron of the poor." His tomb is one of the holiest places in India, where pilgrims—Moslems as well as Hindus—come from every corner of South Asia to pay their homage. Those who came in touch with him, especially the poor and downtrodden, received kindest treatment and blessings from him, and many became his disciples. His simple teaching made a great impact on the crowds, and his message of universal love and peace encompassed the entire human race without the distinction of creed or caste. His strong faith in the unity of God provided the necessary ideological background to his mission of bringing about an emotional integration of the people among whom he lived.

Generosity to others, especially through sharing of food and wealth, and tolerance and respect for different religions, were the cardinal points of Moinuddin Chishti's teachings.

In order to continue his mission of service to humanity, Gharib Nawaz Khwaja Moinuddin Chishti founded the Chishti Silsila (Order of Sufis) in India and sent his disciples to different parts of India to carry on his mission.

Some sayings of Gharib Nawaz Khwaja Moinuddin Chishti:

A friend of God must have affection like the Sun. Because when it rises, it is beneficial to all irrespective of whether they are Muslim, Christian, or Hindu.

A friend of God must be generous like a river. We all get water from the river to quench our thirst. It does not discriminate whether we are good or bad or whether we are a relation or a stranger.

A friend of God must display the hospitality like the earth. It raises and cradles us in its lap, and yet it is always under our feet.

THE PRINCE

Chole Khan was born in 1833 into a family of respected landowners and, orphaned at an early age, was raised by his uncle. Strong and athletic, the boy had a talent for wrestling, but this predisposition was to change when he reached the age of fifteen. That is when his path crossed that of a holy man, a wandering dervish. This pilgrim was not one of the whirling dervishes of Turkey, but was a follower of the esoteric and mystical school of the Sufis known as the Chishti Order. The Chisti path is one of meditation, poetry and music, as well as the cultivation of adoration of the ideal or the Beloved, which is God. One of their ideals is to be found in the person of Gharib Nawaz Khwaja Moinuddin Chishti.

The dervish asked the adolescent: "My soul longs for music, would you sing to me?" (A) The boy retorted that he was no singer, but he would do what he could. Following the amateur rendition, the saintly man thanked him, saying: "I am a poor man and a pilgrim upon the face of the earth, nevertheless it is in my power to give you a treasure. I will baptize you with a new name: Maula Bakhsh—God-gifted—and this name shall be known throughout this land of India and your music shall make it famous." (A) Chole received the blessing with reverence and kept the holy man's words treasured in his heart, immediately changing his name to Maula Bakhsh.

Since his grandfather Anwar Khan had been a successful singer, several years after this important incident Maula Bakhsh's uncle agreed to allow his ward to wander about, attempting to find a suitable teacher. At that time in India it was not simple to learn a trade, especially since art was considered sacred—practically a hereditary possession. A singer or musician viewed his knowledge and expertise, even his talent, as his family honor, something to pass on to an heir. In other words, it was the teacher who would choose his pupil rather than the reverse.

One of the most accomplished singers in India at that time was Ghasit Khan, a great master who refused to divulge his art to any pupil. Young Maula Bakhsh, leading a hand-to-mouth existence, eventually arrived at Ghasit Khan's grand home. To study under this accomplished singer is what the boy yearned for the most, but he had no idea how to approach this idol. Spending much time in front of the house, hoping to occasionally catch a glimpse of Ghasit Khan, the boy was soon befriended by the gatekeeper. Sitting for hours in the porter's shelter, Maula Bakhsh was close enough to the master's house to hear him practice. Day after day, for hours on end in the cool of the evening or during the night, Maula Bakhsh soaked up the singer's warming-up techniques and reveled in the delivery of classical pieces as very few other singers were able to do. Months passed (one version claims two years passed) while the boy drank up every sound that emanated from Ghasit Khan's window above.

At home Maula Bakhsh would practice what he had learned, executing pieces that he had learned by heart from a master who had never even set eyes on him.

As destiny would have it, one day while Maula Bakhsh was rehearsing as usual, Ghasit Khan happened by the boy's home. Intrigued to hear his own style and personal songs, he entered the house. Confronting the boy he asked who his teacher was. Maula Bakhsh replied: "My teacher is great, truly. But if I reveal his name to you, then indeed my hope of progressing further under him must be given up." "Whoever heard of such a teacher!" said Ghasit Khan impatiently, "what teacher forbids his pupil to speak of him?"[(A)] Upon discovering how ingeniously the young man had soaked up this expertise, patiently and industriously from below his own window, Ghasit Khan was impressed.

"But now what chiefly grieves me is the thought that when I leave—for now I cannot go on listening to you as I did before—I must say that it is from you that I have learned; for indeed I have not studied enough nor gained enough of your knowledge to be worthy of being called the pupil of such a master as yourself." [(A)] Maula Bakhsh's humble attitude is what prompted Ghasit Khan to invite the boy to come and learn from him. His only pupil, Maula Bakhsh absorbed everything that his master could impart and he remained with him till his teacher's passing.

After Ghasit Khan's death, the young singer triumphed at one princely court after another, meeting with the highest praise and rewards in the form of gold medals. Though versed in the music of the north, the Hindustani style with influences of Persian and Arabic music, Maula Bakhsh built a close friendship with Subramani Ayar, the most respected Brahmin musician of the time. These southern musicians jealously guarded their Carnatic musical tradition. However, so great was this Brahmin master's respect for Maula Bakhsh that, disregarding cultural and religious barriers, he taught the Moslem all he knew of the ancient classical music of southern India and the Sanskrit songs.

Along his travels, Maula Bakhsh frequented the Court of Mysore, where he gained the personal friendship of the ruling monarch. In recognition of Maula Bakhsh's undisputed mastery in song and technique, the Hindu Maharaja awarded him the highest mark of honor that was possible to obtain in India: the rank of prince. Among the regalia befitting his conferred status, he was given a jewel for his turban, ceremonial robes, a gold canopy to be held over the prince's head, a scepter of worldly authority, and a torch to be lit and carried ahead of the prince at night. When the Hindus at the Maharaja's court questioned and contested this gesture, a ten-month musical competition was held, pitting Maula Bakhsh against the elite of the Brahmin musicians and singers. Again he was acknowledged as having surpassed all others. Not only was a great procession held in his honor, but a young girl was presented to him in marriage.

Though Maula Bakhsh's bride Kasime-Biy's background was kept secret, it is family knowledge that her grandfather (or great-grandfather) was no other than India's freedom fighter, Sultan Tipu. The descendants of the former great Mogul ruler kept their origins secret for two reasons. First of all, they feared persecution or reprisals from the British rulers, whose policy was to avoid any possible uprisings against their colonial rule. Secondly, they were ashamed to be reduced to a humble lifestyle compared to the opulence their forefathers had known. The girl had lived in hiding since her birth and had been protected by two "devoted adherents to her house, with whom Maula Bakhsh became acquainted and after his marriage he took these two loyal and devoted guardians as part of his household, and even after their death their families lived under his roof." [(A)]

At the time that Maula Bakhsh met Kasime-Biy, she and her family had lived under the protection of the Maharajah. Now settled in Maula Bakhsh's home, Kasime-Biy remained in strict seclusion; yet her strong presence was felt throughout the family household. Showing regal courtesy and grace to the few she allowed in her presence, she "felt so deeply the tragedy of life as she knew it in the history and fate of her 'house.'" (A) This same atmosphere of mystery and aristocratic bearing was imparted to her daughter, Khatidja-Bibi, as well. Her children knew that they were expected to behave with dignity and courtesy to all, ever "maintaining noble traditions of an ancient and great line." (A) Kasime-Biy encouraged her husband to take on more wives, as was the custom in wealthy Moslem families at that time. Revealing his religious open-mindedness, Maula Bakhsh chose to wed two Hindu ladies.

He was now received and rewarded by the princes of many noble courts of India and settled for a while at the famous Court of Hyderabad. The Nizam was so impressed with Maula Bakhsh that, one day, he was awarded an elephant by the Court of Hyderabad, a rare and costly status symbol similar to what a VIP's expensive car might represent today.

Maula Bakhsh was the only musician of his time who had mastered both the music of the south and of the north, two very different styles and techniques. During the course of his travels throughout India, he began developing a system of musical notation that would be acceptable to all musicians, whether from the north or the south. In preparation for a meeting with the Viceroy of India, Maula Bakhsh also began learning the principles of Western music. He felt that if he better understood the art of the West, it would become easier to explain to the British monarch the art of the East.

Traveling from palace to palace, Maula Bakhsh built close ties with the maharajahs and princes throughout the Indian Empire. However, it was Maharajah Sayaji Rao Gaekwar of Baroda who backed Maula Bakhsh's project: that of creating an academy of music. He was appointed director of what came to be called the Gayanshala, where not only musicians were welcomed from schools of varying styles, but every caste or creed and—unheard of at the time—even girls were allowed to attend. He felt that music should represent the basis of education of every child, as it plays an important role in forming the character and thought pattern of developing youths. He also introduced the study of poetry, "feeling that the beauty of their words and thoughts must animate the minds of the students and inspire them with a sense of the divine in life and so form a fitting accompaniment to instruction in the divine art." (A)

Two of Maula Bakhsh's sons followed in their father's footsteps. The eldest was Murtaza Khan, who studied Eastern music and succeeded his father as the head of the Gayanshala Music Academy, assuming his position at the royal court. Of majestic appearance, it is said that he bore a striking resemblance to Tipu Sultan! A patriarch in his own right, he commanded respect from all whom he met. This was not only due to his noble bearing and the place of honor he earned for himself at the Maharajah's court, but also because of his own musical accomplishments.

The second son was Alauddin Khan who, choosing Western music, spent five years at the Royal Academy of Music in London, from which he graduated with a doctorate. Dr. A. M. Pathan, he then called himself, linking himself with the chivalrous warrior castes of Islam. His nephew Inayat was to use that name, as well, until WWI. After his return to India, Alauddin assumed a number of functions for the court orchestra and state military bands, and supervised about 500 musicians. He showed talent as an administrator, orchestral conductor and musical director. He also introduced Western music to the numerous festivals and public events of the state.

Dr. Pathan retired early from his stately functions, as he found it difficult to accept the political reality of India as a British Protectorate, and moved to the then free Kingdom of Nepal. Returning to Baroda in his old age, Dr. Pathan rebuilt a small part of Maula Bakhsh House that, due to decades of vacancy following Maula Bakhsh's death, had fallen into ruin and disrepair. During his last years he revived the sacred Indian and Islamic tradition of feeding the poor: large amounts of food were cooked on Thursdays and Fridays and charitably distributed to the needy.

Following decades of great accomplishments during which the highest honors were bestowed upon Maula Bakhsh, he spent the latter years of his life placing high hopes on his eldest grandson, Inayat. The young boy spent much time at the feet of his grandfather, listening to him speak or perform at the regular gatherings of musicians and erudite visitors that were held at Maula Bakhsh's home. The house in Baroda was called Maula Bakhsh Khaneh and stood in spacious grounds adjoining his and his family's main estates. At least 40 people resided in the Khaneh. The Maharajah at Baroda's Court awarded Maula Bakhsh the rank of Nauratan, an honor bestowed on the noblest and most august members of the realm. This was to be understood as a northern acknowledgment and counterpart of the princely status he had been conferred in the south. Not only did the local population bow down before this larger-than-life personality, but the religious and royal leaders did as well. Maula Bakhsh achieved the greatest of positions in his lifetime: "he became the outstanding national symbol of India's independent greatness in music." (A)

When Maula Bakhsh died, his funeral was attended by Hindus and Moslems alike. Though he had been raised in an orthodox manner, his broad views and free thinking attitude allowed him to see the beauty in all religions. Many of his pupils were of the Hindu faith. Having excelled in music, created a national musical notation system and achieved mastery of life as a person, Maula Bakhsh can be regarded as one of India's greatest men, a pioneer in the dawning era of educational, religious and cultural change.

THE PARENTS

Born in 1868 to Maula Bakhsh and Kasime-Biy, Khatidja-Bibi showed a keen interest in learning, acquiring a good knowledge of Arabic, Persian and Urdu. She also learned noble behavior, in all senses of the term, from her mother, a descendant of the royal house of Tipu Sultan. Quiet, reserved and modest, she was also patient with all, never allowing herself to be angered.

Married at fifteen, she reared four children: Inayat, Maheboob, Musharaff and Karamat, a girl. Before the birth of Inayat, she dreamt that Christ came to heal her. In other dreams the Prophet Mohammed blessed Khatidja-Bibi, or she saw herself surrounded by saints and prophets who seemed to take care of her and appeared to be waiting for a time or an event that had been predicted. Confiding these dreams only to her aged grandmother, she was told that she must tell no one but ask for God's protection. Khatidja-Bibi not only invoked the protection of God but of every saint and prophet known to her, including Jesus, Moses, Abraham and the Prophet Mohammed.

Totally devoted to her children, Khatidja-Bibi embodied the ideals of motherhood, ever nurturing and caring for her four treasures. Her husband Rahmat Khan, born in 1843, hailed from a family that not only boasted musicians and poets but, apparently, in every generation had one mystic in their midst. Rahmat's great uncle, for instance, was venerated as a saint and a mystic in Panjab, a man of great spiritual power.

Rahmat learned classical Indian music from Saint Alias, a holy man living in Panjab. Saint Alias was a Sufi who led the ascetic life of a mystic, content with a small hut as an abode. His principle was to never ask for anything, not even food; but he would accept anything given to him, using it the same day. One day a Maharajah left him a large sum of money as an offering. Here again, Saint Alias would not allow the money to remain with him overnight; the residents of all the neighboring villages were invited to a huge feast so that no money would remain with him.

The saint's personality had a deep and lasting effect on Rahmat, bringing about a profound understanding of life's values. In his youth, Rahmat traveled a lot but was unsure about where he should settle. One day he met a saint who, for many years, had stood on the same spot, unsheltered from the elements, except for a small roof that had been recently erected over his head. Rahmat asked the saint where he should go. The saint waved his hand in a certain direction, which led Rahmat to Baroda and, by fate, to Maula Bakhsh. Their friendship grew so close that Maula Bakhsh first gave him his eldest daughter, Fatima-Biy, in marriage and—after her untimely death—Rahmat married Khatidja-Bibi.

Rahmat assisted Maula Bakhsh at the Gayanshala Music Academy and excelled as a singer of classical ragas. Well-respected by all, he helped to maintain the high level of responsibility and dignity that was fitting to both Maula Bakhsh's school of music and his home. Though essentially strict toward his children, Rahmat was nonetheless a kind and loving father, doing whatever it took to grant his children's wishes.

INAYAT, THE MUSICIAN

Inayat Khan was born in Maula Bakhsh House, Baroda, in the state of Gujarat on July 5th, 1882. His mother was Khatija-Bibi, his father was Rahmat Khan.

At the request of his mother's dying aunt Inayat-Bibi, the baby was named after her: Inayat, meaning kindness. Before Inayat alighted on this planet, his mother would invoke her faith to Jesus (the "Spirit of God"), Moses (the "Word of God"), Abraham (the "Friend of God") and Mohammed (the "Prophet of God"). According to family lore, when Inayat was born, a dove flew from a mighty fortress and alighted at the home where the newborn lay, delivering a noble blessing to Inayat's family.

Inayat's home was vibrant with the sound of music, as many members of his family were musicians. The patriarch was, of course, Inayat's grandfather Maula Bakhsh, who later took it upon himself to teach the boy music. A deep bond grew between the master and his pupil.

Inayat was gifted in all the arts but remained indifferent to school grammar and mathematics. He showed signs of being a genius in song and playing the vina, as well as in poetry. Inayat had three siblings, two boys and one girl. His mother loved all her children equally but had a special bond with Inayat. She was demure and lived up to the precept of "Love, Harmony and Beauty." Inayat's voice was considered to be superb. Being gifted in classical Indian music, he was encouraged from every side. His father was extremely attentive and kind; and when Inayat was still very young, he taught him philosophy, courtesy and morals. At times, close to forty musicians gathered in the courtyard of Maula Bakhsh House, sharing the skill and beauty of their playing. Inayat considered his home to be his security and also the best place in the world but, though he loved all the members of his family, he always wished to be alone.

In his adolescent years, Inayat accompanied his father, Rahmat Khan, on a yearlong trip that included the court of the King of Nepal. The long months that Inayat spent on this voyage represented one of the most formative times of his youth. On the way, they experienced many places of interest, including Benares on the sacred Ganges River. Places of worship—even though not Moslem—were as holy to Inayat as those considered sacred in the world of Islam. This journey opened the young boy's eyes not only to the world of musical mastery but also to the woes of humankind. Jealousy, greed, cruelty, illness, poverty, starvation and even death were constant discoveries that the innocent lad had not experienced in the protected realm of his grandfather's home.

With time, Inayat not only mastered the vina and classical ragas but, under the influence of his uncle Alauddin (Dr Pathan) who had studied music in London, he learned to play the harmonium and the violin, even writing manuals for the teaching of these Western instruments.

Carrying on Maula Bakhkh's open approach to musical traditions beyond the limitation of background or religion, Inayat's many years of musical education were in both northern Indian, or Mogul, music and in southern Indian Carnatic music, that is, that of the Brahmin Hindus. To emphasize this tolerance even beyond music, Inayat's best childhood friend was a Hindu.

Around the age of twenty, Inayat embarked on a series of trips throughout India. He was received by the rich and the titled, carrying on the traditions of his grandfather Maula Bakhsh. Concerts of voice and vina would be preceded or followed by a lecture on some aspect of music, along with philosophic themes. Inayat performed for learned circles in society and for rich and powerful people, such as maharajas. His success was stunning, perhaps not only due to his expertise in vina and his mastery of the voice, but also because of the diversity of styles from which he could choose. Musicians of his time were limited to the classical style of the region where they had studied, whereas Inayat's knowledge of music was eclectic. Above all, his listeners were enraptured by his presence and by his talks. He spoke about the state of Indian music at the time and what should be done to improve it. All the while, not only did he impart his knowledge and ideas, but gave his public a glimpse of the wisdom and mysticism that was developing in his soul.

As a young man, Inayat continued learning at the Gayanshala Music Academy in Baroda, while teaching there at the same time. In time, he was given the title of Professor of Music. Working energetically at the Gayanshala, he produced a textbook for learning to sing, including some 75 songs in different languages and styles. On the textbook's back cover one can read a letter of appreciation on behalf of "the public of Madras":

> *To Professor Inayat Khan Rahmat Pathan (Musician of Baroda).*
>
> *Dear Sir,*
>
> *We, on behalf of the public of Madras, have assembled here to express our deepfelt joy at having had you in our midst for some time past. The public entertainment given by you on 12th of July 1902, has led us to form a very high opinion of your attainments in the theory and practice of Music. It is no wonder that, young as you are, you have acquired such pre-eminent skill in your art and display a wonderful insight into its intricacies, for a ready explanation is to be found in the fact that you are descended from that great and famous Musician Professor Moula Baksh who is renowned throughout India as the inventor of a system of notation after the English Model for Hindu Music.*

> *You have not only given us exquisite pleasure by the sweet melody and the scientific Harmony of your songs but you have created in us an insatiable appetite for the dalect symphonies of the celestial art of Music. It is highly gratifying to us that you have made your life's work to improve the Music of India and to endeavour to introduce a uniform system for the whole of India so that some sort of friendly understanding may be established between Hindustan and Carnatic Musicians.*
>
> *We sincerely wish you every success in this, your noble undertaking and trust that the princes and potentates of this mighty land, as well as the British Government, will render you all assistance to enable you to carry out the laudable object to which you have set before yourself.*
>
> *We request you to accept this gold Medal as a slight token of our sincere gratitude for the entertainment you have given us and of the high esteem in which we hold your talents and attainments.*
>
> *We are very proud to note that H.H. Gaekwar of Baroda has done a great deal for the encouragement of Music in this state and we are sure that, if under his fostering care, men of rare ability like you have been successfully trained, the future of Indian Music would be indeed grand. We sincerely trust that the noble example set by His Highness will be imitated by the other princes and nobles of this country. We are, dear Sir, your Well-wishers,*
>
> *THE PUBLIC OF MADRAS*

Perhaps Inayat's greatest musical triumph was to be allowed to perform for the Nizam of Hyderabad on April 8th, 1903. His Highness Rustam-i-Dauran, Mahbub Ali Khan was the sixth in line of the Asaf Jahi rulers, a direct male descendant of Shaikh Shihabud-din Suhrawardy, the acclaimed Sufi from Kurdistan. The Asaf Jahi rulers, also called the Nizams, ruled over the vast territory of the State of Hyderabad and were known to be great patrons of the arts. It was under strange circumstances that Inayat's meeting with the Nizam took place: Inayat and a couple of friends were spending the night at the camp of the ailing Prime Minister, Krishna Prasad, in the coolness of the hills near Hyderabad. Inayat was invited to sing for the Prime Minister who, after a short time, began to recover. An ensuing conversation was dominated by Inayat's exuberant description of his plans to uplift the country through the revival of its music.

Suddenly word came that the Nizam would be arriving shortly to visit the Prime Minister. No sooner had His Highness arrived at the camp, than Inayat was urged to perform for the Nizam. For three hours, one of the world's richest and most powerful statesmen listened in rapture to the young man's performance. The next morning, the Nizam summoned Inayat to his splendid palace, where, after further singing and a long discussion on esoteric matters, the sovereign removed the emerald ring from his finger and offered it to the young musician. "Tansen of the Modern World" is how the Nizam of Hyderabad described the singer, referring to Miyan Tansen, the 16th century singer considered to be one of the greatest composer-musicians of Hindustani classical music, and who starred at the court of Akbar, the Mogul Emperor of India.

Yet somehow, being acclaimed the new Tansen of India did not satisfy Inayat. His longing was for something deeper. The professor of music longed to become a student again, in search of knowledge that is granted only to an ardent and patient seeker.

INAYAT, THE MYSTIC

He spoke four Indian languages, and had a good command of English. He had mastered musical and vocal art and received the highest recognition and acclaim. But Inayat's soul yearned for the peace and the ecstasy that can only be found within. Perhaps this desire was sparked when he was a boy traveling to the Himalayas with his father. One day Inayat had ridden a horse out into the forest where he encountered a muni, a holy man who—totally withdrawn from the world—never utters a word. To Inayat, this person who could claim no earthly pleasures or possessions appeared to be "the happiest man in the world." [(A)]

After quietly sitting in meditation one evening, as he was now making his habit, Inayat awoke in the middle of the night to a bright light in the room, as if the sun had risen too soon. In the midst of music and voices, he glimpsed a dignified elderly man observing him with radiant eyes. Inayat understood this as a sign that he should set out to find his teacher, his murshid.

Inayat presented himself to various sages and spiritual peers, but they would not accept him as a pupil, claiming they were not qualified to teach someone like him. When Inayat least expected it, at the home of a theologian who had once turned him down as a disciple, he met the old, bearded man of his vision. During the course of the evening the man commented about Inayat to his friend, "He appeals intensely to my spirit." [(A)] Syed Mohammed Abu Hashim Madani was no silent muni in the Himalayas, nor a wandering dervish in rags, but a well-to-do member of society at whose feet numerous disciples drank in every word and instruction.

Surprising as it may seem, Murshid Madani's first objective was to reinforce Inayat's faith and self-confidence. He tested the disciple's faith by waiting long months before broaching any subject of depth and meaning. When, at long last, the teacher touched upon the topic of metaphysics, Inayat leaped at the opportunity to finally record meaningful instruction on his notepad. Murshid Madani immediately changed the topic, indicating that this knowledge was to be recorded in the mind and the heart, not on paper.

For several years Inayat was able to absorb the wisdom that emanated from his master's words and presence. Sadly, the day arrived when Murshid Madani departed this world. To Inayat, the loss was great and, after his teacher's passing, instead of returning home to Baroda, he embarked on a pilgrimage to the holy men of India, including acclaimed gurus such as the Brahmin leader Manek Prabhu, and also sought the company of ragged dervishes. He also offered up his respects and prayers at the tombs of Moslem saints such as Khwaja Moinuddin Chishti, India's most celebrated Sufi saint. Despite the noise of the bustling crowd at the tomb, Inayat experienced a great sense of peace there. That night he realized while meditating that "the world was neither a stage set up for our amusement, nor a bazaar to satisfy our vanity and hunger, but a school, wherein to learn a hard lesson."[(A)]

INAYAT, THE MASTER

As a young boy, perhaps about the age of thirteen, Inayat had been praying with devotion and humility as he had been taught. Suddenly the doubt came upon him as to whether "it was wise to go on worshipping one whom he did not see or know." [A] Asking his grandfather, Maula Bakhsh smiled and replied by quoting the Koran: "We will show them our signs in the world and in themselves, that the truth may be manifested to them" before adding, "The signs of God are seen in the world, and the world is seen in thyself." [A] These words impressed Inayat for life so that he always sought God in his surroundings, in his fellow men and in himself.

Inayat realized the deep message of the Chishti Sufi's way: singing of the perfection of God and the limitation of man, while at the same time seeking and recognizing the presence of God in man. Embracing a religion of the heart, these Sufis create an image of God as the Beloved.

Before leaving this plane, Inayat's murshid, Hashim Madani, blessed him and instructed him to "Fare forth into the world, my child, and harmonize the East and the West with the harmony of thy music. Spread the wisdom of Sufism abroad, for to this end art thou gifted by Allah, the most merciful and compassionate." [A]

Through Murshid Syed Mohammed Abu Hashim Madani and the revered line of Pirs and Murshids preceding him, Inayat now embodied the link in an important chain of spiritual heritage that hailed from the source of Chishti ascendancy—back to Khwaja Moinuddin Chishti himself.

During the three years of travel around India that then ensued, Inayat decided to live as an ascetic musician, shunning comfort and possession, wealth and acclaim. Received by a host of religious and secular leaders, he was repeatedly recognized as one whose musical art had reached excellence and whose presence commanded the deepest respect.

In the presence of the Nawab of Bahadur, Inayat was approached by a Brahmin who was gifted in predicting people's future through palm-reading. Upon looking at Inayat's hand he jumped back and, after long moments of heavy silence, he bowed down to touch Inayat's feet and apologized for having attempted to foretell his fate. On another occasion, a great Sufi speaker referred to Inayat, claiming: "Here is a hidden soul, in whom the divine expression is now budding." Another master, working under the guise of a crazy, nonsensical dervish, a madzub, called at Inayat's dwelling, asking, "Where is my Lord and Master?"

One day a great Brahmin arrived in Inayat's home town, Baroda. He was most impressive both in spiritual presence and in size. The master was known to be a seer and could easily read minds. Inayat joined the group gathered around the Brahmin, but the master, though friendly and talkative to all, refused to look at him. Finally, when all the disciples and visitors had left, Inayat sat alone with the Brahmin, who said: "Welcome, Mahatma (one of divine soul)! I am sorry I could not speak to you before all the others, but I can do so now. I can see you are depressed at this moment and clouds have surrounded your life; but it is the dawn, look forward to the rising sun. You are to go to the Western world… And there you will do a great work which cannot be told to you just now. It will not bring wealth, but it is work which is beyond imagination…." [A]

AMERICA

By 1910, Inayat had embodied the perfection of music and mysticism. From his teacher and from his inner heritage and self-discipline, Inayat had learned the art of listening to others and reacting towards them with empathy. His mastery and spirituality had brought him so far that he could achieve a state of spiritual ecstasy practically at will: it was a matter of inner attunement in order to commune with the Beloved. This Inayat could achieve at will. Mind reading, as well as mind control, even over others, had not been a goal to achieve in training, but a useful byproduct of his years of instruction and meditative exercise.

His master had moved on to another plane, his father had recently passed away and, sadly, his first wife then passed away. Encouraged by his family, Inayat remarried; but, tragically, his second wife died within months of their marriage. One day Inayat decided to follow his calling and he embarked on his mission to the Western world. Armed with his vina, he would take a universal—one could even say New Age—message of Love, Harmony and Beauty to America and Europe.

Though well established in their lives and careers, Inayat's brother Maheboob and his cousin Mohammed Ali did not hesitate for a moment to accept his invitation to accompany him, both physically and musically, on a venture that would forever sever them from their home and roots in India. Inayat's younger brother, Musharaff, still attending school at the time of departure, joined up with the others later on, once they had found their bearings.

During the one and one half years that Inayat, his brother, and his cousin traveled throughout the United States, they were known as The Royal Musicians of Hindustan. Establishing themselves proved to be extremely difficult, and due to their darker skin, they were generally treated with the contempt that American society displayed to those of African origins at the time.

A breakthrough came in the form of Ruth St. Denis, who was famed for Oriental dances that she invented. They ranged from Egyptian to Japanese, but at the time when she met the Khan family, she was in her Indian phase. The Royal Musicians of Hindustan accompanied Ruth St. Denis on her tours throughout the United States, playing "on call," something which was totally unfamiliar to them. Though all three were musically proficient—in fact, Maheboob and Mohammed Ali had superbly beautiful voices—they needed a tabla player in order to complete the orchestra of stringed instruments. Providence gave them a Hindu percussionist, Ramaswami, who not only played the tabla, but performed an important role in bridging the gaps between the Indian newcomers and the Western world. Ramaswami had already spent several years in New York and helped to "show them the ropes.'"

One of the main problems the Khan family complained of was the fact that they could not grow accustomed to Western food, which they found to be bland, unpleasant and prepared in an unhygienic way. Mohammed Ali jumped to the occasion by teaching himself to cook the Indian (Moslem) way. Later in Fazal Manzil, Suresnes, his weekly cooking would be fondly remembered by the younger generation.

Eventually the musicians set off on their own, independent of Ruth St. Denis, who was pondering a change of theme. Though they traveled extensively, performing in St. Louis, Los Angeles, Seattle and Chicago, it was in San Francisco and New York that the musicians were their most active. Whenever possible, Inayat addressed the listeners on the subjects closest to his heart: philosophy and mysticism. By so doing, he not only tuned the audience to a higher level through the harmony of music, but also through the harmony of his words. In this way, the master attracted his first mureed, the first of thousands of disciples or students that would soon follow. Interestingly, this first follower of his Sufi Message, Mrs. Ada Martin, was of Jewish descent. The musician had become a mystic; the mystic had developed into a master. But now, by initiating his first mureed, the master became the murshid: the Pir-o-Murshid.

Among the regular venues where the Royal Musicians of Hindustan were welcome was the Sanskrit College in New York. There Inayat met its founder, a man extremely interested in promoting Eastern philosophies, practices, language and culture. This man was to be both a blessing and the source of suffering for Inayat: his name was Pierre Arnold Bernard, Ora Ray's half-brother and guardian.

FORBIDDEN LOVE

Ora Ray had traveled to San Francisco, one of her regular destinations. It was either to meet with her distant cousin Mary Baker Eddy, the founder of Christian Science, or perhaps to accompany her half-brother Pierre Bernard, that she attended a lecture and concert at the Ramakrishna Ashram. The speaker of the evening was a certain Inayat Khan Rahmat Pathan, who would also play the vina, accompanied by the other three members of the Royal Musicians of Hindustan.

Inayat entered with regal poise and a majestic gait. Young and stunning, he brought the magic of his precious vina to life, wearing a pastel turban pinned in the front by a jewel. While the instruments were being tuned—thereby tuning the listeners—there arose an atmosphere of deep stillness. As the evening proceeded the Khan family filled the enraptured hall with the fragrance of classical Indian music.

Just days before, Ora Ray had witnessed the vision of an Indian master. Today she knew that the premonition was taking shape. Her heart made her feel like kneeling down to thank the Almighty. The atmosphere was highly sacred, and the listeners were entranced by the music of the heart.

> **Claire Harper:** Mother told me that she danced on air while being introduced to Inayat. Pierre Bernard suggested that the Indian teach his sister the vina. As she looked at the dark stranger, she imagined a thousand lotus petals shining in his eyes. The grace of love was being celebrated at the pseudo-Indian buffet while, unnoticed to most, a tiny flag of happiness beckoned to the young couple from the future!

For several weeks, Ora Ray took vina lessons from her handsome Indian teacher, all the while getting to know this Indian prince and his relatives. During one of the lessons, Ora Ray told her teacher of her vision and described the elderly gentleman who had appeared to her. Inayat immediately confirmed that she had been visited by his murshid, a sign of destiny.

Inevitably, she fell totally in love with Inayat, and he with her. Inayat realized in his heart that this was the main reason he was in the United States. He later wrote: "If I can recall any great achievement in America, it was to have found the soul who was destined to be my life's partner." [(A)] Spending the next few months traveling through the States with repeated lectures and performances in Los Angeles, Seattle, San Francisco and even at New York's famed Carnegie Hall, Inayat and his relatives sought to introduce mystical Indian music as well as the esoteric principles of Sufism. All the while, Inayat maintained close communication with his beloved Ora Ray by letter and by telephone.

Even though Ora Ray's half-brother and guardian was allegedly an open-minded proponent of all things Eastern, as an advocate of yoga, tantric practices and Eastern philosophies, he became infuriated at the thought that his ward was in love with an Indian. Inayat noted about Americans in 1910 that: "He is accustomed to look with contempt at a dark skin, in spite of the many most unclean, ignorant, and ill-mannered specimens of white people… but, Indians, when insulted abroad, can do nothing but bear it patiently."[(A)]

Pierre Bernard forbade any contact between Ora Ray and Inayat, so the lovers were forced to meet in secret whenever possible. Then Inayat and his companions needed to move on, finally sailing for Europe.

Ora Ray wrote just under 60 letters to her beloved during the long months preceding her escape. In the sixth letter to her "Daya," as she called Inayat, she wrote:

> *My Daya,*
>
> *Could not find a chance my love, to write you these few days, and how long it has seemed to 'Sharda' no one but God knows. Oh, my soul, my soul, how can I ever live through this separation and how is my Daya? If I could only know that, but it seems that I am writing to the winds, for it will still be a month and a half before I can hear from my loved one.*
>
> *I shall try to tell you, my own, how this separation came about. You remember the Saturday I was with you all evening until one o'clock and the Sunday all day and evening, in fact the last days I saw my Daya. The next day Monday I saw my brother, and someone had told him I was away, so he wanted to know where I was that I should be away so late, and of course I told him what*

falsehood I could. Well he could not understand how I could possibly be out so late and really thought I must be doing something wrong, so he said he would have my trunk moved over to Jersey and that I could never see New York again, unless of course I really loved someone, then he would do all he could to help me, and if this one I love, really loves me.

I knew the climax had come, and I could not communicate with my Daya again unless I told my brother I was in love and remembering that he has always lived up to his word with me in everything, and also remembering that my Daya had always said 'if we could only have my brother's consent it would be much better,' I thought the only thing to do was to tell him that I love you and want to marry you, and so I did after about nine hours constant talk, or until I thought, after all he told me, that he really had sympathy for me and after all, if I really love some one, what matters is who it is.

Well he changed immediately, and said your blood would never mix with his and oh, my Daya, I cannot tell you what all happened but he said you could not live, and when those words were spoken, I felt myself going backward in a faint, but I held to consciousness as best I could, thinking he might go over and kill you and so that night, Mon. night, I would not go to bed and tried my best to run away, if only to warn you of your danger.

Well my brother sent for several people that night and the whole house was in an uproar. Will tell you more next time my love, I must stop now. And when you are well I will tell you why my brother would rather have me die than marry you. But my love, I must say I am thankful to God that I did tell him for if we had of married and gone away, it is positively sure that he would have found us and have killed you. For he told me so and I honestly believe it. He said I saved your life by a hair's breadth. He destroyed all of my clothes which I wore up to see you and many things I will tell you later my Daya. In the meantime love and a thousand kisses from the saddest girl in the world.

Claire Harper: From then on, Ora Ray received no more letters from Inayat. She began to wonder why time was going by so slowly, while awaiting a letter to reply to. Ora Ray's nights were starved of sleep. The echo of love's call could be heard in the dark blue sky. The stars twinkled brightly but remained silent. The silence and separation made her ill.

She wrote her Beloved:

> *My love, my first letter to you was written on the fourteenth of August—that being two and a half months after our last happy meeting during which time I was ill. Yes, dearest heart these poor feet should have some consideration as you have said in your letter for they have ran many times to mail letters to you when they were not strong enough to hold this body up. You see my whole system was so low that it took several months to become strong again and the least exertion would exhaust me therefore the first month or so I wrote you my love, under many difficulties as it was so hard for me to be alone, I was watched so closely you know. But I do not wish to worry you with such things. . .*

One morning, as was her habit, Ora Ray was tidying her brother Pierre Bernard's desk when she could not believe her luck. Staring up at her was Inayat's home address in India! She swiftly took note of this distant but hopeful door to her Beloved and sent Inayat not just one, but 21 letters to Baroda, hoping that his family would forward her words on to him. In turn, she asked him to address her only via a personal post office box number in Tenafly, New Jersey, a place she occasionally was allowed to visit. In those days the mail was slow, but the mystery was solved when Inayat told Ora Ray of all the letters he had sent her—Pierre Bernard had simply kept them all from his sister!

Discovering this, she asked Inayat:

> *Dear heart, can you not put a different name on your envelopes' return address, so your real name will not be on 'the outside'—then no one can trace them.*

Inayat had written to ask for Ora Ray's hand, but his request was flatly refused. Inayat, accompanied by his brothers and cousin, had been traveling through France, Holland and Switzerland, holding Sufi meetings and giving concerts for the spreading of the Message. Whenever Ora wrote, it was in the privacy of the Ladies' Parlor at one of the department stores, such as Gimbels. She would then mail it off as soon as it was written.

The Escape

Claire Harper: Greatly relieved that Inayat was safely in Europe, the lovers made arrangements to meet…a plan was in the making: escape! Such a hazardous theory needed to be put into practice. She maneuvered the getaway with keen thinking and great skill; while the implementation of this plan whispered possible success, Inayat warned her of the hardships that she'd be likely to face. She assured him—and herself—that any adversity could be mastered. Her youthful zest made light of Inayat's warning.

In her 43rd letter Ora Ray wrote Inayat:

> *It will be about two months before I leave for Europe. I think it best that I take a steamer at Philadelphia on my return to N.Y. So my love with these later plans of going West it will not do for one to write my folks that I have committed suicide for they may receive the letter before I could board the steamer so I think it best to just disappear taking my grip with a few things in it as is natural in traveling and leaving my trunk at the station. They will locate my trunk and may perhaps think I have been killed by some man or that I may have been stolen in some way or other and for some purpose as you oft times read of some crimes.*
>
> *Of course I know they will go to much trouble and it may appear in the papers in order to locate me. But my love if you really want your Sharda you can have her. I will come to you no matter what happens. If you can trust your landlady, it is well for her to meet me but in that case I would be going to Paris, direct, and my love do you not think it best for me to stay in London a while. Paris would be the first place they would look for me my love, it is sure that my brother knows where you are, you being in public life and Baba could easily locate you.*
>
> *Dear heart, my brother even knew your address at the last place where you were in N.Y. he even knew of the short illness you had there for a few days, how he knew, I do not know, some one certainly told him.*

Inexorably, the hours grew into days and the weeks into months. Ora Ray's 54th letter ended with this heartrending lament:

> *Far away is my Daya:*
> *My heart, my soul, my life, my all,*
> *Sad the day the parting came,*
> *Where is my love, where is he now.*
> *Just to see his face again,*
> *His voice to hear, his lips to kiss,*
> *I would die a thousand deaths,*
> *Where is Daya, where is he now?*

Young as she was, Ora Ray realized that the only way she could be united with her soul mate was to travel to him. We sense this resoluteness in the following lines:

> *Love has a will and a will has a way; so there is much hope for us. May the iron bonds of love keep our hearts always together and I am sure our bodies shall unite sooner or later. Who could be so heartless as to keep us apart very long... My eyes are blind with tears, my love. Good bye, good bye.*

Claire Harper: Ora Ray booked her passage on the next ship from Philadelphia to Europe.[(8)] On one of those country club theater evenings, Ora Ray eloped as she had planned, inconspicuous, clad in a beautiful evening gown. Nightfall was her sole helper as she attempted to conceal a rather questionable looking bag tucked under her cape.

On the way to the dock, she stopped to change into a plain black suit. She pulled back her shiny golden hair, tied it back tightly and hid it under a hat. How and where she managed this transformation remains a puzzle. All that she carried with her was a small toiletry case in which she had packed her lovely silver toilet set.

Clutching the ticket bought in New York in utter secrecy, she embarked and, having found the safety of her private cabin, somehow felt unattainable. To avoid being noticed, she bade the attendant bring all her meals to the cabin. Adventure was now singing to the tune of "I know not whence I'm bound, but I'm on my way."

Two weeks previously she had sent her last letter to her Beloved:

> *My love, you will receive this letter about two weeks before my leaving so I do not think it is necessary for me to cable except before leaving. After reading this letter you will know that I will be leaving here about the 28th of Feb, and I would rather cable you under another name if I receive word from you in answer to the letter I wrote you about it, if not then I shall cable you Anayatkhan, Varma, Paris. But wherever I land, my love, I would rather you would have someone other than yourself meet me, for I am afraid of making a scene at the landing. You know I have not regained my health yet and my excitement may cause me to faint as I have in the summer owing to my weakness. I do not know what might happen so I would rather have our first meeting in doors, my love, we must not have any trouble there. Dear heart did Mohammed Ali receive the Xmas candy I sent him? I think my 54th letter better be the last*

one you answer dear heart, so there will not be any letters here after I leave.

Good-bye, dear heart; remember, I shall be sailing in about three weeks. Love and longing from your own.

One final message of warning was sent to her Beloved in Europe:

Dear heart, I do not want to endanger your life, you must always be well guarded from the day I leave here and when I arrive on the other side, you must not see me. . . for I am sure my brother will have detectives trying to find me.

Claire Harper: Ora Ray kept to her cabin for the duration of the journey. Here she dwelt in a palace of dreams where sleep cradled her in his arms. As the ship slowly moved on into the distance she opened her porthole; darkness fell, lighting her view with a show of stars—even the full moon appeared bright and happy. Above the ship, like seagulls, cherubs followed the voyage, holding hands and announcing the reunion of two hearts.

Words cannot describe the joy of the lovers' long awaited celebration. Inayat had suggested that Ora leave the ship in Antwerp, Belgium, rather than at the riskier ports of England, where she may be snatched up by her brother's detectives. Inayat met his beloved there, and they discreetly made their way to London.

Their marriage took place in London on March 20th, 1913. "Ora Ray Baker, otherwise Ora Bernard," as she registered herself at the marriage registry, was known from now on as Ameena Begum (a Begum is a lady of high rank). Soon afterwards, Mohammed Ali organized a Moslem wedding for the young couple—not as he would have been able to do had they been in India, but at least as authentic and traditional a celebration as was permissible in Western society and with the limited funds available.

The next few months were spent between London and Paris, even enjoying a close exchange with the great Indian thinker and writer Rabindranath Tagore in London. In Paris, the police came to the door one day looking for a young American girl who had "run away." There was nothing they could do as the girl was, in fact, already twenty-five years old and legally married.

Soon after this event, Inayat received an invitation to perform in Russia. Hardly had Ora Ray begun to settle into her new family than she was faced with the reality of her husband's situation: his livelihood depended on his extensive travel. His long absences would be sorely felt throughout their marriage.

RUSSIA

Claire Harper: Long before Murshid, accompanied by his Begum and his brothers, settled in Suresnes, they traveled extensively together giving concerts. In the West, Indian music was little known at the time and, therefore, much sought after. Murshid's musical genius and his brothers' accompaniment met with great success.

Inayat met such famous divas of the day as Mata Hari, as well as Emma Nevada and her daughter Mignon Nevada, among the greatest opera singers of the time. The composers Debussy and Alexander Nikolayevich Scriabin were among those famed personalities that Inayat frequented. Very soon, news of his renown resounded within the musical circles of Paris, and Murshid was encouraged by a Russian socialite, Princess Bartinov, to join in Moscow's innumerable seasonal festivals and to meet great Russian musicians, poets and artists.

Through the princess, Inayat's brilliance reached the attention of Count Sergei L'vovich Tolstoy, a talented musician and composer and son of the famed Leo Tolstoy. He was also able to meet the great Russian performers, such as the opera singer Feodor Ivanovich Chaliapin, and to take part in numerous music festivals.

The curve of Inayat's musical genius reached its zenith. Inayat and his family were received with great enthusiasm; crowds gathered at the overflowing music halls, stunned upon listening to original classical Indian music and seeing this impressive group wearing the national dress. Inayat received so much recognition that, one day, the three-horse drawn carriage he was riding in was unhitched and pulled by eager students and music lovers to the overcrowded concert hall. A few months of such events continued to celebrate Inayat's contribution to the Russian music annals.

The New Year Star

Claire Harper: At the turning of the old and new years, within the shadows of the Kremlin's walls, as an already thick white carpet grew even deeper with heaven's confetti, a New Year soul alighted on planet earth: Noor-un-nisa ("light among women"). In Indian families it was traditional to give a child a second, more familiar or affectionate name. This little one was thus also named Babuli (father's daughter). Her arrival was bathed in light which, to her parents, shone brighter than bright. Thus she was later named

However a stir of unrest was felt throughout the land; a political cloud was weighing heavy overhead: the revolution was brewing. Very soon, the country's turmoil grew to greater proportions in the capital. Music, art, and the luxury of good living, all blew up and swayed like giant bubbles of bygone splendor. The snow-white winter became a black smudge of dismay. Mobs multiplied by word of mouth, and one could hear the rushing hooves of horses whilst barricades were hauled into position and the terror of revolt began.

Inayat and his family were conducted by friends and admirers in a large carriage towards the border. On the way, a group of angry rebels had blocked the free passage, and the horses were brought to a halt. At that very moment Inayat threw open the carriage hood and stood lofty, his cloak flapping about him, his black hat towering tall upon his head. In Inayat's arms lay baby Noor, whom he now lifted with both hands high above his shoulders, presenting this little treasure to the screaming crowds. In the deep blue of the night, there came a sudden hush...for a gesture of this kind happens but once. The mob drew back and watched the carriage slip into the future...only to meet with war—for this was to be their next destination in the West.

GENEVA

Murshid and his brothers arrived in Paris just in time to represent Indian music at the International Music Congress in 1914. During the summer months that followed, they lived at 39, Rue Singer, in the heart of Paris. One day, Murshid felt the sudden call to travel to Geneva. With barely a penny in his pocket and a one-way ticket, he arrived alone in Switzerland.

He walked a lot, exploring and taking in the views of the lakeshore town, when he was eventually noticed and taken in by people who treated him with great honor and respect. It was then that he began visualizing the ideas of the Sufi Movement infrastructure. Eventually, the Sufi Movement headquarters were officially established in Geneva. Murshid's connection to Switzerland became stronger in the 1920s, when an ever increasing number of followers flocked to him throughout the country, among them some wealthy and powerful people. He ended up giving a number of talks in various Swiss towns and even being invited to dinner once by Paderewsky who, after the other dinner guests had left, treated Inayat to a private concert in his home.

On this first, improvised visit in June 1914, an amusing note was sent to him by his wife, always concerned for his person and his well-being and which underlined his human dimension:

> *My Love,*
>
> *I am wondering how you are today and if you intend coming home. My precious, how I miss you, words cannot tell you. I know you must be suffering much, being alone and no one to help you and so much walking to do. I hope you will never go away alone again my love. Do write me a letter every day, I am always longing for your letters. I see nothing but clouds when you are away, my own… My precious take good care of your pin, ring, etc. as it would be so bad to lose them. And in case you send your soiled clothes to the laundry be sure to get them before leaving Geneva, do not leave them behind as they are your best clothes… Good-bye dear heart, take good care of yourself and write (Sharda) all about yourself… Always your most faithful (Sharda).*

To which he briefly replied by telegram: "Quite well. Murshid."

Part Two: Four Rubies in the Sufi Garden, 1914–1927

WAR OF PAPER

Claire Harper: London served as an oasis—as well as a source of challenge—to the family until the First World War ended. Noor was destined to celebrate her New Year's Day birthday five times in the havoc of war. Could this have been a preparation, an initiation? Of her thirty New Year's Day birthdays, how many were going to be spent alone on battlefields?

During the war years from 1914 to 1918, the family lived first in Ladbroke Road and later Addison Road. Poverty was the order of the day, and living meant a constant battle for survival. Members of the Sufi organization would come and go; however, not many knew the real truth about the family's conditions. Noor, our mother, father and uncles experienced the sting of want.

Having left Russia, though, Noor was relieved of the treatment she had received there from the Tartar wet nurse: a daily dose of black coffee, a harsh brushing of the body and a tight band tied around her feet. At last she could relax into a feeling of freedom. Day and night, Noor heard the horrifying sound of zeppelins overhead and bombs dropping in the neighborhood. Though she received a great deal of love from her parents, this made for an unstable life, especially for sensitive little Noor. Meals were scanty: dividing and sharing a loaf of bread was often the daily diet. At times, the offering was rice and dhal (lentils). There was next to no supply of milk or dairy food. Drinking water came out of lead pipes, the only means of refreshment.

At that time, traveling was suspended until the end of the war. Murshid and his brothers attempted to play at universities or at art and music festivals. In 1915 they worked for Richard Wagner & Co, an "International Theatrical & Musical Agency" that secured them an occasional venue. In 1916 they performed at the London Opera House in Kingsway, on the occasion of a season of Russian and French Opera, in this case for a series of performances of Leo Delibes' Opera *Lakme*. Besides this, the members of the Sufi Movement eventually realized the situation and gave whatever they could. Vilayat's birth was expected while the sounds of bugles, drums and soldiers' marching steps could be heard on London's streets; there were no radios in those days to inform one of the surrounding chaos.

Claire Harper: However, there was a faithful and angelic young lady who was devoted to our father and his mission, Raden Ayou Jodjana. Her love for the family grew deeper each day and, with this to hold on to, she became a gifted musician and a spiritual teacher. In the home she performed wonders as well. Out of sheer affection, Raden ran the household from morning till night and received the Sufi followers when music recitals and lectures took place. Not a better person could have accomplished her task so discreetly—she was the blessing from above for the little family. As she moved about each day, the family could not help but notice Raden's use of 'magic wands." The enchantment that surrounded her would one day bring about her marriage with a prince from Java. Raden Ayou sums up life at our parents' home in her memoirs:

> *Inayat Khan, my Guru, foretold my future meeting with another being with whom I was to enter the path of destiny. He told me exactly the sign that would be given to me, and to that other human being. It was a symbol of seven crowns with seven stars.*
>
> *It was in Ladbroke Road in London that I came to Inayat Khan for the first music lesson. I entered the room with a book and pencil. He asked why I brought that book and pencil. And when I said that I wished to take notes of all he was going to teach me, he seemed amazed and said: 'Have you not received the gift of memory? Learn to listen well to all I am going to teach you. Let it enter and impress you. Then you will forget to 'remember.' What will be forever stored in your memory must for some time stay in oblivion, until it can serve you in creative expression at a certain moment. Only what you need to remember in the moment should mount in the consciousness of the brain. Never come to me with a book and pencil.*
>
> *One should not use crutches on the path to Being. When you are with me, dive deep within yourself. Try to become at-one with that all-pervading, Infinite Being. That you may live to know the end of separation.'*

Inayat Khan was the head of a family group stranded in London when the First World War broke out, without any means of a livelihood. The group of adepts in London began to lay down restraining rules for those becoming members of their circle. They fixed a contribution, imposing the responsibility of paying for housing the centre, sheltering Inayat Khan's family, and assuring their livelihood.

In the intimate circle of Inayat Khan's family in Addison Road, we formed the first group in England of initiated adepts. Begum, his young wife, and I were the only women in this circle. Inayat Khan taught us all to master emotional states causing reactions in conduct and expression. And he submitted all of us to severe tests. Maheboob was the most advanced murid. He showed me the way to listen towards within for the answer to the problems we met in daily life. Mohammed never arrived at mastering his emotions. Inayat was very severe with him. He came to the West too young, and was never able to cope with the experience of intimate contact with a people so different from his own.

The other murids giving me little attention treated me as the servant of the family. Inayat Khan often left the house in order to avoid meeting the always intruding murids. He made me answer the door. I trained myself to meet them understanding their Western outlook and conduct. In Ladbroke Road no one ever came to the top floor where the family wished its privacy to be respected. Inayat lived in the front room with his wife and child. The three 'boys' (Murshid's brothers and cousin) stayed in the back room with a view on the garden. I had to clean the rooms, took out the child, as Begum no longer went out in the world. She started to live in Purdah. The 'boys' never entered the front room. I was the only person to serve Inayat and his wife in their room.

Within the family circle of Inayat Khan there was no 'talk.' Silence was a very expressive and necessary state in order to listen towards within, and to cultivate inner silence.

Raden Ayou Jodjana (Kurshid)

Claire Harper: The month of June announced relief after the spring's heavy rains, bringing flowers and birdsong, and affording solace to all the sufferers of the cruel war—thus a measure of peace. No one knew when the war would come to an end and wished it would immediately—and forever. However, the sun illuminated the world and every soul's hope. The true cause of the war was anger, resulting in sorrow and dismay to the innocent.

Birth of Vilayat

Claire Harper: On June 19th, 1916, Vilayat (affectionately known as Baijan, meaning big brother) was born under the challenge of an uncertain future. A baby boy spirited to a high pitch, he blessed the universe with his presence on earth. Hallowed to his parents, he aspired to the promise of Love, Harmony and Beauty, awareness, courage and hope.

Noor was delighted to hug her new brother. She was surprised and elated over his magical arrival! He was his parents' pride, and Noor's as well. She would await his awakening and lovingly caress him while watching his eyes beam. Vilayat manifested a spiritual beauty. Noor would smile and whisper to her little brother in baby talk. She was happy to find a new friend, asking Mother and Father lots of questions, such as "how and where did he come from?" She treated him delicately, like a fragile flower, watching him at every moment of his wakefulness. She was speechless in her wonderment, bewildered and comforted by his close presence. A most blissful companion was he.

Yet the loud sounds of war were still in vigor, disturbing the peaceful rhythm of life. Especially as poverty lingered, having found its habitation on the empty shelves, there was no foreseeable solution to this traumatic state.

So different a setting was this from Murshid's vocation in India; he constantly made efforts to give concerts and talks, but these seldom happened. Murshid surely thought about his childhood at the feet of his grandfather, Maula Bakhsh, who had entertained numerous musicians each evening. Long ago were the performances before the Maharajas in their splendor. Far away were the days when concerts were rewarded with gold medals. In another life, it seemed, were the days when finances were abundant enough so as not to have to think of them. Concurrently, Ora Ray's America had been on par with Inayat's India.

Claire Harper: The war dragged on; no one could predict the end of it, and hunger followed its course. When going out, Mother felt somewhat inhibited; she felt conspicuous wearing a sari and veil, yet safe from passersby. A western lady dressed in Indian clothes attracted attention. Though she must have looked radiant, Mother disliked being noticed.

Often enough, Sufi meetings were held within the walls of Murshid's small room, where many people attended. Some were monks, and many regarded his work from their own point of view, considering it their mission to teach Inayat. Others were simply curious; few were those who could appreciate the beauty of Murshid's Message of Love, Harmony and Beauty.

Finally, the family moved to Addison Road. The scene changed, and here there were rules to be strictly observed. Lovely lady Raden Ayen Jodjana seemed to assume the role of messenger and enforced silence as the house rule. The doors were kept closed, and Raden guarded the entrance to the house. Meetings were followed by plays and, after some interviews, music was played. It was at this time that Miss Goodenough and Miss Williams were initiated.

In the new house there was no family life, the atmosphere was confined, sad and bleak. The seasons passed by, behind closed doors; questions remained unanswered.

Birth of Hidayat

Claire Harper: Another fairytale was soon told: "Once upon a time, on a hot summer's morning, a third little being stepped into the family circle, finding its way into Amma's arms." On August 6th, 1917, a baby brother chose to join the family. Vilayat enjoyed the idea of there being more children at home; his Abba and Amma blessed the newcomer with the name Hidayat, meaning guide and, affectionately, Baiyajan, little brother.

As for war, only time would right the wrong. In Ladbroke Road the fastest way to muster courage was by looking at the small garden, so eager to survive the ill-fated war.

Murshid referred to the First World War as the "war of paper, blazing brightly, yet burning out swiftly like paper." He also said: "The Second World War will be one of wood, and the Third World War will be one of coal." This was, and remains, a warning for those who monger war. If one learns something from it, only then can one derive a benefit. If one has learnt nothing from an episode, then all is lost.

Claire Harper: Days came and went with just a few wooden blocks and some books to amuse and busy the children. The house at Ladbroke Road was as shabby inside as it was outside, although the children were happy to have a roof over their heads; so many had fared less well during the war years.

Each fruit of summer was a festival and made for a celebration. Smiles were passed around by the hungry family. Sufi adepts now often shared their meager prosperity with the family. Gratitude abounded inexplicably. Noor was nearly five, Vilayat turned two and Hidayat was barely one. Children's sounds could be heard in a romping and play corner. Summer packed up for another year, opening the gates for autumn to enter. The gifts that autumn brought arrived just in time to fill the barren shelves. They were packed during the harvest season with a store of nuts, apples, legumes and preserves. As the shops stocked their supplies for winter, it was jam-making time and there was much to do. All of England was eager to stock up. The instinct of survival was much at play.

Schoolchildren ran along the streets, picking up horse chestnuts. Cold wind blew in circles, making the golden leaves fall and dance on the wet streets. The fallen leaves resembled the palette of an inspired artist. Autumn became a major event; colored carpets spread in gardens and on pathways.

One day Noor asked her Amma for a baby sister. Mother took Noor in her arms and said: "Yes, you will have a baby sister, but you will have to wait. Do not tell the secret to anyone." "I won't," she promised.

Soon after, a lady came to visit and, in her intense excitement, Noor could not help divulging her secret to the lady. Ora Ray heard Noor's secret revealed out loud to the lady. She had forgotten not to say it and she was in a quandary about what to do. Crying bitterly, Noor was frightened that her telling would obliterate the happening. What to do? She asked her mother. Mother told her to ask the lady to forget—which she promptly said she would—and the great worry was over. Noor's tears dried instantly.

During the month of November, there were rumors of the disdainful war coming to an end. November 11th was the decisive date. The first agreements were signed, the return of peace was declared. It was hard to believe, to comprehend, but it was happening, truly right then and there. That day it was also raining buckets, cleaning away the past. The roar of zeppelins could still be heard here and there. The rush into the cold and cobwebby damp cellar for nights on end was over. The country was in mourning! Rather than victory flags being hoisted with shouts, there was a feeling of relief, a chance to start living normally. All were astonished at this unforeseen armistice, however, and could barely dare to believe that it was here for keeps!

At last everyone could breathe easy again and set about their plans, after all the setbacks and denials. On the streets one saw tears on the cheeks of those who had lost dear ones within their own families and circles of friends. Joy was not standing so upright. To the onlooker, consolation was hard to express. Starvation took a back seat. The children needed time to gaze—once in a while—at empty blue skies void of threatening planes. The pale sun warmed heads and hearts.

Murshid again did the rounds to find concert or lecture halls for the spreading of the Message. His brothers and cousin accompanied him. Success was around the corner. People needed consolation more than food. This they found by listening to music. Murshid and his family could now eat nearly the same as what they had been accustomed to, and the children could exercise their little legs outdoors. Life was blessing them with a sense of freedom. They could not explain it but it showed in their mannerisms. The little ones were busy invading the world with freedom.

Noor's birthday was on New Year's Day. She turned five years old. There was a cake and candles; her little face cheered as she opened a real birthday present with lots of kisses and love. She took her gift with her to bed and slept the whole night through. She was a little sleepwalker and would open doors. For this reason she had to be closely watched by her parents at night.

Birth of Khair-un-nisa

Claire Harper: Spring approached on padded feet, showing signs of nature's budding wealth. As life can be like a jigsaw puzzle, we each had a place in the picture. The family's identity was all there, save a piece of rosebush. The French say that girls come into the world from rosebushes. This little baby girl, Khair-un-nisa, was blessed by the family tree; lovingly known as Mamuli (mother's child), she weighed close to 10 pounds and stared at her Amma through bright eyes. All the children watched her, tucked into her mother's embrace on June 3rd, 1919.

Noor had a lot to say until feeding time. She was so happy that her secret dream had come true that she jumped around the room, finally banging her head under the table.

Mother and Father prayed to the Almighty for blessings from above. Amma was frail and undernourished. Each birth had required either a Caesarian or a great many stitches. Abba was drained and thoroughly depleted. In those days, patients subject to hospital care were without medicine to alleviate the pains and discomforts.

Fortunately, though, Mother and Father were together, to solve the demands of the hour. Abba and his two brothers were always able to obtain some funds designed to purchase food. Everyone had their part to play, from the oldest to the youngest. During this unforeseen display of circumstances, each one tried their utmost to help. The devoted adepts had been angels on earth, despite their own problems, which were often hard to bear. The Sufi spirit was very much present. The mutual rhythm of each one, in time, gave peace.

Though tranquility had returned to everyone's lives following World War I, there was unrest in India. The centuries of British rule and colonization were no longer viewed by all as acceptable and desirable in the long run. Self-rule and independence were increasingly becoming the bywords of the times in India. Great Britain viewed with suspicion any Indian who commanded a following, be it spiritual, intellectual or political. At this unstable time, any prominent Indian was closely monitored for fear he might influence others in the cause of freedom—viewed by Great Britain as conspiracy against the existing law and order.

Inayat's brother Shaikh-ul-Masheik Maheboob recounted the following amusing and revealing incident:

> *During the war of 1914–18 Murshid lived in London. He used to spend hours in his room meditating in the evenings. Somehow Murshid drew the attention of the police, who wanted to know what this Indian was up to in these days of war.*
>
> *One evening there was a ring at his house. Two policemen told Musharaff Khan, who answered the door, that they wanted to search Murshid's room. Musharraff Khan said this was impossible, for on no account did he want to disturb Murshid in his meditations. This, however, made the case even more suspicious, and the policemen said they must be shown into the room.*
>
> *At his wit's end, Musharaff knocked long at Murshid's door, and in the meantime the policemen grew more and more suspicious.*

At last Musharaff entered Murshid's room, apologized greatly for having to disturb him, and told about the policemen. "Let them come in," Murshid said, rising to his full height.

When the policemen came in and saw Murshid's great majesty and felt the wonderful atmosphere of the room in which Murshid had meditated all that time, the expression on their faces changed completely. They just looked about the room, as was their duty, then went to Murshid, One of then said, Master, forgive us; we had our orders." They bowed their heads to him, and Murshid laid his hands upon their heads and blessed them. Then they kissed Murshid's hand and left, full of reverence and deeply impressed.

It was often intimated that Murshid was not only investigated by the police but even spied upon through agents posing as followers. It is believed that the family's departure from England was due to the pressure and confined feeling that these investigations had created for him, thus constraining his freedom of action and speech.

A friend of the family's, Lord Lamington, who had for several years been governor of Bombay, confided to Murshid: "In order to really succeed in England, one must do work quietly." [A] It would appear that the confined atmosphere in which Inayat now found himself was becoming too restrictive to carry out the work he was planning.

FRANCE

Moving to the Paris Region

Claire Harper: The question of leaving England, possibly traveling to France, arose. Need pointed to possible solutions. Murshid had met with several lovely people who were more than willing to assist in spreading the Message. From late 1920 on, our family's first residence was at Le Tremblay-sur-Mauldre, about 20 miles west of Paris, just past Versailles.

Later, there was a small house in Wissous, just southeast of Paris, which was available and in which we stayed for about a year. Vilayat remembered it to be most dilapidated and without heating.

During that time, our father and his brothers traveled to Belgium and Holland where Murshid made the acquaintance of a Dutch lady called Mevrouw Egeling, a former Theosophist. When initiating her, he gave her the name Fazal Mai, which signifies Grace of God. At the Theosophical Society in Holland, Murshid, his brothers and cousin played their beautiful music, after which he gave a lecture that was very well received.

One of the constant angels, Princess Raden Ayou Jodjana, organized numerous meetings in Holland. This was quite a challenge for her to do but Murshid received much acclaim. The papers and reviews accumulated letters of appreciation. People spoke with great recognition of the perfect interpretation of "Professor Inayat Khan."

Time moved on with challenges and rewards that Murshid never expected. Sacrifice was added to these wonders; there is no saying how hard Murshid worked day and night for the spreading of the Message, along with his wife and children. Being constantly low on funds was a contrast to his home in India. He had grown up in Maula Bakhsh's House, at which time the family was never without financial ease; in fact, he had come from a background of prosperity that could be traced back throughout several generations.

The Val d'Or

Claire Harper: The kings at the Chateau de Versailles traveled to Paris regularly in four-horse carriages, stopping en route at the Val d'Or in Suresnes to water the horses at the beneficial springs. Later, this spot came to be known as Croix du Roi (Crossroads of the King) and is but a stone's throw from our home, Fazal Manzil. In fact, it is said that the underground spring of healing water, known as Source Sainte Genevieve, runs directly under Fazal Manzil. As for the name Val d'Or (Golden Vale), Nostradamus writes, "There will stand a great mystic at the Val d'Or. He will breathe from the magnetism of the area." Murshid confirmed that this spot held much magnetism. Murshid referred to the location of Fazal Manzil in Suresnes as the Urs, a place of pilgrimage.

In the West, our father moved throughout a number of countries, always returning to his base in Suresnes, France, happy to be reunited with his Begum and his "Rubies Four." He made his world twirl vivaciously by adhering to the laws of the universe.

Fazal Manzil

Claire Harper: Thanks to Murshida Fazal Mai, the house—later named Fazal Manzil, or House of Blessing—was purchased in 1921, and our family moved there in 1922. The upstairs rooms, on the top floor, were smaller than those of the main floor, each an average of around 300 square feet. They had been planned as children's rooms. There was no kitchen, nor bathroom facilities on that floor, with the exception of a small toilet. The task of deciding upon the use of these sundry rooms was no doubt the responsibility of our parents and of Murshida Fazal Mai. The use of each room was decided after our uncles' subsequent departure from Fazal Manzil. Until then, they had occupied the front center room of the top floor, as well as a side room at the back.

Our parents occupied the front corner room on the top floor. From there, a small passage led into the next front center room, as well as a door leading into the hall. This little passage was no larger than a meter square. Later it became a closet.

The two boys occupied a room at the back, and we girls were allocated the middle room. There was no matching furniture; we had enough beds, but they were all odd and probably came from friends or adjoining houses. They were simple and unobtrusive, except for a typical old-fashioned wooden couch-bed with rounded headboards at each end which could easily be converted into a couch in the daytime. It was exceptionally high and a little hard to climb onto, but whenever any of us was sick, we would be placed in that bed because it was the most comfortable. I remember once, I read Robert Louis Stevenson's poem about the soldier on the counterpane, and I imagined that there were soldiers all over the bumps, hills and valleys of the bed.

Sometimes we were all sick at the same time, as we contracted the usual contagious diseases that children get. We often suffered from an upset stomach, which was a great ordeal for our poor mother. But once I had scarlet fever and I was the only one to have it. For this reason I was quarantined in one of the rooms, and nobody could enter except my mother. I remember that very well, because my mother tried to make me as comfortable as possible. I don't remember having suffered or having had a bad time. I just remember the comforts and I felt isolated from my brothers and sister, and I just wished to be well again quickly. When I recovered, the room was fumigated, as was the custom in those days. They used to fumigate with some sort of disinfectant which was burned in the room; this was done quite often on different occasions.

Before long, by 1923, our parents had a bedroom set: a large cupboard in bird's-eye maple, with a large beveled mirror. It was most elegant and inlaid with borders of another wood. It was enhanced with brass handles and flowery brass decorations above the mirror. I can still remember the squeaking of its doors. Standing upon the golden oak parquet floor, the matching furniture gave an overall impression of warm sunlight. The walls were papered with light yellow and white stripes, no doubt the suggestion of the old-fashioned painter who had chosen a pale yellow for the windows. There was only one window in that room, making it rather dark as that corner of the house never saw the morning or the afternoon sun—only the evening sun as it was fading.

The room that Noor and I shared was simply called "the girls' room." There was great excitement when our mother gathered us together around the table to choose new wallpaper. Neither of us had ever seen—let alone handled—a huge book of wallpaper samples. It was quite voluminous and stunning; turning each page made for a lot of excitement. There were so many colors, patterns, each more beautiful than the other, it seemed; such a medley of choices! Our mother favored red. The red in those days was not bright and gaudy; after a lot of exchanged opinions, our mother chose a deep old rose in two shades. One leaf was old rose, and the other leaf leaned towards a burgundy red. The two shades complemented each other, creating a sort of relief effect. The leaves were outlined with gold, with tiny gold berries joining their stems. The paper had a velvety texture, lending the wall a peaceful play of colors. The window and the door were painted a pastel to subtly match. My sister and I were very happy and we tried hard to keep the room tidy so the wallpaper would show up even more.

Then another big surprise filled our room—and our lives. It was a bedroom set in mahogany, a lovely, dark red, shiny wood. The bed had a very nice headboard and it came with a night table and a large wardrobe with a large mirror. The set filled the room; there was very little space to walk, but it was beautiful and extremely cozy. There was still a small corner for my desk, which was coral surrounded with white flowers, plus a bench.

For a long time Noor and I were hypnotized by this luxury. The lush mattress was such a contrast to the old metal cots with their thin horsehair mattresses, which we had hitherto been accustomed to. On weekends, I had a hard time waking up, and Noor would sing a song from some opera. Her voice was so sweet, clear and high that I would pretend to be sleeping just so that she would continue singing.

Of course those precious times were exceptional. We were usually up early; if not, one of us would be sprinkled with water on our face. But from the early school days on, we always rose by six—our mother earlier, of course, at five; lights were on at five.

The mantelpiece in the Oriental Room was made of white marble, the same as in the salon. Above it hung a large mirror, reaching up to the ceiling. It reflected the light from both windows and gave the room a feeling of expanse and depth. In our father's time, the walls were painted yellow, while featuring molded panels in the French regal style. Originally the Oriental Room was meant to be the master bedroom for the first owner and his wife, overlooking the green span of the Bois de Boulogne and the Eiffel Tower. The other windows gave onto the grand entrance steps. At the far end of the room, a door led to the dressing room and, from there, on into the bathroom. Of course, that door was blocked for practical reasons.

Much of the furniture in Fazal Manzil had been purchased in Paris. Our mother thought there weren't enough chairs to accommodate all the mureeds who gathered to listen to Murshid's teachings. There was a show in Paris called "The Colonial Exhibition," if I remember well. My mother asked us to go there and see if we could find some Oriental furniture, which we did. We found Moroccan furniture and we bought chairs and a small table with a brass top, and poufs—low leather cushions—and other coverings such as an embroidered blanket which could be draped over the screens or the couch. The couch was really a bed, a three-quarter sofa with pillows all around and cushions with Oriental designs. It was meant to be the bed of the duke and his wife. However, the tragic fate of this duke who had commissioned the construction of the house put a sudden stop to everything.

Fazal Manzil was meant to be a home, a family house, the home of our father and his family. But it never really proved to be that way; we never knew privacy. Household management was fragile, and we all had to rely on funding in a complicated way. If our father or any of us needed clothes or other necessities, a request had to be put in so that Murshida Fazal Mai could budget these different items into columns. We had been brought up to live frugally; it was not a matter of being rationed. Nonetheless, we sometimes felt the restraints of dependency

One has to bear in mind, however, that when the family first settled in Fazal Manzil, our three uncles lived in the house as well, which meant that a lot more funds were needed. Who was going to determine the amount of purchasing of anything for any particular family member, from food to clothes to furniture? All the necessities for running the household were, in fact, reckoned by my mother. But when everything was added together, quite understandably, it seemed like a large sum to Murshida Fazal Mai.

When she had lived in Holland, her livelihood was taken care of, because she was from a wealthy background and, perhaps, had little idea of budgets of this measure. But then, neither did our mother. She would never touch money. She didn't have to touch money while she was in America as a young lady. Financial planning and distribution within the household proved to be quite a challenge. It took a while to find out how much food was needed and to what extent material things were necessary in our everyday lives.

Our father had to travel extensively. His program was heavy during the winter and he visited many places. This, too, had to be financed, and I believe it was the Sufi Movement Headquarters in Geneva that approved the expenditures of Murshid's winter programs.

When our mother married our father, she didn't realize or expect that she would be responsible for taking care of his three relatives as well. They felt no need to help her in any way but would spend hours talking together about old times in India, and they'd sing the songs that they were used to singing over there. They would discuss religion, as well as the Sufi Message and the ideals they aspired to at that time. They had no clue as to organizational or household needs. Mother was especially delicate and did not have a background of housekeeping or subservience. It must have been somewhat horrifying to her to be faced with this situation. I don't know how our father thought out a solution, but very soon his brother Piaromia Maheboob Khan met Shadi, the daughter of Ekbal Dawlat van Goens, a lovely lady of French descent who was most enthusiastic about the Sufi Message. Ekbal decided to build a house on the same street as Fazal Manzil and offer it to her daughter Shadi as a dowry for her marriage to Maheboob Khan. Prior to this, Ekbal Dawlat had become good friends with my mother. This friendship continued all Mother's life.

Before too long, Maheboob Khan was living in the new house with his wife, as well as with Ekbal Dawlat in the summer. In the winter, the family would go to Holland, where she already owned two adjoining houses in the Hague. Our uncles always stayed together; they were inseparable, so she agreed to take them under her wing. Also Ekbal was a widow but was always laughing, most pleasant and very happy. I think she enjoyed the company of the uncles. I must say they were entertaining, and this was very new for her: all this Oriental music, day and night, and people speaking exotic languages. I am sure the conversations they had about India and other places must have been quite fascinating to hear. So that's how life worked out for some time, until the pattern of life changed.

On the occasion of her mother's birthday in 1922, Noor, who was eight years old, wrote the following poem on behalf of the four children (the original spelling and punctuation have been respected):

8 mai

Dear Ammah,

I wich you a very happy birthday today I wich a did not need to go to school today because it is your birthday and if we could all go out today to celebrate your birthday to go to Bois-de-boulogne. But it is the gimnastic lesson and sowing lesson especially on your birthday

Love from the fore children
Good health
Long life
Right guidence from above
Prosperity
Succes
Happenesse
And love

Likewise, that same year on July 5th, Noor wrote on behalf of her siblings and herself:

My dear Abba,

We all wich you the happiest birthday possible today and we offer you this little vase which we have spent all our money gladly, for your birthday and we hope you will keep it always in your room in remembrace of your four naughty little children Noorunissa, Kharunissa, Villayat and Hidayat

Under the Kerosene Oil Lamps

Claire Harper: At the stroke of midnight, four little children—Murshid's "Rubies Four"—tiptoed down the massive oak staircase in Fazal Manzil, towards the half-open door of the Oriental Room, where their sweet mother waited to receive them. She wore a fine, light blue, silver-bordered sari, and her complexion glowed rosy; she was simply radiant.

Quietly we entered, one by one. Our father, clothed in an apricot-colored gown, stood very still by a large, blue-green Christmas tree. It was aglow with flickering lights and crowned with an equally bright star that nearly touched the high stucco ceiling.

We all gazed in wonderment! The decorations were so profuse that we did not know where to look first. A multitude of tiny candles, whose twinkling flames pointed to the heavens, whispered tales of Christmas. A tiny glittering treasure had been placed upon each branch; there were fairies, deer, baskets, bells, and cherubs with exquisitely painted faces, as well as numerous other figurines in pastel shades and trimmed with silver and gold. The tree was incandescent with light and it shimmered like transparent crystal. Time stood still.

Had Heaven descended upon earth to offer us this gift? Were we learning the first letters of the meaning of sacredness? Not only did the candles' light emit radiance within and about the entire tree, but it emanated joy. We remained speechless.

This Christmas was one of few where our Amma and Abba were together. In the spirit of Love, Harmony and Beauty, they had presented us children four with a wondrous surprise, announcing that Baby Jesus was born in a Manger. We were delighted that something good was happening, and we also wondered whether Santa Claus had perhaps filled our stockings that hung on the mantelpiece.

In the stillness of the night, before we awoke from this fairyland dream, we leaped up the staircase under the kerosene oil lamps, with starry lights going round and round in our heads.

Letters to Santa Claus:

Santa-Claus do come to me
In your mantle white and red
Down the chimney come and see
Little me, just tucked in bed.

[written by Noor]

My dear Santa-Claus,

I would like a toy motor that I can sit in for Christmas. Everyone in Fazal Manzil believes in you but Bey [note: Bayjan, Vilayat]

Love And kisses from Hidayat

Please do not come through the central heating chimney if not you fall in the fire

My dear santa-clauss,

I would please like a bycyle an Italian one like leonardo's and one for everyone in Fazal-Manzil and for the family Maheboob and I would like a violin also please. And a little piano only for me and an eareoplane and des sabots de salieres.

Love and kisses from Vilayat Khan

And will you please go to tinhouse to our neibourghs

Dear Santa-Clauss

I hope you are well I would like a little bycyle and a new pram and a big doll and a motor car that I can sit in and Bhayajan [note: Hidayat] *is naughty*

[written by Claire]

My dear Santa Clauss—I would like to see you at Christmas. I wuld like a toy motor that I can sit in and I won't break it and it must have pebbles just like the one I had before and I thank you for the things you brought last year

Love and kisses from HIDAYAt

A dear old man is Santa Claus
Of course we all love him
He comes and brings, such pretty things
And charges nothing, nothing.

Dear Santa Claus,

I need a little writing desk and I would appreciate it more than any toy.

Love and kisses from Mamulie [note: Claire] *is a funny girl*

Dear old Santa-Clauss,

We can never thank you enough for all your interest for little children how happy we are when Christmas comes. There is a little boy in Italie who does not believe in you but I have made him believe you so will you please go to his house 4 Porta-Pinciano Roma his name is Leonardo. And there are two little children Emile and Olivier who live in the little house just near our house will you please go there if they are there at Christmas

And there will be in Suresnes a big Christmas tree for the poor children will you please go there in the Mairie [note: town hall]

With all the love from Babulie [note: Noor]

Would you please come and see us on Christmas like in England

Murshid's wishes

In 1921, our father wrote to two of his mureeds the following wedding wish:

May my best wishes reach you
On your wedding day.
May your life be happy
From my heart I pray.

For the birth of a mureed's child he wrote:

Welcome the son
My little sun-shine.
Bring to the earth
Some light Devine.
Eric Inayat
Edward is he.
May he live long
And, successful be.

With hearty blessings
Murshid 30 Oct. 21

About this time he also jotted down (spelling left original):

Don't forget my little familly
If you Kindly for me pray.
God bless you and your dear ones
And protect you night and day.

TRAVELS

Claire Harper: From 1922 on, I remember a near constant absence in our home. Our father traveled most of the year, giving lectures throughout Europe and America. The void created by his absence was painful to our mother. Father dedicated her this poem on her birthday:

At all my busy hours in life,
Everything I do,
You are only my consolation,
And I think of you.
My work keeps me away from home
But I leave my heart,
At home, to be ever with you,
Our souls can never part.
Happiness be with our little ones,
Right guidance from above,
I wish good luck in this house,
And my deepest love.
Prosperity and success,
Long life and good health,
May be yours always Sharda
My treasure, my wealth.
With a world of love

Mari Calleja on your birthday
from your own
1922

Most everywhere he went, Murshid met beautiful people who helped him in his travels and work. Whilst away from home, our father kept in constant communication with our mother by letter. One day he sent her the following poem:

Be not anxious my Sharda,
On his service I must go,
Though parting is hard to bear,
But it's God who meant it so.
I'll carry you in my heart,
Where ever in the world I roam.
His protection is over us,
Rest in peace soon I will come.

Cherbourg, 14 Feb. 1923

Eventually a secretary or organizer accompanied him constantly, in particular Sirkar van Stolk or Kismet Stam. Sirkar reported how, on a long train journey through Italy, he was feeling somewhat sorry for himself through the weariness of travel. He recounts the following educational experience:

That evening the sun set beautifully, and the Italian scenery we passed through was marvellous, but I did not see anything. Murshid said to me, "Look at that wonderful sunset! If the sun appeared to people only once in a thousand years, innumerable thick books would be written about the phenomenon of the sun, and people who lived then would be envied by the others who would not be able to see it. But we, who are able to see the sun every day, don't appreciate it and are not grateful for it."'

And then Murshid said: "You must consider that the mere fact of being allowed to be on earth is an extraordinary opportunity for a human being to develop spiritually. We cannot be grateful enough, if only for this fact. We are not grateful for all the things that even the poorest among us receive daily, because we think we have a right to them. You must understand that when we come on this earth we haven't a right to anything. There are millions of souls waiting for the privilege of being allowed to incarnate on earth. For life on earth is an incredible chance to develop. We cannot be thankful enough for what every man daily receives. For it is all given to us."

And, yet, Murshid was not exempt from the constant demands made of him. Weariness occasionally weighed upon him as well. On February 5th, 1924—oddly enough exactly three years to the day prior to his passing—he wrote to his wife:

5th Feb. 1924

My Mari Calleja

It is most difficult to bear the responsibility as I do and to pay due attention to everybody at all sides and yet keep ones balance. I am getting quite tired of this world.

With all the love there is,
(Inayat)

Murshid made two more trips to the United States: one in 1923, the second one in late 1925. Within a two-week period in April, 1923, Murshid wrote four letters to his wife from San Francisco. He was visiting his very first mureed, Murshida Rabia Martin at the Sufi Order School of Philosophy and Metaphysics at 153 Kearny Street. After over ten years of absence from the United States, he was trying to reestablish interest in the Message. Several comments are of interest:

My difficulty here is that I do not know for some reason or the other Mrs. Martin is not popular here. Maybe that it is a race prejudice or that there is a spirit of jealousy and rivalry… Perhaps I expect more than what should be anticipated, still I cannot help it, I cannot be pleased with small success… No doubt my visit has given a new life to Sufi Movement in America and now I am sure it will grow. (April 16, 1923)

I had another treatment of the dentist… just now I am living on ice cream only and iced soup and ice coffee… have you ever heard of such a thing?... The progress of the Message here is not made in a sensational way and I am glad about it for this slow process may keep it alive and give it continuity. Now I have learned many American words and phrases and when I come home with my added accomplishment you will all be so surprised to see the change. I feel America was the place for work, not France: don't tell Budhi (Fazal Mai), she won't like it. You don't like it too. But I love America perhaps because I love you. (April 21, 1923)

I am beginning to realize that a sensational success perhaps won't be so good for the cause but this way as I am interesting people who are more serious, perhaps will work out to be for the best in the end. (April 25, 1923)

Repeatedly Murshid expresses concern regarding Begum's health. She had been suffering from tiredness and shortness of breath. He also reprimands her for working too hard and not allowing herself time to rest and recover. Several excerpts emphasize this:

I hope you follow the medical advice every (day) without fail and breathing. (April 16, 1923)

My soul, I am so glad now that you have a cook and a nurse for the children. I hope you will take the needed rest and the treatment which I sent in that prescription. Mari, I am so anxious about your health and you cannot help me better than taking good care of your self. (April 21, 1923)

I received your letter, my soul, and was afraid you will use that nurse for pressing clothes or doing some thing other than helping you to relieve you of your work that keeps you on your feet. I am realizing now every day that if we had a hundred servants to help, still you would work just the same, for work is your disease. It is most unfortunate that you ignore my advice and neglect your health… It is my devotion for you which make me so uncomfortable and anxious for your state of health… (April 28, 1923)

Throughout 1923 and 1924, Murshid repeatedly urges his wife to listen to his suggestion for improving her health:

Are you eating malt! The milk, wine and egg! (January 20, 1924)

Please continue all things to take which I am so anxious for you to take. (January 31, 1924)

It was in 1926, during the course of a long lecture tour, that Murshid met the automobile tycoon, Henry Ford. In true journalistic fashion, the Detroit headlines read: "A Magnate and a Mystic Meet." The two leaders compared notes on various topics ranging from meditation, music, the soul and God. "Murshid Khan," Mr. Ford said, "I think you are preaching a gospel that men of all faiths can understand. No matter what form it takes in doctrine, it is the thing Americans need." At the end of their warm meeting and exchange of viewpoints, Henry Ford said: "I agree with you." Upon which Murshid retorted, "And I agree with you." (A)

On that trip, as well, he confided to his wife that he sometimes felt alone and overwhelmed:

7 Jan. 1925

(the Waldorf-Astoria, New York)

Mari my Calleja,

… you must know that your favourable attitude would help me immensely to carry my burden which at present is too heavy for my strength. I told you before leaving that I did not feel up to it. However let us see how it works out.

(Inayat) with all love

In the aftermath of Murshid's meeting with Henry Ford, he received a Model T Ford as a gift from his friend, the industrial tycoon. In fact, he discreetly took driving lessons in Paris in order to obtain a license for his new car. On his travels he wrote on two occasions that: "Ali Khan should learn to drive the motor car in and out of the garage and keep it watered and oiled."

A few months later Murshid suffered from a bad abscess due to his teeth. He wrote his wife the following verses:

To my Sharda,
As pure as the water,
Of a gentle stream,

As near and as dear,
As milk and cream,
As sweet as the honey comb,
As sacred as the church of Rome,
As pretty as the flower,
Of Lover's dream.

Written in bed
April 1925

Sometimes Murshid revealed a humorous side, as well. Ending a letter to his wife he wrote:

Give my love to my brothers, also keep some for yourself.

Claire Harper: We children and, of course, our dear mother, were always thrilled when our father returned home. At last, life returned to normal.

My prayers arose as burning incense and entered into the sky. In Heaven they all had great ecstasy. Thoughts were moved to cry. The Lord awoke from His deep slumber and said, I will grant you all you ask. Humbly lowering my head to the ground I said, God make easy my task.

With hearty blessings
Inayat Khan

MEMORIES OF MUREEDS

Murshida Fazal Mai

Claire Harper: The story of Murshida Fazal Mai is intrinsically tied to our early lives in Fazal Manzil as she lived with us for so many years. Murshida Fazal Mai came into the picture early on in Murshid's life in France. Our father had no permanent place in Paris to settle until Murshida Fazal Mai made this possible by putting the house in Murshid's name. He then named it in her honor: Fazal Manzil (Blessed Home).

Fazal Manzil's two large rooms—we called them the "big rooms"—consisted of a salon or living room and a dining room. The salon was always kept closed, even when Murshid was there in the summer. It used to be separated from the dining room by folding doors and was appointed with Murshida Fazal Mai's furniture that she had brought from Holland: a couch, two armchairs, a buffet, a table with beautiful upholstered chairs to match, and a few other pieces, such as pedestals and a harmonium.

We were not really allowed to enter her room, but I was most tempted because of the small organ, the harmonium, which appealed to me because the sound was very soft. I suppose she had brought it from Holland to play on it herself; but I never heard her play, and she wouldn't allow me to play it either, not even at Christmas. So, basically, it was just another piece of furniture in Murshida Fazal Mai's salon.

A fine-looking gold leaf clock had been placed on the white marble mantelpiece. It had a rounded glass cover and was flanked by statuettes on either side. On one side there was a pretty little statue of the Virgin Mary, and Jesus on the other, probably of white plaster; it could even have been marble, rather shiny. Fortunately, it survived the war. I found it somewhere after the war and kept it as it was a special piece. I remember at some point giving it to Hidayat as he appreciated it so much.

I also remember another attractive statue on the mantelpiece, which was rather tall. It represented a lovely lady, a mother, standing with her little girl of five or six; they were both dressed in beautiful 1920s fashion and wore ribbons in their hair.

All this was crowded into one room, just large enough to accommodate the furniture, which was typical of the old Dutch style. There were no electric lights; but only petrol lamps, instead, which lent an antiquated look. The salon floor was covered with a carpet, a Persian or an Indian rug, I can't remember exactly; but I do remember that our father brought a few carpets back—perhaps from England—one for the Oriental Room and one for the salon.

The reason Murshida Fazal Mai had brought all her furniture was not simply to be surrounded by her things in Suresnes; she wanted to move because she wasn't really settled in her life in Holland. She had just married when her husband died of tuberculosis the day of their wedding. So this was a tragic event in Murshida Fazal Mai's life, and she had come to find Murshid's teachings a great consolation. One can easily understand why she felt the logical solution was to settle in Fazal Manzil upon our father's invitation.

Murshida Fazal Mai also furnished other rooms in the house; she bought the dining room furniture in Suresnes or in a neighboring town, which is why it was in the French style. She had also brought a very large, dark oak buffet for all the dishes. It was placed in the second hallway as one comes in the entrance. The cupboard was very large and had beautiful doors and glass windows. At present it is—thankfully—still in the house, in Hidayat's apartment. It had survived the war, all except for the porcelain it once sheltered. The porcelain was, I think, a set for twelve guests: four or five shelves were fully laden with the finest porcelain, decorated with lavender flowers. Murshida Fazal Mai also brought silver and brass objects for the fireplace, and a few Dutch tiles were inserted inside the mantelpiece. Apart from the salon, Murshida Fazal Mai had her own rooms upstairs: a bedroom and a sitting room. Naturally both were furnished with the items she had brought from Holland.

The children were never allowed in the salon; Murshida Fazal Mai kept the doors closed, and I don't remember our father every receiving in there. He understood the situation and, in fact, he wanted to receive mureeds and visitors in the Oriental Room, which was beautifully arranged and decorated. There he felt more at ease, apart from the fact that he wanted to occupy that room in particular because a tragedy had occurred in there,[(7)] and he must have felt that his presence would help bring new vibrations into the room and, consequently, into the house. So at that time, nobody was upset by the fact that this salon was out of bounds.

Dinners for Mureeds

Claire Harper: The dinners that our mother made and served were taken in the dining room, which was appointed with rustic furniture. The dining room was enhanced by a lovely tiled fireplace which, in a way, looked somewhat regal: the man who had the house built was a duke. In fact, his coat of arms appears on the windows in colored glass of red, green and yellow. There was also a piano there, an upright Pleyel which Murshida Fazal Mai must have bought in Paris. Added to that were four chairs: two large armchairs, and two smaller ones. The smaller ones were a little bit like what one would call carvers. They were made of ebony and upholstered in brown leather. To this day, they have been preserved as best as possible, but some have been lost or just disappeared during or after the war. Two are now still left, and are in the Oriental Room. The two large ones were destined for our father and mother, who sat at each end of the table when they received.

There were many occasions when my mother and father received, sometimes many people. On such occasions, chairs had to be brought in from elsewhere to accommodate the crowd. These dinners and meetings would last from about eight o'clock till midnight. Many of the guests were murshidas such as Murshida Fazal Mai, Murshida Sharifa Goodenough and Murshida Sophia Saintsbury-Green. Then there were mureeds who held positions of responsibility: Sheikha Kefayat Lloyd, Sheikha Sarferaz Meyer, Khalifa Sakina Furnée (Nekbakht), Kismet Stam, Shanavaz van Spengler, Sheikh Sirkar van Stolk and his secretary, Mr. van Essen, Sheikh Sirdar van Tuyll and Khalifa Nargis Dowland.

The list of helpers in those early years is long, and each played an important role in establishing a long-lasting memory of Murshid's presence and work. Among them I still remember Sheikh Craig, Shamcher Beorse, Shadman Dussaq, Mrs van Gool and Ratan; but the list is much longer. Most of these people were responsible for gathering Sufis together and for lecturing, as well. They held titles such as leader, Cherag or Cheraga, Khalif, Khalifa, Sheikh or Sheikha. They were all extremely enthusiastic and helpful. Our father must have given them all a very good sendoff, because they never stopped working or doing their utmost to spread the Message in their own ways, even after the passing of their master. Of course, they had received guidance from Murshid, and each one seemed to be more gifted than the next in carrying out the work. Their dedication to the cause was important: it was a first step toward the spreading of the Message and an encouragement for our father.

Many of the mureeds had been Theosophists at one time—some had belonged to the Theosophical Society in Holland which, in those days, was well known and attended mainly by the educated or wealthy. Most of them, having heard Murshid speak once or twice, were in agreement with the fact that he had more to offer than what they had known up until then. Thus they became adepts of the Sufi Movement.

In the early days, there was no official organizational structure except for Headquarters in Geneva. These were the Sufi Movement headquarters, where most of the responsible members would meet after Summer School and discuss itineraries or plans for the winter and following summer, or publication plans and finances.

Sheikha d'Eichthal

Claire Harper: Baroness M. C. d'Eichthal was a wealthy lady whom our father had met in Paris, and who was very helpful to him already in the early years. I remember my mother speaking a lot of her. Occasionally she came to Fazal Manzil, and I remember her vaguely. She wore very fine clothes, behaved in a very formal manner and spoke beautiful French. She organized many meetings and became the Sufi National Representative for France and editor of a French Sufi journal. She also arranged private, small group meetings in Paris where Murshid would lecture to a closed audience of French cultured people, intellectuals and musicians, at which time he met Debussy. In fact, there is a composition of Debussy's called "The Music Box" ("La Boite a Musique"), which is based on a raga that Murshid sang to him.

Zeb-un-nisa

Claire Harper: I believe that Marquise Farinola, whose Sufi name was Zeb-un-nisa (because she was a musician and poetess), had some friends in Paris society. Murshid had met her in Rome, where she lived and where she had a large room to receive and entertain in, and where she could dance. Her friendship and dedication to the family continued long after our father's passing.

Sheikh Sirkar van Stolk

Claire Harper: De Heer van Stolk's Sufi name was Sirkar. A very tall and wealthy man, he lived in Wassenaar, Holland, known as an industrial town. Sheikh Sirkar came from a family whose main source of income was in the sugar and cotton plantations of Java, Indonesia, making him one of the five richest men in Holland at the time. When I first met him, Sirkar was in his thirties. He would look down at me and greet me most graciously. His clothes were of the finest; I'd even venture to say that he looked like the best dressed man in Holland.

Whenever he came to Suresnes, he was accompanied by his wife, Sargeny, a Dutch lady who had lived in America for some time, long enough to take on an accent. He built a house in the neighborhood of Fazal Manzil in Suresnes, where he stayed each summer with his wife, as well as their two beautiful daughters and his secretary, Mr. Wassir van Essen, and a tall, beautiful governess for the girls. Since Suresnes was very hot in the summer and there were frequent showers, Sirkar was always seen with a gabardine rain coat over his left shoulder. Since I was about the same age as his daughters, I was invited to visit.

Sirkar had a lovely mother. I remember her looking like a queen dressed in the most beautiful attire. Her dresses were close-fitting and draped from the waist down, made of silk and lace, in silver, white or ivory tones. She wore diamonds and pearls, and a fine silver choker to meet the day's fashion and complete her outfit. Her coiffure was always impeccable, and her manners exquisite. She spoke with eloquence and appeared to be a happy woman, and I could not help but admire her beautiful personality.

She was friendly to our mother when she and her husband, Mr. van Stolk, a gentleman farmer, visited for tea in Fazal Manzil. It was a beautiful day, and Summer School was in full swing. During the tea party, I watched the guests and listened to the conversation, fascinated by these visitors.

After they had gone, I asked my mother many questions. Among one of them was why this lady looked so regal. My mother told me that she was from Swedish royalty. Naturally Sirkar van Stolk was their son, but they also had two daughters, Bhakti and Shakti. They all visited Suresnes during the summer to attend the meetings at Summer School as devotees, as admirers and helpers. From morning till late evening, they attended the activities: lectures, lessons, meditation and concerts in the evening.

Sirkar van Stolk was our father's right-hand man in many organizational duties within the Sufi Movement. Publishing, finances and travel were among his main concerns. He would often travel with our father and organize lecture tours. I believe he was one of the pillars at Headquarters in Geneva.

Bhakti

Claire Harper: One of Sirkar van Stolk's sisters, Bhakti, was unusually tall. She was an artist, a painter and, I think, a dancer as well. She had a daughter called Mea. Bhakti is the artist who painted the picture of Vilayat at ten, dressed in Oriental clothes. It is in the salon now and is still very well preserved. The garment that Vilayat wore at the sitting was very transparent and fine, probably silk or cotton voile, and a little tight for him. As these garments did not have buttons, just a tie-around gold ribbon, Bhakti thought it might be artistic to leave it open on one side. My mother wasn't very pleased with that detail and asked Bhakti to close the shirt as far as she could, which she did.

Bhakti also painted two portraits of my mother. One was of my mother wearing an almond green sari, against a background of the setting sun. Unfortunately it could not be found after the war. The second painting was of our mother in a pale blue sari draped over her head, as a profile with yellow background. It was a very beautiful painting and it was indeed on the walls of the salon after the war; at least it was put back, but it was eventually stolen among many other things. However, there is still a photo of it.

Bhakti was a very happy person, always laughing and extremely enthusiastic. I remember her husband was just as tall as she was and also very happy. He wore a monocle. Bhakti always dressed in beautiful pastel clothes; she was very elegant. She wore long necklaces of different shades with large beads of amber.

When the Nazis took their family's wealth, they regretted not having donated it to build the Temple of the Universel. In 1958, I had a chance to visit Bhakti and her sister Shakti in Holland and to talk about the prewar years. They now lived in a very small house, and Bhakti told me how Murshid had appealed to all the mureeds to build a temple. They now were very sorry that they had always tried to put it off because they thought times were bad and they didn't find sufficient funds. They said that, because they hadn't done what he had wished them to do, now after the war, they had nothing. They were living in the caretaker's house and were forced to rent out their former estate. All this was said over a cup of tea. We soon left and, sadly, I never saw them again.

Sirdar and Saida

Claire Harper: Sheikh Sirdar was a most prominent person. He was, in a similar way to Sirkar, a member of the Sufi Movement who became very active. He displayed great reverence and respect for Murshid and showed it in many ways.

Sirdar lived in a beautiful home in The Hague, on the same side as the Peace Palace, which is a very central and prominent area. Born into aristocracy, his full name was Baron Sirdar van Tuyll van Seeroskerken. Murshid encouraged the union of Sirdar and Saida (whose name was Henriette Willebeek Le Mair).

Saida, just as tall as Sirdar, was a brilliant artist and spent many years drawing and painting all she could of Murshid, our mother and us children. She was responsible for the famous painting of Murshid walking with our mother in a wheat field in the evening, when we were all tucked in bed. Prior to having met Murshid, she had a contract with an American firm to illustrate books. Well known amongst the world's illustrators, she always used her maiden name, Willebeek Le Mair, for her work. Saida could dance beautifully. She had learned Indian dances and could also play the vina, as well as other musical instruments. In the evening at the hall, she danced to Indian music and her performances were very much appreciated.

Sirdar helped a lot by finding places where Murshid could speak during the winter months, and he often accompanied him while organizing other activities. When Murshid traveled through Europe and arrived at the Dutch border, Sirdar would take the train right to the border to accompany Murshid to his home in Holland. Thus, when in Holland, our father was a guest of Sirdar and Saida; at least when in The Hague.

Sirdar had a great love of horses and was actively associated with the stables in The Hague where his horses were kept. He and Saida rode together every morning and they knew all about horses; I believe that Murshid was also invited for an outing on horseback. The dunes at Katwyck, near The Hague, are a lovely place to ride horse because of the sandy hills and the sea. They loved it there and enjoyed riding along the beach.

Though Murshid felt a certain magnetism in Katwyck, I do not know whether he ever suggested that this would be a location for the temple. I believe the location for the temple was indeed in Suresnes, in the field where he laid the foundation stone.

The Neighborhood

Claire Harper: At the lower end of Fazal Manzil's garden was the conciergerie or caretaker's house. Monsieur Marcel Codonnié, an electrician by profession, and his wife, Louise, were the official *gardiens* or caretakers of the property. Theirs was the task of gardening and maintenance, and Madame Codonnié occasionally did some cooking. I was frightened of the large black dog they kept in a caged-off pen. I heard that the dog was let out at night to guard the property.

What is commonly called "the field" or "Sufi land" was a plot of ground opposite Fazal Manzil in Suresnes. As far as I know, the field was purchased by members of the Sufi Movement. At the end of the field they built the hall, a fairly functional building tucked at an angle against a wall. It was large enough to hold the mureeds in those days. There weren't more than a hundred, a hundred and fifty at the most, at the time.

I remember the summers being so beautiful in those years. They were always very hot. There were occasional showers, even heavy storms, but we never experienced cool weather, dampness or rain like nowadays; it was weather you could depend on.

Apart from the hall and the Sufi land, there were three other Sufi houses plus the Mureed House behind Fazal Manzil. There was the Nekbakht House, for one, which was practically on the land. Beyond that, there was another house called the Society House, or Goodenough House, which later was bought by Miss Skinner. Then a bit further up the road, there was another house that looked a bit quainter and more ornamentally decorated than the usual French houses in that neighborhood. I can't remember who the owner was, but it was rented out for the summer to visitors such as Marquise Farinola. In other words, there were several Sufi houses, including the Mureed House, around Fazal Manzil.

The grounds were quite large. The actual field looked like a meadow, except that two paths crossed it, one on the right and one on the left, with a lot of space between for a lawn. Further up, near the hall, there were many trees, including walnut trees.

In the autumn, we children had a lot of fun because walnut trees are not so high; they grow more in width and have lots of branches. We picked lots of walnuts and ate them green—absolutely delicious. Of course, we would gather them for the winter and gave some to the neighbors. There were also some apricot trees yielding plenty of fruit for everyone. Those were the sweetest apricots I've ever tasted. Added to these, there were bushes and bushes of white gooseberries and red gooseberries, as well as raspberries, red currants and black currants. These, too, we picked, and our mother made jam out of them.

The street, Rue de la Tuilerie, separated our home from the field. In those days, the streets in the suburbs were usually just dirt paths, dusty and narrow. Our street, though, was cobbled in a beautiful half-circle design. Horses and carts traveled up and down; in those days it was a two-way street, unlike today. We only ever saw horses, work horses pulling heavy loads such as earth, vegetables or coal. They looked tired trudging up that steep hill. The owners would sometimes whip them on, mindless of the poor animals' torment. The sound the drivers made to encourage the horses to advance was "allehop," and to stop them was "whooaa." One heard these commands throughout the day because there were so many carts traveling up and down our street. There were many stray dogs as well, on the loose, looking for food. Some were sick, some were lame and some were wild.

Nearby there were pigs who fed from the garbage dump. They ate whatever they could find, even shoes, I remember. I was always scared of them, dirty and snorting about, and I would cross over to the other side. One had to pass them to get from the house to the shops.

Walking up to nearby Mont Valérian, the old fort on the hill, we would encounter goats everywhere, and that was more fun. We children often went up to the fort to play. The windows were broken; nobody was around and nothing was checked or supervised. So we had the place to ourselves, which was rather dangerous because the fort area was surrounded by a dry moat, and although it was very deep, we didn't seem to care. We were wild—like rabbits.

I don't remember Noor ever coming with us. During Summer School she listened to our father's lectures or helped our mother. Noor was always doing something sensible while the rest of us were into exploring and going on adventures. I was a bit of a tomboy, pretending to be rough and tough, especially around Hidayat.

The area to the right of the field was a slum. There was a set of houses inhabited by the very poor. They really had nothing; how they survived, I don't know. There was a lot of squalor, and I was very scared to pass by. I always stayed on the house side of the street going down.

A few doors down our road stood Maheboob's house, where he often stayed with his family. Although they lived permanently in Holland, they often came to that house, which had been built by Maheboob's mother-in-law, Ekbal Dawlat, in order to be there when our father was there. She was very welcoming and received a lot of Sufis.

From there, the road turned and twisted as it led to the railroad, where one could hear the noisy passage of the train going from one stop to the next. Further on, there was a tower which was rather high and had a flat roof. We children found that area very strange because we never saw anybody walking in the street. We were the only children around trying to explore these odd places. That particular house, where the windows were broken, seemed very uncanny because sometimes we thought we heard noises from inside, and we thought there were ghosts or witches living there. Whenever this happened, we all ran home as fast as we could.

Just around the corner to us lived a Sufi lady, called Mrs. Van Gool, on the Rue des Roses. She lived there most of her life with her two children and I remember her being very nice and kind to the family.

On the street where the Mureed House stood, the Rue de l'Hippodrome, there was also a house towards the top of the hill which is still pretty today. It was built with white and turquoise bricks decorating the windows and doors. I know that, at one time, our parents went there looking for a house. I don't know why our father wanted to buy a house on that street—perhaps to lodge mureeds. In any case, he was very interested in this particular one and, though it wasn't for sale, he asked the lady who lived there many questions about it. Much later on, I spoke to her because I had known her daughter, and she told me she was very impressed when she saw Murshid come and talk to her. She thought he was a king and she didn't quite understand what he was doing there. She had tried to communicate with him by saying that she liked the jewel on his turban, at which he replied that he would give it to her. She was frightened and embarrassed because she was not used to such an offer, and quickly said no, thank you. She said that he had been looking for land. She couldn't understand why he was in a little country town as small as Suresnes.

Sirkar also had a place near the Mureed House, but in the 1950s he decided to sell it to a group of nuns. I don't know what happened; but later he was sorry that he had sold it, and he returned to ask the nuns for the house, but they would not relent. In the month of April 2000, his house was demolished to make way for a new building.

Further up the street was Mr. Leclerc's house. He became a Sufi later, when Murshida Fazal Mai was active. With his family, he built a very large house which now belongs to the Nekbakht Foundation.

INAYAT, THE HEALER

Pir-o-Murshid Hazrat Inayat Khan's gift to humanity was not limited to the level of esoteric teachings and an inspiring message of universal love and understanding. A priceless contribution to those he came in contact with was his ability to heal. We often hear testimonies of those who went to see Murshid with troubles they could not solve—hoping he would be able to help them out of their dilemma. In these cases, he often made it impossible for the agitated person to even start describing their woes; within a short time in his presence, their confusion, grievance or despair had vanished.

Numerous reports also evidence Murshid's miraculous healing powers of the physically ill, notably, in one instance, where he saved a baby from dying. Once he asked a mureed to visit a sick person in Paris. The patient's health immediately improved upon seeing Murshid's messenger, as if his healing power had been transmitted through his envoy. Murshid had developed his inner being to such perfection that he could tune others through his words or his gaze, even by his mere presence.

THE SUMMER SCHOOL

Claire Harper: Summer School in Suresnes was a very lively time of the year, beginning on July 5th, Viladat Day, our father's birthday, and ending on September 13th, Hejirat Day, the date that Murshid and his brothers left India to bring their music and the Sufi Message to the West.

I was always fascinated by the clothes the mureeds wore because, in those days, a lot of lace was worn, as well as silk or fine wool, to wrap around their shoulders on a summer's evening, as a stole. It was all very graceful and colorful. Another thing that impressed me a lot was that instead of wearing straw hats, which some of them did, they carried a parasol against the sun; it was always very picturesque.

Many Sufi mureeds scribbled notes during the lectures, but two of them were responsible for much of the recording of Murshid's words in shorthand. These were Khalifa Sakina Furnée, later called Nekbakht, and Kismet Stam, Nekbakht's cousin. The two shared a house opposite Fazal Manzil, now called the Nekbakht House. Though Nekbakht was principally responsible for writing down the Message, our father later put her in charge of the Biographical Department. She and Kismet were responsible for much of the transcription and editing of Murshid's words. These scribes were very busy all winter long, putting their handwritten notes into type. Nekbakht happened to be very wealthy and she personally arranged the publishing of some of the works, which were sometimes bound in leather.

Many of the mureeds arrived several days or even a week before the beginning of Summer School to settle themselves. They hailed from many different countries: Holland, Germany, Sweden, Norway, England, Belgium, Spain and Italy, as well as North America and South America. Many stayed in the Mureed House, adjacent to Fazal Manzil. Somewhat larger than our home, it was bought by Sufi members and converted into a type of hotel for the mureeds. It was run by a staff and was able to accommodate many of the Sufis, though some of them already had summer houses in Suresnes, and some stayed with friends in the neighborhood. All the rest rented rooms wherever available.

There was some interchange among the Sufis when they had time. But I don't think my father allowed them much time to talk among themselves because he filled in the program of the day very well. The meetings started early in the morning and continued until very late at night. In the evening there was zikr, repetition of sacred words and names; or sometimes concerts were held with various people singing with piano accompaniment, and sometimes the vina could be heard. Murshid's cousin, Ali Khan, was the main singer. He had a rich tenor voice and sang the Sufi songs, usually for the Universal Worship. Sometimes he gave concerts in the evenings which were appreciated by all. Our father encouraged symbolic plays too, such as *Una* and *Living Dead*.

I never went to the meetings except in the latter years, and I do remember attending some of the activities during the last year. Sometimes there were parties, a bit like garden parties, where people would dress up and socialize. On Sunday there was a Universal Worship in the afternoon.

Occasionally, in the evening, meetings were held in the house, in Fazal Manzil itself, where we participated only by peeking through the doors and watching the people come in and out, trying to find out what they were doing and saying. That was quite interesting, especially to Hidayat when he was very young and wanted to know everything. He was curious, as I was too.

Sometimes there seemed to be some very serious meetings, or occasionally dinners, around nine o'clock. I remember several murshidas came in, three or perhaps four, along with other guests. Hidayat and I were as naughty as we could be: I can remember hanging over the banisters to try and see who was coming in and who was going out and what they were saying. We did catch snitches of what we thought to be very funny things that the mureeds said, especially since some had such strong accents. Our evenings were quite entertaining because we snuck out of bed to watch what was going on until about twelve o'clock. We wouldn't miss out on any of these dinners and evening events, of which there were quite a few.

I remember we once were given a small table at which to eat, thus being allowed to join the adults for dinner. It must have been somebody's birthday—perhaps our father's—I don't remember. On that occasion we were very mischievous: Hidayat tried to pull the table cloth off the table—despite the fact it was fully laden—so everything would fall and break. One time, somebody was meant to be looking after us for awhile, but we wouldn't let her. She became absolutely desperate, as she didn't know how to discipline us—we were so wild.

Khatum, a healing service, was held on Thursdays. It took place in the salon after dinner and lasted about half an hour. This service was also conducted by our uncles, and I remember how my mother made halvah to be served after the service.

Summer School was always an eventful time; in addition to the lectures and other activities, our father gave interviews to many people in the Oriental Room, which was intended for this purpose. Throughout his time in Suresnes, Murshid had to cope with administrative issues also; I don't think he liked that very much. He had numerous people in charge of the administration of the Sufi Movement and the various centers, but the organizational side was not always pleasant. I remember there was often a heavy atmosphere in the house; I felt that there were troubles, problems, things that had to be sorted out and talked about, and I always felt that the life surrounding our father and our mother was exceedingly hard. Though usually serious, they say that occasionally our father liked to laugh. When he heard something funny, he would enjoy laughing, though we seldom saw him lighthearted.

Summer School was also a hopeful time for everybody. All these seekers had come to find a key to open the doors that barred them. They were attracted to our house as if it were a shrine. Our father made it a rule that Sufi visitors would not spend time in our garden because he felt that the field was the right place for them to congregate and to talk to each other and that Fazal Manzil's garden was for us children to play in. With the gates open, there might have been a danger in having the freedom to come in uninvited. This he didn't always want; he wasn't always prepared to meet with mureeds or curious visitors. Our father valued the time he set aside for rest or for meditation—sometimes in the garden. He liked to keep the two areas separate: his private life and his public activities; in this way he endeavored to maintain inner harmony.

Toward the end of the summer, most people felt they had been inspired and helped, and many felt that Murshid was their leader, guide or master; others, perhaps, felt differently, I don't know. There were some envious or self-engrossed people who thought they knew just as much or more than him. Hence, one of the poems that our father wrote: "Some did say that I knew nothing; some did say that I knew all."

On the last day of each Summer School, a farewell ceremony was held and a photographer came to take pictures of the group. I can remember tea parties in the field outside, under trees where people had their cake and biscuits and could meet; it was meant to be very pleasant. There is a photo with my father and my mother at one of these ceremonies in which my mother is looking down.

I assume Mother was simply exhausted because she had done so much; she was always in the background, doing whatever she had to do, and I imagine our father was pretty tired, too. Looking back, I think some people were unduly hard on Mother at times. She was a refined and delicate lady who did not know the ways of the world, and had arrived in Europe and founded a family when very young. I know it could not have been easy for her to assume all the responsibilities that she was given. She not only had to take care of four children, two of whom were consistently mischievous (Noor never misbehaved; she always tried to help, the same with Vilayat) but she also wanted to sew all the clothing our father wore. She didn't have a sewing machine but sewed by hand everything he wore: his cloaks and his shervanies. How she managed to do that I don't know, because she never learned to sew and was able to make all these garments without even using a pattern. Everything he needed, even a hat, she would sew by hand at night, when we were all asleep and her chores were done.

At the end of each Summer School, the Mureed House was closed down for the winter and packed up; and everybody left, for another year, till the following summer.

This was a sad time for us because our father would then travel, departing immediately to journey to numerous countries the whole winter long. During those trips, he would stay with various Sufi adepts at their homes, or they would put him up at hotels if necessary. He would give lectures that the Sufis had arranged for him and wouldn't return home to Fazal Manzil until late spring.

Around 1925 our father asked an architect, called Kramer, to work on a plan for building a temple. Its purpose was not to be solely for praying and meditating, but also for creating the right vibrations in one place so that they could be diffused outwardly to the world. Very much like a church, one comes inside and feels much better if one has a problem; maybe one even goes to confession and comes out feeling much better. I believe the idea of the temple was similar: a sacred meeting place. The shape of the temple had to have meaning also. It shouldn't have corners, it should be rounded off. Murshid had drawn it or described it to resemble four persons praying back to back. It was to be shaped like four Buddhas, sitting in the lotus position and facing the four cardinal directions.

THE DEPARTURE

Claire Harper: In the month of September 1926, as Summer School drew to a close, our father called his mureeds to arrange for a ceremony to be held at the Temple's foundation stone which stood in the center of the Sufi garden. A great formality was to be observed: having summoned Vilayat, aged ten, our father appointed him as Head of the Confraternity of the Message and bestowed upon him the Medal of the Confraternity in the presence of the whole family and the dignitaries of the Sufi Movement. He also handed Vilayat his Sufi emblem of heart and wings. This ceremony was held at the inauguration of the laying of the temple's foundation stone; in other words, Murshid gave Vilayat the charge of building the temple.

Prior to this ritual, our father asked our mother to make a yellow robe for Vilayat. Our mother's heart told her that our father would never return—handing over the Sufi robe was a gesture of heritage. It is for this reason that our mother refused. Murshid had mentioned his plan to journey to India, and our mother felt that this was a sign that her beloved would not be returning.

In the Sufi garden, a farewell gathering was held which our mother attended. Whilst Murshid bade all farewell and offered up thanks and appreciation to those present, though she tried to veil her grief, our mother was in tears. An atmosphere of uncertainty permeated the air. At this particular closing of Summer School, who could not have wept? Undertones of unspoken questions wavered in a dead silence.

When Murshid left his beloved mureeds, a great stillness gripped them. Murshid and his Begum walked down the Sufi garden path to Fazal Manzil. Under a starless sky, in deep sorrow, Murshid left his beloved wife and his Rubies Four this side of the world, to return to his motherland. Once arrived, there was no saying how he must have felt to kiss the soil of his beloved India.

MURSHID'S PASSING

On August 28th, 1926, Mother received a telegram from Venice stating:

Sailing today. Murshid

A letter from him arrived a few days later in which he noted:

Venice, Tuesday

Mari Calleja, I am leaving today at five o'clock. It seems there are more houses here than human beings and every house is built in Moorish style, very oriental but it is damp everywhere. I would never live here for anything—this place is beautiful to pass through. Good bye my soul. With all love...

On October 17th, 1926 a telegram from Karachi announced:

Arrived

Claire Harper: During the first week of February 1927, Mother received a telegram from Kismet—who was the only person to accompany our father to in India—informing her that Murshid was very ill. Mother could not eat or sleep from worry. Another telegram was received to announce that Murshid had passed away. This news was the greatest sorrow on earth. Mother was inconsolable, and Noor took charge of us. We children began to consider her our "Little Mother."

Our father's sudden death brought up many questions. Multiple signs had indicated that he would not be returning. Would we ever learn the full truth, the mystery of his passing? Ambiguity will always remain because so many hypotheses have been put forward. Yet, another official one is evident. Pneumonia could be a suitable reason to succumb, and Murshid had previously contracted the pulmonary illness twice. Apparently, he had spent the night enraptured by the sounds of some Qawali singers, seated on the cold stone floor of a small house, called Tilak Lodge, just north of Delhi's Red Fort. Seeming to be in a type of trance, it was difficult for Kismet to know if our father was in a state of deepest meditation or, on the contrary, whether his physical body had succumbed to an ongoing chronic weakness of the lungs.

In those dreadfully sad days when we had accepted that our father would not be coming home, our mother experienced a serious nervous breakdown and was told by the doctor to stay in bed for three months. Nonetheless, she did leave her bed. As a young girl, she had contracted typhoid fever, and the doctor said that she survived only because she had such a strong will. Her escape from America confirms her tremendous courage and her strong will. This inborn trait of hers was still present under the weight of her overwhelming sorrow. For our sake, she tried her best to overcome her grief. She had gone through years of need, as well as four pregnancies. But life has a way of restoring everything to its natural state. Many mureeds came and went, trying to console her. Some were friends, some were not. The house was open to all; there was no check on visitors.

Our mother was aware of a sense of enmity, no doubt from the past, which was quasi-dormant while our father was still with us. This materialized itself more vigorously in the form of indifference. Our mother realized that now, more than ever, she needed to be down-to-earth in order to survive and to adjust to the new life she was now obliged to lead. The worry of supporting four children became more and more overbearing.

Murshida Fazal Mai felt the loss of Murshid greatly, but quite differently. Some invisible feeling would rise in her heart and leave its mark in our midst. She was not only under shock at the loss of her master but, as a Murshida, she had a role to play and felt somewhat at a loss without Murshid's guidance. Other leaders encountered this same problem; these were the early days of adjustment and suspense.

Kismet Stam returned from India. She seldom went out and usually confined herself to her house. She dressed in black, wearing a thick veil over her face whenever she went out. At times she visited at night, after we children were meant to be asleep, to tell my mother the details of the trip to India and of Murshid's illness: the doctor, the medicines, Murshid's words after the medicine had been ingested. Both sitting on the floor in her room in front of the mantelpiece, my mother would cry bitterly. Kismet reported that Murshid was administered the wrong medicine and had succumbed to it. She also stated that he was aware of this and had said so. Of all the Sufi followers, Kismet was the only one to witness his passing through the threshold of this life into the hereafter.

Noor was the angel who helped our mother. When Noor was able to console our mother, I felt that Murshid was coming through. When Murshid couldn't help a person with their illness, sorrow or mishap, he wished at that moment that he could be the greatest consoler.

Concerning the questions surrounding Murshid's death, the versions and viewpoints vary. Unless one can find other leads to follow, we simply have to accept what we know, which is not very much, and the evidence is rather vague. It has occasionally been alluded to that somebody in India poisoned Murshid, that he was sick indeed, but that someone administered him poison instead of medicine. How much truth can there be in such a rumor? Only God knows. What people say could also be a source of the imagination. Let us say that the story has no end.

The following letter from Dr Pathan shows that Murshid was already ill by November 7th, 1926, suffering enough to write to his uncle for advice. This leads to the presumption that Murshid was ill for at least three months before his death. A response from Uncle Allaudin Pathan in Nepal dated November 17th, 1926, reads as follows:

> *My dear Inayat Khan,*
>
> *I am so very pleased to receive your letter of 7th inst. but at the same time much grieved to hear you are not well and you are under treatment. Anyhow pray let me know about your trouble and I will try my best to ask the Baidwas here if they can give me some advice for medicine for you.*
>
> *I have already applied for leave, in the meantime please let me know about your health so that I may fly and see you soon and we may, by the grace of God, go together to Baroda. Your auntie tells me that if she had wings she would fly at once to nurse you.*
>
> *Now my dearest one we sincerely pray God for your quick recovery and may God listen to our united prayer to see each other as soon as possible and give you very long life and prosperity and happiness—may God bless you.*
>
> *(signed) Your most affectionate and loving uncle A.M. Pathan*

Claire Harper: It is difficult to understand the real reason why our father left for India all of a sudden, when we were so young, and also, did he really die? He may have been threatened. Perhaps not he himself, but his family could have been threatened if he didn't leave for India. Or, perhaps, he had to go there for some calling, hoping to return. There was no reason why he had to return to India after being in the West for ten years. He still had many things to do. In fact, he told one of our uncles, I think it was his closest brother, Maheboob Khan, whom we called Bouwa, that if he returned, he would have a different way of spreading the Message. I believe he intended to spread the Messsage by writing instead: writing books and staying in one place. In other words, he intended to come back, but why did he go in the first place? That is a big question, and he never really gave a clear reason. Mother said, "Had I gone with him, he would not have died, but I could not have left the children."

Later Kalyani van Gool wrote:

> *During that Summer School* [1926] *I did not attend many classes, being too busy with our new home; however I attended the inauguration of the first stone for the temple and thereafter Murshid's farewell gathering which turned out to be his taking leave of us.*
>
> *Murshid looked tired, so did Begum, the atmosphere was melancholy. Murshid had a special word for each of us. He said to me: "Keep in touch with Murshida Fazal Mai," pointing out that she would replace him in Suresnes, knowing that he would not return. Murshida Fazal Mai has indeed been my spiritual mother and a great friend throughout.*
>
> *In February 1927, as I returned from a visit to Holland, I heard from a neighbor the terrible news of Murshid's passing away. I did not believe it and immediately ran to Fazal Manzil with Yetty at my hand and met Musharaff who confirmed the sad news. At Fazal Manzil, Murshida Fazal Mai was awaiting me. I said to her: "That's the end of our Movement," but in her grief she told me that the message would continue and that she would take care of Murshid's children.*

PILGRIMAGE TO INDIA

The Boat Journey

Claire Harper: I was eight years old, and there was a great deal of excitement in Fazal Manzil, at least amongst us children, because a trip to India seemed like a big affair. We were going to take a ship and we'd already seen pictures of it: a beautiful vessel called the Rawalpindi. It was an incredible thrill to know that we would be traveling on that steamer, and even more of a delight to know that we would be staying on the ship for several weeks. I thought that sounded like a very long time to be on a boat, and I wondered how we would be able to play in the garden on the ship. The whole excitement of traveling seemed to be like a dream.

After much planning came a time of careful packing. Lots of clothes were arranged in trunks which were sent off in advance, and I was told that we wouldn't see them until the other end. Some smaller trunks were called cabin trunks, and those would travel with us in a standing position in our cabins.

Murshida Fazal Mai, who lived with us, stayed behind. To me, she appeared to be almost indifferent about the journey; perhaps she wanted to go but could not neglect the responsibilities of the Sufi work for such a long time. Perhaps this made her seem somewhat aloof; I suspect, however, that she financed the whole trip for us.

Finally the departure day came, and I remember waiting downstairs for my mother to put my new coat on. It was such a comfortable coat, made of dark blue wool with gold buttons, and the lining was dark blue with white squares. I loved those squares and I loved the feeling of my mother putting it on me; I remember feeling so good and being more excited about my coat than I was about the journey.

Then we were off; I don't know how we all managed to get it together. The traveling party consisted of our mother, Noor, Vilayat, Hidayat and myself, as well as our three uncles: Maheboob or Bouwa, meaning uncle; Musharaff or ChaCha, meaning young uncle; and Mohammad Ali or Taya, which means either uncle or cousin-uncle.

We traveled to England to board the ship, because it was run by the Cunard line. Upon boarding the ship, I was impressed by its huge size. I can remember steps after steps after steps continuing up and up, turning right and left, and then finally arriving on the level where we found our cabin. Our cabin was rather small considering that there were five of us, together with our mother. But we were most excited because the brass porthole was round; we weren't used to looking out a round window. We gazed at the water and we were extremely excited about viewing the open sea and embarking on such a long journey but, for my part, forgetting the purpose of our voyage: to visit our father's tomb.

Noor was always quiet; we never really saw her, and I didn't know where she was. She probably kept to the cabin with our mother, whereas my two brothers and I ran around the ship like mad, exploring the lounges, the dining rooms, the halls full of suitcases and other people's cabins.

It finally grew dark, and we kept looking out that round porthole at the shining stars. The important thing to me was being on the ship and being all together. At one point, the ship started to move, and we could feel the vibrations while the smokestacks gave a number of blasts. It sounded utterly majestic to hear this ship begin to move, making a sonorous declaration that it was embarking on a long journey, a meaningful pilgrimage.

The days passed pretty quickly. We always ended up playing around most of the time. Our mother let us have the freedom of the ship, so long as we stayed together. I remember one meal in particular with Taya. He told us we were going to be served a magic meal, and we all believed it. I puzzled over what a magic meal might mean. It finally appeared: spinach with a poached egg. I wondered how that meal could come to our table without a waiter arriving.

The food on board was excellent. I remember being most excited about the turtle soup, which I had never tasted before. We started off the journey in the month of October so as to spend three months in India, three of the coolest months—October, November and December—so we wouldn't suffer from too much heat. For this reason, it was rather cold on the ship during the first part of the journey.

We made a stop in Aden, though I don't remember if we got off or not. During the crossing, I remember hearing talk of a fancy masquerade ball and I wondered what a masquerade ball might be. So we three, my brothers and I, peeked in. The festivities took place in a large hall, and everyone was dressed up and laughing; and I, naturally, wanted to dress up, too. But children weren't allowed to join in—it was only for the adults.

We urged our mother to go on deck to take in some fresh air and see the sea and relax on a deckchair, but she wouldn't. She kept to her cabin, looking exceedingly sad and remaining very quiet. Mother was our backbone, our security, our government; any questions we asked her, any wishes we asked her, any problems we asked her. She was always there. We wished she could be happy, but how could she be happy with our father gone? Perhaps that's why we were such naughty children, because we felt there was something wrong, something broken in our lives, in our family. The happiness we knew as children had gone for some reason. We didn't talk about it with each other; we just got wilder. The uncles attempted to keep an eye on us; they tried to keep us tame, but we ran away and we kept away, hiding from them. We did everything to make things difficult for them. Our mother would have been very lonely had Noor not remained by her side: she was the consoling factor.

On the ship, we would look out at the moon shining brightly as it became fuller each night. The water shimmered with the reflection of a long silver line. The closer we got to India, the lower the moon seemed to hang in the sky. Our mother would say it looked so much like a lantern. It became a deep yellow moon, not the white moons we see in the West. It gave the whole of the sky a different atmosphere, the atmosphere of the East, I suppose, and we liked that ambiance; it was a somewhat peaceful feeling.

Upon arriving in Delhi, we were introduced to several Indian friends who had known our father, who had seen him while he was there. My mother cried a lot. From that time on, things became rather grim and sad. I kept quiet, and my brothers were very quiet, too, as much as young boys can be.

The Dargah

Claire Harper: I remember entering our hotel which, to me, looked very cold because the ceilings were high and the hotel was large. We were given a spacious room, almost like a hall, where we were to sleep, all five of us. To me, the beds looked strange because they were covered with netting suspended from four posts. I didn't know exactly what the netting was for but I thought it was nice. There was a very sad moment shortly after entering that room: our mother burst into tears and remained most upset in that hotel room throughout the night. According to Hidayat, our mother had opened a drawer and found her husband's passport. She couldn't understand how, after so many months since he was considered deceased—about eight months—his passport would still be in that drawer. It is possible that he stayed in the same hotel, in the very room that we occupied.

We soon went to visit what we were told was our father's grave, his dargah, on the western side of Delhi. The grave was a patch of ground, soil overturned, under which our dear father was meant to lie unguarded, unknown, unidentified. There was not a name to be seen, not a flower, not a prayer. He had apparently succumbed to pneumonia a few miles away from here, but the plot was donated by a Sufi friend of our father's, Pir Nizami. According to hearsay, our father had visited this man and, gesturing towards the family's burial grounds, exclaimed that he would like to remain there forever.

It was a very tense moment and it became tenser during our time there. The impact of actually stopping and surrounding the grave by our presence, standing defenseless, was more than fearful, more than awesome: unthinkable. Our mother fell to the ground, crying bitterly. A dark cloud had fallen, showering tears of oblivion. I remained almost indifferent; I seem to have been untouched. I couldn't believe it was possible that my father was under that piece of ground, so I refused to believe it. The sound of our mother's crying was too much for the human heart to bear.

Noor suddenly said, "He's not there." My mother believed her statement; I was silent and shocked. We returned to the car looking down, feeling utterly lost. Noor was too old for me to talk to at this time, and my brothers were talking to each other, possibly about Noor's declaration. A cocoon of numbness surrounded me—an absence of communication—protecting me from pain and sorrow. My feet dragged along the ground. Why did my father have to die, and why so far away? Why did he have to go to India anyway? But nobody heard me; I didn't expect answers. The world could have come and gone, and I would still have been there wondering. I turned lifeless; somebody would have had to pinch me if they wanted me to blink. I felt as light as a feather, and yet my feet trod the ground, following the family. Only the song of a bird could have awakened me to reality. My thoughts were that something terrible had happened. I was angry. The past was buried in the present; there seemed to be no future to hope for, to nourish us or to dream of.

The Heartbeat of India

Claire Harper: From there on ,we toured the country mostly by car, in a large vehicle that accommodated my mother and the four children. The chauffeur was not a very good driver; I don't think any driver in that part of the world had much sense of safety in those days. He was extremely reckless and would just run right into bullocks in the street, as well as nearly run over people and children.

We had entered a world of noise and pandemonium. Our driver would constantly lean on the horn while all the other cars hooted as well. Life in the streets was exceptionally raucous and frenzied, chaotic—a hopeless muddle. The roads were full of curves, the streets were muddy; hardly a stretch was paved. Having no sidewalks, people walked all over the roads.

Though our uncles traveled separately in another car, we stayed together. We went all through Delhi and for miles around. The weather was perfect, and the flowers were beautiful. There were exotic plants everywhere, and I remember admiring all of nature, which was striking there, exceedingly green below a glowing sun and a sky of azure.

We embarked on a number of extensive tours. One excursion took us to the Taj Mahal. Walking towards it, I was most impressed at its colossal size, as well as the stunning beauty of the edifice: I'd never seen anything like that, not even in a picture. It was gleaming white with fine blue veins running through it. Being small, I was closer to the fountains, which were about my height. To me, the interesting feature of these fountains was that each was designed to hold a lime; each fountain had a lime in its center, held up by the stream of water, or so it appeared.

I wanted to share this with my mother, but she was always serious and spent much of her time grieving, so I couldn't really engage in a direct conversation with her. My brothers were always talking about other things, and Noor was trying to console my mother. So I felt a little on my own in India, admiring all these exciting things that I couldn't really talk about with anyone.

When we arrived at the top of the path, there was a step where everybody stopped before entering the Taj Mahal. Being a child, I was not allowed to go in; none of us children were allowed to visit. I wonder if my mother went in; I don't remember. All I know is that my uncles entered, and we waited. They had to take off their shoes and step into a basin of water before they could enter the sanctity of the Taj Mahal mausoleum. I was very curious to know what was inside, but it wasn't possible.

Claire Harper: The morning sky was deep blue, as usual, and the air was fresh and cool. A distinct silence reigned in the vicinity along with an atmosphere of prayer and devotion. Grandeur and beauty, past, present and future could have been its keynote. Everything felt utterly alive; it looked as if the surroundings were telling a tale. A single lifetime did not seem to be long enough to tell the story, so perhaps this place belonged to eternity. It was a feeling I could not explain in words, but it felt like it had always been there and would always be.

Our uncles kept to themselves, but we saw them daily; wherever we went, they were there too. They had more or less arranged the tour together with an uncle of theirs, Maula Bakhsh's second son who came to meet us. This uncle was called Dr. Allaudin Pathan, an extremely hospitable person who showed us around India and welcomed us warmly as close members of the family. It was with him that we toured the important places that he thought we should see.

Indian delicacies were offered to us regularly between our various visits. One of these delicacies was particularly interesting because it was handed to us in a leaf, and in the leaf were a lot of sweet goodies that made one's lips red—this did a lot to a young girl's vanity!

I also remember the famous Red Fort, which I didn't think much of. I found it too red and, to me, it didn't fit into the setting—it did not appear to look Oriental enough. It was straight, austere and devoid of decoration; perhaps, in fact, I was a bit frightened of it.

One day, we were surrounded by palm trees—incredibly tall, almost touching the deep blue sky. I observed a tiny boy wearing a turban run up a tree, so fast I couldn't believe it and, when he reached the top, he cut down coconuts. The coconuts fell, and then he came back down, not quite as fast as he went up, since he had to descend backwards. I was amazed to see such an acrobatic number as part of everyday life. Nobody praised him, nor did he get a reward. He ran away, as if it was just a natural thing. One of our guides opened a coconut and gave us a piece, along with some coconut milk as well. It was delicious.

We passed by lots of bazaars; they were very intriguing with all their jingle-jangling bracelets and jewelry, as well as food and kites, and little paper lanterns and reams of silk for saris. Apart from the bazaars, there were marketplaces bustling with activity. People had to really promote their merchandise, even if it were only a coconut; they had to remind people that they were selling them, and that theirs were better than what the neighbor had on offer. So it was an incredibly exciting time in the streets of India. The weather was mostly fine, except for thunderstorms at night, which were rather frightening. But somehow we always managed to get indoors in time.

On one of the endlessly long journeys we made by train, with continual drafts and hundreds of people hankering for a seat, I got sick. Mother noticed that I had developed a high fever, so we had to get off the train and stay overnight in the station sleeping quarters. In those days in India people could sleep in the stations, and this is what happened. I wasn't aware of what became of the rest of the family; I only remember that my mother took care of me, and had me lie down. She had made up a bed on a table, and I can remember that I felt awful and very hot. I must have had a very high fever because she looked worried. She managed to get oranges, and all I know is that I would doze off, and she woke me up throughout the night to give me some warm orange juice. By the morning I was much better; the fever had subsided and Mother was relieved. We boarded the train again and continued to our destination.

Often, in the morning, we went out walking or sightseeing. Sometimes we would take a car or a cab. Many of the cabs were horse-drawn and we would be jostled around. Everywhere we saw people lying in the streets and mothers with their babies begging, sick and crying. Some people were dying, and I asked my mother why they were there. She told me they were very poor, but I couldn't understand. I was always wondering why they had to be in the street when we're in a house. My questions were never properly answered because there was too much sorrow in my mother's heart. She didn't seem to be able to answer all my questions.

We didn't stay very long in one place. During the course of our travels, we went to the Ganges. The thing that interested me the most there was the Ganges itself, which looked very different from any river I had seen. It was different from the Seine River which I was used to looking at when we crossed over the bridge in Suresnes. The river Seine is very dark green and calm, whereas the Ganges is very agitated and grey in color. I saw many people going in, getting their feet wet or even going right into the Ganges, quietly and silently.

We children played a little on the shore, taking off our shoes and running around. We discovered a strip, about a yard wide, of lovely pink shells; it was incredible, the combination of rose-colored shells on the silver sand was beautiful. The sun glistened on the water, creating an image never to be forgotten.

One of the hotels we stayed at impressed me more than most others. The walls were painted a shrill green, and what seemed to be fluorescent lights lent it a cold, unfriendly look. I know it looked very miserable, but that was the price we had to pay to be inside for the night, at least. Just moments before, we had passed lots of people sleeping outside in the streets, and I was horrified to see families and an array of people of all ages sleeping out just anywhere on sidewalks, in alleyways or in doorways. I would feel more protected and comforted to be in the hotel, no matter how poor it looked. At least I was with my mother and I felt her presence very much there.

Then we made our way to Baroda, the family hometown. The family house, Moula Bakhsh's house, where our father grew up, had greatly diminished in size since the grand days of old. Much of it had collapsed through neglect before our great uncle, Dr. Pathan, saved what he could.

Murshid's Appearance

Claire Harper: Staying at Maula Bakhsh House, we spent a lot of time on the balcony. I remember my mother trying to put mosquito netting up there. On one occasion, she heard singing in the street and she recognized our father's singing voice. She said to us, "Children! That's Abba. You must take him these hot towels. Quickly go!" And we all ran down. Hidayat said he rushed down like a shot because he was always the fastest of all of us; and he said that, as soon as he reached the street, there was nobody to be seen. We looked around everywhere and there was no one in sight. Hidayat said he'll never forget that event. When Mother had peered over the balcony, the person she saw looked up. She affirmed that that person was, without a doubt, Murshid. But no sooner seen, had he vanished. There was another instance when our father was seen and heard singing in Baroda. So it might be well to call his parting a "disappearance."

Part Three: Growing Up, 1928–1939

OUR YOUNG YEARS

Visalat Day

Claire Harper: After our father passed away, the Oriental Room remained closed. It was no longer a welcoming room to go into, and as we were still young, we never said anything to each other about that room. But each year, Visalat Day, the 5th of February, the day that Murshid left this world, was commemorated in the Oriental Room with prayers and with silence.

Our mother asked us to take out all the furniture and carpets. We found brooms and buckets, and floor polish and steel wool as well as copper and brass polish. There was no vacuum cleaner then so we used a straw broom. Noor was the manager, and we adhered to her instructions. We all had to keep silent and we were barefoot as a symbol of respect. It took a full day, and we each had our project, according to our age and ability.

After the windows were washed with vinegar water and newspaper, and all the dust was wiped away, we polished the chairs, tables and wooden screens. Some of the chairs were studded with mother-of-pearl or ivory. The pictures were also polished, but the large mirror was quite a challenge. All the handmade Indian shawls were shaken or dry-cleaned before we could throw them over the screens. Much care was taken in every way. In this room, our father had received his mureeds. We were very glad to do this work; to us it was a gratifying chore.

As we all know, there is no end to work but the result is rewarding. We dusted the walls as far up as we could. All the copper, brass and glass were collected on a tray to be taken upstairs and cleaned. My job was to polish the brass and the chairs. Anything to throw out was laid on a newspaper in the hall. After some time the room looked very clean, and then there were lots of little objects to put back in place. When everything was ready, Mother was very proud of us. We all hoped the Oriental Room would look like that forever.

When the big day came, our mother arose early to make a large wreath of yellow roses which was hung on a large photograph of our father. She took hours to make it because roses have their thorns. The white marble fireplace looked very grand. We children were given the responsibility of welcoming the mureeds, who would take off their shoes before entering the room, now perfumed with incense. There was a constant procession of mureeds bringing beautiful bouquets of flowers, mostly roses. One after the other, they paid their respects and left.

Murshid's golden shoes, which he had left behind, were placed on a chair. A lovely mureed had skillfully made two tea-color roses out of silk; they looked very real, and we laid them on the shoes. Most of the visitors did not really wish to leave, but others were waiting. The room was small, and time was running out. Often our mother was too upset to come downstairs. We all stayed close to her that day, and often Mother could not stop weeping.

That day, she was our treasure to care for. We knew not how to console her excepting to try to be quiet and good. But starting the next day, the daily routine had to resume: there was shopping to do and dinner to prepare.

Mother's Troubles

Claire Harper: After our father left, our mother spent many years in a state of depression, often keeping to her bed. She often cried and was very weak; sometimes she would hardly eat for days: she had no appetite. When Noor realized that our mother wasn't eating, she made a big fuss about it and we all joined in and agreed. We laid down some rules: "All right, Amma, if you don't eat, we won't eat, either!" we decided all together, in unison. Eventually it worked.

Though our mother had not learned to sew professionally, she managed to sew dresses for me. I can still remember a beautiful white silk outfit she made for me. I was very careful when I wore that dress because she asked me to be, but sometimes I couldn't help getting it soiled. The concierge, Madame Codonnié, ironed it for me in the summer, and I used to feel sorry for her because of all the pleats that she was ironing meticulously; there were so many of them, and I didn't know what to do to show my appreciation. I must have been about ten at the time, but I still remember very clearly how happy I was with that dress.

Those were very difficult times. Mother didn't have enough money to take the dirty clothes to the laundry so she washed all the clothes and bedding herself in cold water. I remember her washing the sheets with her bare hands, rubbing till her knuckles bled. I said, "Mother, your hands are bleeding," and she said, "Yes." And I asked, "Why don't you use a brush?" "No," she replied, "it will wear the sheets out." I thought to myself, she's already worn her hands out, how terrible! Life seemed terrible witnessing my mother's sacrifice. She squeezed the big sheets by hand and hung them up on wire lines. The other children were at school and they didn't know. But I saw these things happening in the house and I felt very sorry for Mother.

Between her periods of hard work or of tears, Mother wrote poetry. Her beautiful poems were to fill a collection that she called *Thy Rosary of a Hundred Beads*. I believe only two-thirds of them were completed at her passing. Mother said she didn't want them published to make money; she didn't want money in return. I think they deserve to be shared because each one is more beautiful than the other. This was her tribute to her departed husband and to love itself.

Dissension after Murshid's Passing

Claire Harper: When our father was no longer there, Summer School still continued; but many things changed, including the atmosphere. Many of the followers changed, some of the regulars no longer came; new ones arrived. Some people attempted to assume leading positions, and our mother had her hands full in trying to protect and fight for justice; and she was all alone to do it.

Murshida Fazal Mai, who had gifted Fazal Manzil to our father, remained in the house until her passing. In certain ways, she adopted a grandmother's role towards us, as well as providing an allowance for food and for the general running of the household.

As long as our father had been there, it had been an acceptable fact that Murshida Fazal Mai would help the family survive financially, but afterwards, it was another story. Being proud, our mother wanted to be as independent as possible. We children were still rather young, and my mother wondered what to do to gain more financial freedom. Our mother wrote to her uncle, George W. Baker, in New Mexico, an uncle who loved her very much and who was delighted to hear from her. He was a lawyer and a cattle rancher—a wealthy man—and he helped her for awhile. For a number of years this economic support trickled in, until the war cut off all contact.

After our father's disappearance, there was some confusion regarding the leadership of the Sufi Movement. I remember that a number of people, among them our uncles, expressed varying views as to how the Sufi Message should continue to be presented.

Shaikh-ul-Mashaikh Pyaromir Maheboob Khan became Murshid's first successor as a "protector and caretaker of Inayat Khan's Sufism."(B) He carried out devotion to the work in his own way for 21 years until his passing. He was also an excellent singer and composer, most beautifully putting to music some of Murshid's most inspiring poetry. Maheboob, who respected, protected and loved his elder brother, stated: "Pir-o-Murshid was a spiritual giant."

Murshid Mohammad Ali Khan's service to humanity was essentially that of a healer. This gift, along with training in various healing practices, began already in Baroda, before setting out with his cousin Inayat to the Western world. It is said that, at times, his gift of healing could be as miraculous as that of our father. Along with his contribution, Mohammad Ali Khan's rich singing voice effectively combined the music of the East and the West in carrying on the musical heritage of the Chishti Sufis.

Murshid Musharaff Moulamia Khan, the youngest of the four Royal Musicians of Hindustan became Mohammad Ali Khan's successor in 1958, carrying on activities in healing and counseling in various centers of the Sufi Movement. He was most emotionally inclined; I remember Uncle Musharaff as being easily moved to tears in many daily situations.

Claire Harper: At the age of fifteen, my brother Vilayat started to array his surroundings with whatever he could collect in the way of Sufi books and "sacred papers" which he was given by Sufi center leaders. He transformed the main dining room into an office and, one day, managed to bring back a giant oak bookcase, picked up at a flea market. Long hours were spent assembling this mammoth.

The dining room table was turned into a desk, and this room was now out of bounds; Vilayat was plunged deep in study. Though school studies were also part of his daily program, Vilayat found time to write an eighty-page spiritual drama entitled *The Light of Truth* at the age of fifteen. Our uncle Maheboob, in charge of the Sufi Movement, told Vilayat that he would safeguard this responsibility until Vilayat was old enough to assume leadership. On the other hand, I remember that Mohammad Ali Khan did all he could to prevent Vilayat from succeeding in this endeavor.

As Vilayat developed into a thoughtful young man, he became increasingly aware of his father's work and legacy. This was a theme in which he showed much interest and would sometimes engage in animated conversations with his uncles. On one occasion, an argument regarding the Sufi message arose between Vilayat and our Uncle Musharaff who, furious, dragged his nephew into the garden, tied him to a tree and began beating him with a stick. The neighbors came to Vilayat's rescue, threatening that if Musharaff did not stop, they would call the police.

At times, it appears that some of the uncles adhered to orthodox Islamic aspects of the Sufi tradition, perhaps not daring to fully embrace the universality of their late brother's Sufi Message. One such example occurred when one of them called for the worship room's yellow curtains to be replaced by green ones, the color of Islam. This so upset our mother that Hidayat tore down the green curtains and threw them in the river.

Mother was often unhappy about mureeds who were unkind to her. Some of these "spiritually-minded" people, who had been so enamored of our father, were occasionally unkind to our mother. They were sometimes rude, made nasty remarks, some even attempted to take on positions of power within the larger Sufi Khankah. One of these people, a man who was a leading member of the Sufi Movement administration, wanted to purchase Fazal Manzil. Our mother fought for us, because the house had been given to the children, and we had the right to live in our home for life. Our father had especially insisted that ownership would be in his and his wife's names, which was important because, under French law, if a husband is deceased, the spouse only has the right to live in the house for life, but the children own it. However, in practice, it appears that things did not work out this way. Uncle Maheboob took the matter in hand by employing an English lawyer, who proved to be very expensive.

Strangely enough, before Murshid left for India, the Sufi Movement asked him to sign over the rights of the Sufi publications to the Sufi Movement. It was his mind, his inspiration that had written all these words of wisdom, and yet they didn't want him to have any rights or power over the books. I discovered this fact when coming across one of the documents pertaining to this issue and, upon asking Vilayat, he confirmed that our father had been forced to relinquish the rights to the books.

Viladat Day

The second birthday in the absence of Murshid was celebrated in the Sufi hall and in the Oriental Room, for prayers and silence. Despite her immeasurable grief, Ora Ray prepared and delivered the following address to the mureeds:

July 5th, 1928

Most devoted mureeds of our Beloved Pir-o-Murshid, I am most grateful to have the privilege of conveying to you a few heart-felt thoughts on this blessed and ever living day as we unite on this sacred ground; thoughts that are so simple yet so true, for Truth lies in simplicity. Was not our Master simple, yet so deep?

May our hearts dictate to us the true and simple object of the summer school. Is it not to unite us all in Love, Harmony and Beauty, which is our Master's Message and which alone will spread the Message over the whole world. Thereby we fulfil sacred duty to our Master, proving our devotion to Him, and in so doing we purify our hearts, which alone allows our souls to receive the light for which we are striving, that we may see through the darkness of the earth.

As our Master has helped us in the past, to purify our hearts and to make our minds clear, that we may have right understanding, even so is He now helping us and will continue helping us until our hearts become pure enough to receive the Light which is the aim of our life on this earth, our eternal goal.

We have but to think in our Master's words, allow our actions to be guided by His words and our speech controlled by His words, then only are we His true devotees and then only can we spread His Message in the world.

I wish to express to you our deepest appreciation for all the help given to us, prompted by the sacred thought of your love and devotion for our Master.

With blessings from above.
(Begum Ameena)

My Schooling

Claire Harper: When I was about four, there was a question of my going to kindergarten but it did not happen. For this reason, I was alone with my mother for a whole winter while the other three children went to school. I must have been seven when I started at the same school. Not speaking French made it a challenge, and the teacher relegated me to the back of the class, which made things very difficult for me. In the last rows of the classroom is where the naughty children sat, as well as those who didn't want to study. They all talked a lot, and I had difficulty in understanding and hearing the teacher. This made me unhappy.

I remember starting the first class in the middle of the year; the other pupils seemed to know their work, but I was lost—everything just went too fast for me. Unexpectedly, the teacher had to leave, and some of the girls cried because they loved her; then a new one came. This, too, upset my rhythm and my hopes. I had difficulty in adjusting to what was expected of me; I sat at my little desk trying with utmost difficulty to understand what I was meant to learn.

I couldn't bother Noor because she was exceedingly busy with her homework, which was much more difficult. I was at a loss, and didn't quite know what to do. My mother wouldn't have been able to help me because she didn't speak French well. As for my brothers, I didn't dare ask them. Each night I would fall asleep on my reading books. I had to learn history and math and so on, but it was all very complicated. So I fell asleep, and was found asleep and put to bed.

But the real punishment came the next day because I didn't know my lessons. I was supposed to read out aloud, stand up and read what I learned, and I couldn't do it. I was very unhappy, and there was a lot of whispering. The children laughed at me, and I was miserable; this was the beginning of a big problem. After some time, I managed to make friends but it was difficult. I needed help from the teacher but I was not given the chance to learn.

Our Musical Education

Claire Harper: As the years passed, life in Fazal Manzil certainly changed. The question of schooling and our children's future was paramount. One year, as usual, we were preparing for a new school year and the eventual onslaught of winter. All four of us were busy choosing and getting enrolled in various schools. At that time, I didn't care for the French schools because I didn't feel at home with the language, so for a time I attended an English school in Paris. Unfortunately, this too proved to be a disappointment.

Kismet suggested helping us with our musical education, which must have helped to console our mother because we would all receive a musical education as well. It is possible that this is what our father had wished for, although ultimately, such a strong focus on musical education did not contribute much to preparing us for professional careers.

And so I simply started to study at the music school with full-day instruction. I took piano lessons and training in composition with Nadia Boulanger, a famous and accomplished pianist. This was an excellent private school, for which the tuition fees were entirely gifted by Kismet. I also studied harmony, musical theory and musical appreciation. In those days, our other activities included listening to the classical music available throughout Paris, thanks to a plethora of concerts.

Of the numerous concert halls, the Salle Pleyel, which had just been built in 1930, was the most well-known. It was small but sympathetic and warm, and here we could applaud such masters as Segovia, Casals, Heifetz, Ezenberg and others, such as Marian Anderson, whose voice was sublime. One shouldn't forget Kreisler or Rubinstein—all those great masters we were lucky enough to hear and see in person. We were even introduced to some of them, thanks to our teachers who took us backstage to meet these stars. Among the famed performers was also Joseph Szigeti, whose nephew was a friend of Hidayat's because he played the violin. Szigeti's nephew was practically adopted by our mother as one of the children. Kismet also learned the violin from Joseph Szigeti. Twenty years later he played in Manhattan on a Sunday afternoon. I attended the concert and, our family having known him, I introduced myself at the end of the concert. Though crowds of people wanted to see him, he would see no one—yet I was called to meet him and he took me to his motor home. We had a brief conversation and then he was gone. Joseph's nephew, Yanchi, became a good friend of Hidayat's at the music school. Our mother often invited him to stay with us in Fazal Manzil. The music conservatory told Yanchi they had nothing more to teach him, such was his genius.

We youngsters became increasingly involved in the musical world. I was very young at the time and didn't realize just what opportunities were offered to me then; I really should have taken them more seriously but, at that age, it was difficult. The fact that our mother was unwell represented a constant worry to me. I would lie in bed before going to sleep, sweating profusely from the thought that, if our mother passed on, we would be alone in the world. I lived with that terrible fear, and it made me dreadfully nervous. I didn't want to share this with either my sister or my brothers. This was a grave matter for me and I simply lived in a constant state of fear.

Noor began studying the harp. I, too, took up the harp with her, but then I found that if I practiced on her harp, I would deprive her of playing on it. A difficult decision had to be made. Only angels and saints play on the harp, so when I glimpsed the piano at the far end of the room, I chose to study the piano. Vilayat studied the cello, and Hidayat the violin. We all attended the same music school, l'Ecole Normale de Musique.

There was a concert hall within the music school complex. As there were so many pupils at the school, this concert hall was full when, for instance, Nadia Boulanger gave us lessons on Gregorian chant or on counterpoint. At first I didn't understand much but, eventually, I came to understand more by trial and error.

Hidayat studied in the violin class of Bernard Sinsheimer and, like the rest of us, the composition class of Nadia Boulanger. He also was part of Diran Alexanian's orchestra class and later he attended chamber music courses given by the Lener Quartet in Budapest. Hidayat eventually became musically active in Holland and worked as a conductor in Haarlem, Holland.

In his early adolescence, Hidayat showed a talent for poetry, writing several poems in French. At the age of fourteen he wrote some romantic verses:

Mon Coeur Languit Pour Toi
Ne sait tu pas, ma bien-aimée
Qu'un cœur languit pour toi ?
Dans l'océan de ta beauté,
Ce cœur languissant se noie.
Ne sait tu pas, O ma chérie
Que languir tous les jours
Est un plaisir qui me réjouit
Et m'exalte d'amour ?

Literal translation:

My Heart Yearns For You
Do you not know, my beloved
That a heart yearns for you?
In the ocean of your beauty,
This yearning heart drowns.
Do you not know, o my dear one,
That to yearn every day
Is a pleasure that rejoices me
And exalts me with love?

Claire Harper: Noor practiced the harp for hours on end. It is a difficult instrument to master and it is also painful to the fingers. Noor's harp was extremely beautiful. Mother bought it at Erard, the manufacturer. I remember how beautiful it looked when it was delivered to the house. Normally a harp has brown wood edgings on the corners of its frame. But these moldings were covered with gold; the whole harp was gold. Two dogs sat at the foot of the harp—small wood carvings — for protection. There were also saints around the crown of the harp. My mother had those saints removed, for what reason I don't really know. It may be related to the fact that my mother was brought up a Methodist. The harp stood in the salon where Noor practiced.

Occasionally, we gathered together and played the music of Mozart, because he had composed for cello, piano, violin and flute. The flute parts could usually be played on the harp. This was an easy way to play together, though it was a rare occasion when we did. Sometimes, when mureeds would wish to see my mother but she didn't feel well enough to receive them or talk to them, we would take over and entertain them with music, making them feel comfortable, welcome and happy, and offering them freshly squeezed orange juice.

The 1930s were days of rigid studies. But they were complemented by plenty of cultural rewards; music, theatre and ballet were in fashion. There was a shortage of concert halls in Paris, which led many churches to rent out space; and standing at the back of the church was free of charge.

Awakening Responsibility

Claire Harper: Birthday occasions were one of the times when I was aware of Noor's influence over us as children. She possessed a guiding hand, and her power—her loving power—was a motherly strength and protection which we sorely needed. It must have been very hard for her. We didn't realize this at the time, so I don't think I was ever very appreciative. I lived in a world of my own and had this power of my own, which I did not hesitate to demonstrate. This is why I was called the "ruling power" by our father, and I'm sorry to say that I made Noor cry quite often because of it, because of that stubborn streak in me. Yet I don't remember ever being punished or reprimanded for this behavior.

Noor's will power, as well, was very much present—especially when she wrote her stories, her poetry and her compositions. We never knew where she really was. At times I would be surprised to find her in the Oriental Room, sitting at one of the round Oriental tables, particularly a dark brown one, inlaid with mother of pearl. Here she would busy herself writing poetry on the typewriter. I wouldn't say anything, knowing she was occupied and deep in thought; so I would just quietly leave the room.

Noor's atmosphere was sad and, in a way, we were all sad. We were extremely serious, except on occasions when Hidayat and I were a little more jovial. We were very much aware of the fact that duty and responsibility came first. Sacrificing for each other also had to come into play. This was hard to do. When we were rewarded, it encouraged us to continue in this way of feeling and doing.

Life was a serious business. When I failed—something that happened very often with me—I was strongly reprimanded by the other three. I felt shamed. Vilayat was the strongest male element in Fazal Manzil and he came to feel a sense of responsibility around the household as well. He became a kind of ally with Noor, and the two established themselves in the dining room.

Mother's Music

Claire Harper: Our mother enjoyed the music of Massenet, especially the opera *Thais* and the song *Berceuse*. Offenbach's *The Tales of Hoffman* was also among her favorites. In fact, sometimes Mother played on the piano herself. She could also play the guitar. Having left all her belongings behind when she escaped to Europe, she had no guitar with her; but her joy in America had been to play the guitar. For Mother's birthday, we children found a Guadanini at Rue de Rome in Paris. The street was famous for its sheet music and also for musical instrument makers, because it was located around the corner from the Conservatory of Music. Normally a very expensive guitar, this one was affordable and was a surprise and a consolation to our mother.

Mother's graceful hands touched and played this beautiful instrument with a deep feeling of wonder. The guitar survived the war. It was found in the attic in perfect condition but, unfortunately, through the years it was stolen in the end, just like so many other things, especially those that were kept in the Oriental Room.

Easter in Suresnes in 1930

Claire Harper: We children awoke early with spring in the air. Outside, the chill of an April morning still lingered. For us, Easter signified a sacred day. As we looked out of the window, we discovered a powder blue sky, and the sun shone with all its might, announcing a beautiful day.

Our young lives were able to see this beauty better than a camera—we took it all in. We children were all budding like the spring flowers in the garden. The white carnations' fragrance wafted into the open windows. The dew on the grass resembled diamond chips. No cars disturbed the stillness; only the clop-clop of horse-drawn carts hauling the food to market could be heard. A warm breeze softly caressed our cheeks, crocuses and pansies strewed the ground. Orange blossom could be scented; the quince tree and Abba's pear tree were in bloom as well. The acacia's drooping yellow blooms were fairy-like. The hilltop fort of Mont Valérien clearly came to view. Mother was very pleased to know that Noor and Vilayat had planned out an Easter goody hunt in the garden.

But Easter Sunday was also market day, and our mother had made a long shopping list. The townsfolk bought cakes and flowers, as was the custom. The church bells echoed their repeated invitation as the locals filled up the brick churches. Most everyone was clad in their Sunday best, and families would go to market as a group. In those days, shopping bags on wheels did not exist. Every member of the family helped carry the customary cloth bags and wicker baskets. The stores and market stalls overflowed with every type of fresh produce: lettuce, farm eggs, garden vegetables, fresh fruit, herbs and homemade pastries. Our market farmers had begun harvesting their produce at five in the morning and were extremely proud of their bounty. As we drifted from stall to stall, the market folk sought to draw our attention by shouting out the prices of their wares, adding to the din and animation.

Of course our shopping list included baguette, regional cheeses, and fresh dairy milk (Mother always delighted at the sight of the layer of cream topping the milk). Once our mission completed, Mother and Noor began preparing Easter lunch. I asked Mother the meaning of Easter. She told me it was a celebration in the memory of the Lord Jesus Christ.

In the afternoon, Hidayat and I helped Murshida Fazal Mai with the service arrangements in the reception rooms. We balked at the idea of closing all the shutters, making the room as dark as night. The dining room table had to be moved from the center of the room to one end, against the window. Electric lights were switched on in the room, and we draped a yellow altar cloth over the table. The candlestick holders had to be cleaned and the books of each great religion placed on the altar—one on Sufism was in the center. We moved all the chairs to face the altar, and the piano was moved from one room to another. While we were taking care of all this, our black pet salamander fell out of its fishbowl and couldn't be found. We brought out vases in expectation of the flowers that some of the Sufis would bring. Now there was little time to change before the mureeds' arrival.

When Murshida Fazal Mai came down from her quarters and solemnly began the service, I wished her to hurry through the sermon; to me it seemed an eternity to have to sit quietly in the darkened room, heavy with gravity. As soon as the service was over and the mureeds departed, we began to reopen the shutters and tidy up.

It was only after the service was over that we were allowed to go out into the garden to see what the Easter Bunny had brought us. We were all so eager and happy that we could hardly wait for Mother to join us outside. While waiting for her, I was startled to spot a little robin redbreast perched on the same branch where I had discovered it the year before. He enjoyed being spoken to and remained transfixed as I whispered to him.

When everyone was present, we set off on our Easter egg hunt. I was indeed delighted to find home-colored eggs on windowsills and behind bushes, as well as little foil-wrapped goodies hidden among the flowers. Though the tragedy of Murshid's absence still weighed heavily upon our family, this particular day was brightened by the joy of spring and by the promise of rebirth that Easter conveys.

Holidays in Holland

Claire Harper: After Father's passing, we did not keep up much correspondence with any of the mureeds. Some were quite condoling and endeavored to remain in contact. Not being well, our mother preferred being on her own. There came a time, however, around 1933, when Saida and Sirdar showed increased interest in helping us children. They started with Noor, inviting her to Holland for a few weeks and then a few months. Eventually I was invited as well. I remember the first summer when we went together; they had organized an extensive program for our stay. Being in Holland was a very new adventure for me, new in every way, and looking back, I can say that we were spoilt after the hard times we had often had in Suresnes.

The first thing on our agenda was for me to learn horseback riding. Naturally, we first shopped for riding clothes and gear. Both Noor and I were allowed to try on whatever suited us or whatever came in our size. I remember Saida and Sirdar helping to pull off my riding boots; I had tried them on and couldn't get them off. Now that we had our complete outfits, no time was wasted. The very next morning, we went to the stables and spent the morning at the riding school. They had provided us with carrots to reward the horses. I remember also receiving bicycles as gifts and riding to the stables.

The second part of the plan was for Noor to work together with Saida in the choice of illustrations for Noor's book, *Twenty Jakata Tales*. This was a large task, as Saida—being such a fine artist—wanted the illustrations to be as beautiful as possible. Discussions and work went on for a long time until, finally, the book was published. This was a great achievement for Noor, and we joined in her happiness and feeling of satisfaction.

Noor took lessons on the vina, and Sirdar and Saida also rented a harp so that Noor could play in the evenings or whenever she had time. They were very enterprising in helping us. Noor was the most important at that time because she had done so much to bring us up, and she needed a break.

Noor and I were also taken on trips to see other Dutch towns, such as Leiden. We visited various exhibitions, such as flower shows—we'd never seen a flower exhibition—it was gorgeous. At various seasons of the year, there were different flowers, of course, so there was always a variety and a change in the displays of the numerous exhibitions; Holland being the cradle for cultivated flowers, there were numerous beautiful arrangements.

Sirdar and Saida invited our mother, Vilayat and Hidayat also. They spent a short time there, maybe a week or two, and returned to Suresnes. During that time, it was very nice to all be together in that beautiful house.

The house had two floors as well as a roof garden. The ground floor entrance had black and white square tiles, just as in one of the Vermeer paintings, and rustic looking wood as well as a large wooden bench with a high back. In the center of the hall stood a long, impressive table. Opposite the entrance, a few stairs led up to what was called the music room. It had beautiful paintings lining the walls and Persian carpets on the floor and on the table, thus creating a cozy atmosphere. Further on, one came to the entrance to the church; Sirdar had built a church hall at the back of the house. Expansive and boasting a high ceiling, the hall offered seating for, perhaps, up to a hundred visitors.

Upstairs were bedrooms. The first room was Saida's bedroom; very tastefully arranged with a four-poster bed and a lovely wardrobe and an armchair. The floors were covered with Persian carpets. Further on along through the doorway was Saida's workroom, a sort of living room/workroom where she would be quiet, looking out the windows that lined the room. One window gave onto the roof garden; another looked out onto the Peace Palace. So it was a very beautiful and comfortable room. Back toward the stairs was the guestroom that Noor and I occupied. Sirdar's room was further toward the back of the house. Downstairs was a very spacious kitchen and pantry. The dining room was also very elegant, its walls covered with old Dutch paintings. It had two large windows; one gave onto the street, the other onto the garden. In the center was a great big round table, the dining room table. There was also a large fireplace which was sometimes used in the winter. All the furniture was handmade in the old Dutch style in dark brown, highly polished, rustic wood.

Sirdar and Saida had help: Paula the housekeeper. She was German but had probably gone to school in Holland. She was there already during the First World War so she was more Dutch than German, except she remembered how to make German pies, which were delicious. She was a nice person and I liked her very much. She was always working and I felt sorry for her, but there was nothing I could do. She also had a helper to do other things, as there was a lot of work to be done every day to run a household of that size.

Whenever Vilayat visited, he spoke at length with Sirdar. He must have been about fifteen or sixteen at the time and was eager to learn all he could about Sufism and the Sufi activities, and the thoughts and ideas of other people, too. It was his opportunity to draw closer to what proved to become his life's calling. Vilayat often wore a brown shervani that our mother had made for him in Paris, and it suited him well. He and Sirdar conversed in the library. There, the walls were lined with books, and large windows shed light onto a huge table.

Sirdar was a scholar, and it was interesting to speak with him, although I was only in my teens. I confess, I really didn't know much about anything, but I wasn't shy with Sirdar and Saida because they were so friendly.

As a token of appreciation for having invited him, Vilayat gave Sirdar his favorite pen. I believe it was gold-plated. Vilayat also rode horses and there are a few pictures of him on horseback.

Sirdar was spreading the Message in Dutch in his church and drew a large and enthusiastic public. Sirdar van Tuyll eventually broke away from the Sufi Movement and ran his church independently.

Sirkar von Stolk and Sirdar von Tuyll were never close friends. While he was still there, Murshid had tried to make these two powerful men active in the Sufi Movement in such as way as to bring them closer together. However, somewhere there seemed to be some kind of rivalry or enmity between them, but they did meet to talk and convey their thoughts.

Making Do

Claire Harper: During the 1930s, I grew to the age when I realized to what extent my mother needed help. My sister was older and therefore busy, doing more important things, and my brothers were constantly off somewhere. Hidayat drove his new car around, a vehicle that Murshida Fazal Mai had given him with the understanding that he would also chauffeur her places when needed. Vilayat was always at the Quartier Latin, the student district of Paris; whether it was to study or to meet friends, he loved that neighborhood and he was involved in his studies there summer and winter.

The result was that I was the only one at home and I wondered how I could assist my mother in her work around the house. I adapted myself quite fast to the household chores, and they were many. The one would lead to another, and before I knew it, there was a lot to do. My health was pretty good, apart from a year-round allergy which made me lose energy. I would have to blow my nose almost constantly. My mother gave me old torn-up sheets, huge squares as large as headscarves. Nonetheless, I helped her as best I could.

While Vilayat occupied our former dining room, Hidayat decided that, as he had watched the electrician do work in Fazal Manzil, he would put in switches and additional electric connections everywhere to make it easier for us to turn lights on and off. He managed to get everything together to undertake this project and spent hours doing electrical work. He was proud indeed whenever he succeeded. I was worried about him because I felt that there was some danger, but he assured me there was none. I still think it was dangerous in those days, because the cables were questionable, especially the old wires that he would cut with scissors. So I kept watching him, just in case he got electrocuted, so I could do something, not really knowing exactly what.

The cellar was full of old odds and ends that had accumulated for years. Hidayat and I teamed up and put everything outside in the garden to see what there was. We would keep some of the bits and pieces, and throw the rest away.

We were always tidying and reducing the amount of excess junk in the cellar so we could put large tables in there and create some kind of order. We kept ourselves busy. One day I had the bright idea of using the bathroom on the ground floor, where the maids were meant to be living. In fact, it wasn't much of a bathroom because the room housed a huge heater which occupied practically half the space of the bathroom. But I used the bath to wash everything that I thought should be kept. I also used the bath for "dry-cleaning." That is where I cleaned my brothers' suits, ties, scarves and hats. I put them in the bath to soak them in petrol and then I ran out quickly to hang everything outside to dry, because the smell was horribly strong. I became quite an expert, and my mother was very pleased because everything would come up clean.

Hidayat seemed to understand the practical problems and needs in the house; he possessed a knack for fixing things or putting things in order and he seemed interested in household amenities. We had to just make do with what little we had.

Memories of Noor

Claire Harper: Noor-un-nisa signifies the "light of womanhood"; the lantern of her soul shone Divine Light on earth. Her writing poured down like rain through rainbow hues. At the age of seven, she wrote a birthday wish to our mother:

> *Ammah jan, I wish you the happiest happy birthday you have ever had and I hope you will have no work to do but get out in the beautiful parks and play with us. And I hope Allah will make it a beautiful day. And I hope you will have hundreds of presents and hundreds of birthday cards. With all the love and kisses from your loving little daughter. Noorunissa Inayat Khan*

Just two months later, in July 1922, Ora Ray was taken ill, and it was thought best to keep her at a mureed's house in Paris, far from a mother's duties at home. Noor wrote:

> *Ammah jan, Every night we all ask Allah to make you quite well and strong and to bring you home quickly and safely. I know you are in Paris but I don't know where. Please will you right and tell me were you are living. I am sending you these little children* [drawing of children] *to remind you of us. When Abbah brings me to see you I will bring you something that Miss Strauss has brought us… The children are very good and have been making photographs… With all the love and a hundred kisses, Noorunissa*

Claire Harper: Because French children had trouble spelling and pronouncing my name, Khair-un-nisa, Noor exclaimed "From now on, we will call you Claire."

At dawn, Noor would sometimes wake me by singing a most appropriate and beautiful aria from a well-known opera: "Paresseuse fille, qui someille encore. Déja le jour brille dans son manteau d'or…" Listening to her angelic, crystal soprano voice, one could well imagine her wearing a fairytale dress to match it.

After our father's passing, Noor and I would never mention the past; it was too sad a reminder of his absence. We grasped and held on to the present—it was the only staff to hold onto.

Noor's studies and homework often occupied her till midnight. Our mother, by her presence, gave Noor moral support at night so that she wouldn't be alone. Noor had to go to school early each morning and know her lessons well. Despite the language challenges, Noor excelled in many subjects, especially French and literature.

Baroness Sarah Agnes Sophia van Pallandt, whose Sufi name was Sarojeni, was a dear lady of the Dutch aristocracy, and a most devoted, beautiful soul. Her son, Floris,[(6)] whose Sufi name was Huzurnawaz, was in his mid-twenties at the time and studying to become a diplomat. Sarojeni had plans for her son to marry Noor, who was about eighteen at the time. Sarojeni van Pallandt encouraged the union in a very subtle way. My mother knew of this, as did Noor, who was very happy. She looked forward to this friendship developing.

Each summer Baroness Sarojeni van Pallandt came, with her son Huzurnawaz, to visit our mother. This became a custom; and she made it her duty and her pleasure to take Noor and me to Paris to one of the department stores—which in those days were more exclusive than they are now—either Le Printemps or the Galeries Lafayette. She chose with us the material we wanted to select for summer dresses to be made or evening dresses for parties. They were pink silk or whatever color we wanted, and these clothes were made for us. Our sizes were measured and the dresses were ready within a week. Noor chose a beautiful silk of some lighter pastel shade of pink, whereas I preferred tea pink. I remember my dress was very pretty, with a gold lace band across the front. It reminded me of India with its ever-present gold embroideries. These were gifts that Sarojeni wanted us to have; perhaps a token of appreciation for Murshid's work and effort, as well as for our mother. Sarojeni loved our mother; she was always kind to her and wanted to do her utmost for the whole family. I vaguely recall the boys receiving beautiful clothes as well. Hidayat wore a silver silk suit with a pink collar; I used to think that combination was most beautiful. Vilayat wore a brown suit with shorts. I believe the outfit was also a present from Sarojeni.

I was too young to really follow the development between Noor and Huzurnawaz. I wouldn't know exactly when they would have had the opportunity to talk or go for walks or play music together or visit. What I do remember is that there came a time when the relationship was leaking out, and a few people knew about it; our uncles were told as well. It is possible that Huzurnawaz asked Maheboob Khan for his approval, as he was our legal guardian, and eventually, Mohammad Ali got to know about it. The sad thing was that we received a phone call—it was usual for the eldest to answer the phone, so Noor did. Mohammad Ali was on the phone and he told her that he disapproved of the friendship. This had been more than a friendship; Noor collapsed right at the telephone. To her this refusal was a terrible blow.

It was about this time that Noor wrote:

> *The four little children of Murshid were named: Noor, Vilayat, Hidayat and Khair. They called their father Abba and their mother Amma.*
>
> *The first lesson Abba taught to his little ones was to open their eyes to selfless love and devotion and constant sacrifice of their Amma. He painted in our little hearts the ideal of motherhood, in all its beauty and purity. "Heaven lies at the mother's feet." He taught us to show our gratitude in the smallest little way, to renounce gladly to a game or amusement if we saw the least little thing which we could do to give joy to our Amma or if we felt that our playing caused her the least displeasure. When playtime was over just before the night covered our solitary house in the fields, the four little ones went off to sleep. Abba would gather, most times little Khair-un-nisa on his knees and he told them stories of his childhood, he told them of his love for his mother and the sweet deeds which that love brought about. He rooted in our souls the feeling that our first and most sacred duty was towards our mother and even our prayers to God were secondary; for the prayers of the child which does not consider its mother are not heard by God.*

Claire Harper: Noor composed musical pieces for her golden harp, as well as songs dedicated to the sages of the East. When she heard me play my compositions for piano, she would sometimes sing the melodies with her celestial voice, thus bringing inspiration closer to our hearts. One of Noor's own songs was:

SONG TO THE MADZUB

At Thy Feet, O Madzub, I come to seek Rest,
In the Fire of Thy Glance, may this yearning Soul be blessed.
Thy Footprints of Crushed Thorns are strewn with Pearls Divine,
And Lo! Their Glory unveils, these dazzled eyes of mine.
Thro' Life's Test, may this heart, O Thou Living Shrine,

As a Lotus once bloom, Bloom in these Rays of Thine.
At Thy Feet, O Madzub, I come to seek for Rest,
In the fire of Thy Glance, may this yearning Soul be blessed.

Claire Harper: When Noor and I would return from having attended a concert in Paris, we remained speechless; music lent us consolation and courage. To listen to the masterpieces of the great composers was like magic. The musicians seemed to exceed their own technique and talent in their interpretation. Having listened to these wonders helped us in our studies, and we realized that music was a language of its own.

Noor liked to type stories and poems or simply visit her school friends. She had many projects, so we let her do whatever she felt she needed to do. I always felt sorry for her because she was exceptionally studious and utterly devoted to everything she undertook, while remaining sweet to everyone. As Noor was older than the rest of us and more responsible, our mother told us that we must let her do what she had to do. We all loved our sister, respected her and left her alone. In addition to writing over a dozen stories, Noor rewrote and adapted the famed *Jataka Tales*, based on stories of Buddha. Noor also wrote extensively in French and was able to have some of the stories and poems published in the famed French newspaper, *Le Figaro des Enfants*. She was also busy creating a newspaper for children, called *Eureka*. Noor excelled at poetry and would not fail to write exquisite messages in rhyme for our mother and us on special occasions, such as birthdays. At the age of 16 she wrote the following:

To Our Amma

See your four little ones
Unfold in your heart's bright ray
As buds with teardrops bedewed
Unfold at the dawn of day.
Even if the whole world,
Would serve us and help us e'er,
Still it could not equal
Your tender motherly care.
Forgive us, dear Amma,
For often we lose our way,
How oft' in this vast world,
You kept us from going astray.
Hidden within our hearts,

In deep gratitude for you,
May it bloom more and more,
For none can be so true.
Lo! His thoughts so deep
In sparks are manifest,
To console your heart
Throughout life's painful test.
Ah! Beloved Amma,
E'er keep this before your eyes:
"My sorrow, forget not,
Once again joy will arise."

In the late 1930s, Noor felt that she could write better for children if she understood their world, their psychology. She undertook studies in child psychology at the university in Paris. In one of her dissertations she wrote:

> *Children require a wide area open to them that they may think and act freely… There is reason to believe that traces of the higher planes are disclosed to little children, whereas they are veiled from the eyes of the parents…We might help the little ones by studying their thoughts and actions, giving to each thought and action the same importance as to those of our own, thus not only helping them but also lending a new trend to our own thoughts.*

It was around 1934 that Noor was courted by Azeem Goldenberg. An outstanding pianist of Turkish Jewish origin, he worked with Noor on her musical compositions, harmonizing their accompaniment on piano. This companionship turned into a close friendship and, despite much opposition from the uncles, a six-year romance. Sadly, the war would put an end to the relationship.

Noor, ever the poet, wrote the following lines in June 1936, on the occasion of Vilayat's twentieth birthday:

Just listen to what the birdies say
That twenty years ago this day
From heaven came a little boy
And brought on earth a world of joy.
And long was he awaited here
To be his father's sonny dear,
And all along the way, His love
Will bring him blessings from above.

Claire Harper: Bringing to mind our sisterly love and friendship, I would say that Noor was an unending source of inspiration. She set an unattainable example for me, as well as for countless others, not only while she was living but also long after her untimely departure from this plane.

While the declaration of WWII was blaring overhead, in a rush, Noor took me to a well-known and fashionable shop in Paris. She asked me to wait for her while she chose something in secret. Very shortly thereafter, we were in the process of packing up our home, Fazal Manzil, en route for England, when Noor pinned a badge onto my jacket pocket. It was decorated with America's stars and stripes, and embroidered with gold. I was very touched. I had forgotten it was my birthday—but she remembered and took it to heart.

Part Four: The War Years, 1939–1946

FLIGHT TO ENGLAND

Escaping the Nazis

Only two decades had passed since the end of WWI, which Murshid had described as the "War of Paper," before the next war was ignited. Murshid had referred to WWII as the "War of Wood," burning hotter and longer than the previous one.

Claire Harper: In 1939, there reigned an element of unrest in France and throughout the world, but principally in England. There seemed to be a sort of agitation between England and Germany. At the time, I didn't realize how serious it was. I thought these were just passing misunderstandings between countries. Being older, Vilayat and Noor listened more attentively to the radio and they followed the developments on the news. The headlines were not promising, nor were the activities of the German Reich.

After Germany's annexation of Austria the year before, followed shortly by Hitler's takeover of Czechoslovakia, the rest of Europe stood on guard. We knew that Germany's leadership was kind to its own countrymen; it was producing a lot of Volkswagen cars. Hitler promised the Nazi Party members many things: a house, a car, vacation plans, etc. Germany was beginning to become very strong and was reinforcing its military force. Things were becoming a bit frightening.

By late summer of 1939, we learned of a direct threat from Germany due to its invasion of Poland. The taking of Danzig would affect a lot of shipping companies, so England felt most concerned.

At that time, we were scattered around Europe. Hidayat was married to Leni (later named Iman) and spent much of his time in Holland. I happened to be in Holland as well, whereas Noor and Vilayat were in Spain. It was around this time that Murshida Fazal Mai, who had been living in the house, left for Holland with us; sadly, shortly after, she passed away.

With the reality of war imminent, we children decided to return home quickly to discuss what to do about this threat. Reunited in Fazal Manzil we decided that Noor and I would learn nursing so that we could help on the front in the event of war. We attended a course that lasted six months and, as it was a very intense course in Red Cross nursing, we graduated as full-fledged nurses. During that time, world events worsened. We thought, if the fighting came to France, we couldn't stay in Suresnes. If the Germans invaded France, we wouldn't be allowed to fight, so our idea was to go to England; we all had British passports, so travel to England would be no problem, and there we would be free to become involved.

We had made a positive decision, but we didn't talk to each other about it, just about the situation. Hidayat was worried because the safety of Holland was threatened as well: it seemed that Germany was about to invade Holland, Belgium and France. At that time we heard that Belgium had given up; that the king had abdicated, and Belgium had capitulated to Germany. We were furious. Everything happened so quickly. With Belgium taken, the next country would be France.

In June 1940, we had nearly completed our preparations. Our mother had tried to pack the minimum that we needed for our trip to England. We had to travel but we couldn't depend on trains as they were not running on schedule; nor could we depend on buses. Vilayat had a small sports car, an MG which was only a two-seater, but we decided that we could squeeze four passengers in his car. Hidayat also had a car and he fled Holland as soon as he could. There was a threat that any British subject would be imprisoned or killed, so we thought, "We British have to get back to Britain." Hidayat, his wife and, I think, one uncle arrived by car and continued towards the relative safety of the south of France.

What precipitated our departure was the sound of guns heard in the distance. On June 10th, panic was breaking out, shops had closed and there was a smokescreen over Suresnes. Soldiers at the bottom of our street had used artificial smoke to fog out the people who were leaving. We realized that it was high time we left too, before it was too late. Vilayat led the way south, and Hidayat followed in his car as a convoy. Our mother sat in the front with Vilayat, and we two, Noor and I, squeezed in the jump seat. It was extremely cramped but it didn't matter; we were together.

Despite all the careful packing of suitcases, there was no room in the car, so we just took what we had on us: no suitcases, nothing. We headed southwest of Paris in the direction of Tours, where the trains were reportedly still running and might take us towards Great Britain. On the way, the roads became more and more congested with cars, and there were multitudes walking along the highway. Everywhere, we encountered people with children, old people, animals, carts—everyone and everything seemed to be moving along the roads.

We ran into very bad traffic jams; we had to wait and wait. Then, in the midst of this chaos, we lost Hidayat. When we reached the train station in Tours, pandemonium reigned. The station had been targeted by an incendiary bomb which caused a fire, resulting in some of the enormous glass roof breaking. The noise of the glass shattering caused the crowds to panic. People were being pushed over and trampled on in their panic, their desperate rush to get away.

We were fortunate that we managed to hold on to each other and leave the station unscathed. Later we found out that the reason for this bombing was that most of the government had left Paris at the same time as us—we were, in fact, escaping alongside the political leaders of France, and that was the reason why they had put up a smokescreen in Paris. Tours was a military base and for that reason it was being bombed, as well as to keep people from taking trains.

In Tours, we managed to obtain a letter of introduction from Mademoiselle Guérineau, a Red Cross friend who worked for the Childrens' Social Services in Paris. Like us, she happened to be on the run in Tours and provided us with a recommendation addressed to Mademoiselle Fritsch, the president of the Social Services in Bordeaux. With this in hand, we continued south to Bordeaux. Upon arrival in Bordeaux on June 12th, we were not allowed to get off the train as the station, as well as the city, was overcrowded with people trying to escape. Many were headed towards the south of France and Spain. We were obliged to pursue our journey to the small port town of Le Verdon, approximately 50 miles north of Bordeaux's harbor.

Suddenly Noor said: "If there's a war on, there are people being killed. I am a nurse and I have to help them." She blurted this out at a moment when we had to decide whether we were going to take the boat or not. "Also we need copies of our Croix Rouge (French Red

Cross) Nursing Certificates." It is true that we had failed to bring these along when we left home in a hurry.

She also talked about her traveling to La Rochelle, Brest or St. Nazaire to report to the British Red Cross. I said, "No, you can't go there alone; I'm coming with you." So we left together, and our mother was in despair to see us go. We said, "We'll come back. If it's too hard where we're going, we'll come back; so wait for us." Vilayat said, "Well, hurry up, because there aren't so many boats left to take us."

So we hurried. We went to different places. We jumped on a bus to see if we could go to La Rochelle but, apparently, it had been bombed. So we continued far towards the north to Saint Nazaire, a port in Brittany, in the dark—and the area was being bombed. We didn't know exactly where to go, but Noor seemed to know. She said, "Oh, look; there's a British Red Cross ship." I said, "So what's the difference? We're supposed to be helping the French wounded, but there's nobody around." Just then, the air raid increased. We took shelter in a warehouse near the Red Cross ship. From somewhere in that same warehouse, lights flashed on and off. I believe these were collaborators—people who backed the Germans and who were sending signals.

I started to complain, saying, "Mother is waiting for us, Vilayat is waiting for us; we must get back."

We were in a very dangerous spot there. It was pitch black, and we were hiding behind large sacks in the warehouse. The people who were flashing the lights were very close to us, probably telling the Germans where to bomb. The Red Cross ship was illuminated with a large red cross on its side so as to be protected. Somehow we got away and found a hotel. I was frightened because it was late at night and all the lights were off. We went up in an elevator, and I was scared because the people in the elevator looked shifty.

Finally alone, we agreed that those people might be collaborators, and I suggested, "Let's get out of here quickly." But when we went down and tried to leave, they wouldn't let us. They said, "Who are you?" We said, "Just normal people." They kept us prisoner. We waited to see what they would do, whether they would question us as to who we really were. We had to show our passports and we were very scared. Suddenly another round of bombs fell. Taking advantage of this element of surprise, we ran for our lives.

Noor said "It's really impossible here. Let's get on that ship; at least we'll be safe there. Maybe we can go over to England in that ship." We saw British naval officers there, and they asked to see our passports. When they saw we were British, they said they could take us over when they left, but if the bombing continued, they wouldn't be leaving. I said to Noor, "I'm not going. I'm going back down to Mother." So there was a little bit of a dispute between Noor and me, because she said, "They're going to join us from there; they're taking a boat. Vilayat is definitely going to take a boat to England with Mother. So if they take a boat and we don't go, we'll be completely stuck." I retorted, "No. We're going down. If we don't find them, then we'll know they've gone, and we'll see what chances we still have."

It took us about twenty-four hours, if not two days, to return to Le Verdon because there were few buses. We jumped on buses and walked a lot; our shoes were terribly worn and we never ate: there was no bread, nothing to eat and no chance to sleep. We just walked and walked and tried to find our way by asking people, but they couldn't care less. It was wartime and nobody knew what was going on; they had just left their homes—Lord knows where they were heading. At night, all was black.

We were stuck somewhere with no conceivable way of continuing our journey. Suddenly we found one bus that was going to leave for the south. We managed to squeeze aboard though it was already full of passengers: we snuck in through the back door. The people on the bus didn't approve, but we didn't care. We were in and we were together, that was the main thing.

Then we waited a long time, and the driver said, "We must wait here because there are dogfights overhead and we won't be able to leave as long as the bombing continues." So we stood waiting for eight hours, wondering whether the bus would finally go; at last it did. The bus did not take us all the way to our destination, though. We still had another journey; we had to take a ferry and we weren't sure if the ferryboat to Le Verdon was still running. As we waited at the dock, night fell. All kinds of people came, but still there was no ferry. We thought, well, if it's not tonight then maybe it will come tomorrow morning. We wanted to spend the night in the waiting room of the ferry dock but couldn't sleep because lots of Polish men were bothering us. We escaped for the rest of the night into the privacy of a small fishing boat on the dock. In the morning around eight o'clock, it was a relief to see the ferry show up. We were so tired by then, we didn't know if we were standing or sitting but we were extremely relieved to board that ferry. Finally it left, taking us towards our destination.

When we arrived at Le Verdon it was midday, and the Germans had announced on the radio that anyone seen on the streets would be shot. We thought that we had better run. I don't think I ran so fast in all my young years as at that moment. When we finally found our mother, she cried bitterly, and Vilayat was angry. He said, "Where have you been? We thought we'd never get across." We didn't say anything; we were just happy to be reunited.

Vilayat said, "There is still one last boat leaving and it's waiting for us." He had already worked out a plan to get us all to the freight docks because he had somehow found a motorcycle (the car had run out of fuel). First he took our mother, who sat on the back—I don't suppose she'd ever been on a motorcycle in her life—and he drove rather fast because of the rush to catch the boat. It was about ten or fifteen minutes' ride to the cargo boat that was waiting. Vilayat left our mother there with the captain and returned to fetch Noor, take her to the boat, and then returned to get me.

Vilayat also managed to buy some bread because the people on the boat asked us to bring as much food as possible, as they didn't know how long we would be traveling and didn't know how many people there would be to feed. Finally, leaving the motorcycle on the beach, Vilayat boarded the boat with us. We were all together at last and could hardly believe it! I believe we were the last passengers to board.

The cargo ship sailed towards freedom and a new life for us all on June 19th, 1940: coincidentally Vilayat's 24th birthday! What a celebration! We conversed with the other passengers, exchanging news of the war developments. Everybody told their side of the story; how they had escaped. We also discussed our plans should we arrive safely in England. But there weren't many plans to be made, as we weren't sure we would ever reach dry land. Danger lurked even on the high seas from both the air and from underwater.

I didn't have to worry much about our future because Vilayat did all the thinking. He had already been in England, spending considerable time studying at college in Oxford. He knew where he was going to take us once we landed. On the boat, my mother was delighted to be talking to English-speaking people, because for many years she had so often been forced to communicate in French. Her mastery of French was poor because she had never had the time to learn the language properly.

Mother was more relaxed and could explain what she'd gone through to whomever she was talking, and we were pleased that she was communicating with people and not feeling upset or, at least, not showing it. Noor made friends with the daughter of a Belgian politician—I believe he was the foreign minister. Everything seemed to go easier for a while.

Noor put in words her sentiment regarding the plight of the French people under German occupation. The ideas and ideals she expressed were to prove prophetic for the heroism and dedication she would soon reveal. Some excerpts from her essay entitled "Escape from St. Nazaire (1940)":

> *At the docks of St. Nazaire... All had changed. The town was stunned stiff. Wild eyes... tensed chins. Their throats were choked. I sat and waited for the next ferry. The dock was crowded.*
>
> *I understood that the news of France on fire, in flames... Paris! Gates open, the tomb of their unknown soldier guarded by the enemy... God! It was worse than death!*
>
> *In a flash, 20 glorious generations passed through every mind, Charlemagne, Joan of Arc, Napoleon, Foch ... as the whole life of a man passes before him when he sees death.*
>
> *"Tell this to our English comrades," said the soldier. "Tell them that we'll fight for it back, every acre of it. We'll go to the other end of the world but we'll fight for it back."*
>
> *The will of a whole nation was spoken on his quivering lips. Can the will of a nation be crushed? Perhaps suppressed momentarily... Material can be crushed, that's all. Simple are those who believe that all is peace in France. Of all with whom I have come in contact, not one is ready to submit. I can challenge that, at this very moment, thousands are giving their lives "pour la patrie" (for the homeland). Their secret hope is Britain across the sea. We hold a task never in history a land has held before. No, France shall not die! France shall live again.*

Claire Harper: After a long journey, we arrived at last on June 22nd, 1940, hardly daring to believe that British soil was in sight. Narrowly escaping the enemy, our boat-crossing from Le Verdon, France, to Falmouth, England, had lasted three full days.

At the dock, we found that we were just a few amongst the multitudes who had been doing the same thing: taking boats, even their own small boats to escape to England because it was still a free country.

A New Life

After having set foot on British soil, the family must have thanked the heavens. A great many people stood in endless lines or busied themselves on the docks: at least one thousand people were waiting their turn at immigration. The family was limp with exhaustion and dehydrated. Not only British nationals were there, but French, Polish and many other travelers waited patiently. Whoever had managed to flee to freedom was corralled under huge tents. A tense silence spread around those waiting and praying at the immigration booths.

Claire Harper: A registration system had been set up to process all the travelers into Great Britain. After having waited our turn for hours, our family was finally called to immigration. Mother signed her name as Baker, whereas Noor and Vilayat registered as Inayat-Khan. Vilayat's name was too complicated for the clerk to write, so being asked for a shorter name, Vilayat thought of "Victor," which the clerk shortened to "Vic." I followed Mother's Western example and signed in as Claire Baker.

Only towards evening could we move on; we had spent most of the day in the long queues at the dock but, after a three-hour train ride, we reached Oxford at last, where Vilayat said, "We're all together here now; we'll find a bed and breakfast." We were very tired, thirsty and hungry. Finally Vilayat found us a bed and breakfast, where the kind landlady served us tea and snacks. It took quite an effort to maintain a polite disposition. Very generously, the landlady's daughter gave up her own room to accommodate us. A big bed accommodated my mother, Noor and me. Vilayat occupied a small room equally as quaint. We all awoke 24 hours later, which must have been the first time something quite so uncivilized had occurred in the landlady's respectable house, set in a central area looking out on Cowley Street. We were most surprised that we had slept so long. As we were getting ready, we were happy to find one another. Without saying much, Vilayat was pleased that we had found accommodation, especially in time of war.

WAR OF WOOD

Oxford 1940

Claire Harper: Since it was summertime, we were free from having to bundle up. After some tea and toast, we were ready for action; none of us had any more than pennies in our pockets. Noor had a friend visit her in the sitting-room, while Vilayat was out looking up his friends from Oxford University. He also volunteered his services at the Royal Air Force base in Oxford.

Noor went here and there looking for work, including soliciting the BBC to broadcast her stories. Vilayat busied himself looking for work, as well as a study course. To make money, Mother helped out as a nurse at the mental asylum, where the everyday scenes were horrifying. Sensitive and delicate as she was, Mother was not suited for this type of occupation. As for me, I registered with the town's hospital, Radcliffe, in my capacity of nurse.

Soon after our arrival in Oxford, Vilayat took us to visit the Mitchell family, who had invited us all. Mrs. Mitchell was confined to her bed which could be rolled out onto the streets. She had two daughters, Myrtle and Betty, and one son, Basil. Mr. and Mrs. Mitchell had known Murshid and were prepared to help our family as best they could. Noor had already made a number of friends and was, therefore, often away. Mother taught me how to make clothes, because we had left Fazal Manzil empty-handed. Vilayat still had many friends from his college days.

Having been accepted by the British Red Cross, Babs (our nickname for Noor) and I were issued Red Cross uniforms which we wore proudly. Fortunately, we had not needed to produce any French training certificates: all we were asked to do was to take a two-week first aid course.

German reconnaissance had somehow overlooked the existence of Oxford and Cambridge. No sirens wailed here, although the beautiful town was a tempting target to be shattered to pieces. With the exception of military uniforms, no one in Oxford could have suspected that England was at war. Many of the big city children were evacuated to the countryside. Oranges, orange juice, baby food and dairy products were kept for the little ones so as to ensure a healthy generation to come. Adults were nourished with packaged food, but on Fridays we were allowed an inexpensive lunch of fish and chips wrapped in newspaper. Shop owners were horrified when one spoke of the war situation. Everybody was concerned about their loved ones. Should Oxford be hit by bombs, one would consider it a navigational mistake: London was Hitler's prime target. The capital's great religious and historical monument, St Paul's cathedral, was bombed intentionally. As a house of God, its targeting was an act that would not bring the perpetrator any luck.

On August 18, 1940, Hidayat sent us a reassuring letter from Solignac, France:

> *Dearest Vilayat,*
>
> *Since receiving your telegram from Le Verdon we have been living in anxiousness about you all. What a blessing it was for us to receive news from you through our dear Mahtab. We left La Tranche the day after the Armistice and arrived as far as our reserve of essence brought us. We are now at Solignac (Haute Vienne) in the "Chateau Marbouty." This is a little village near Limoges... Nekbakht has returned to Suresnes and taken over to her home every important thing in Fazal Manzil. Fazal Manzil is occupied by the Germans. We heard that the Uncles in the Hague are well, we know not more about them... Please give my deepest love to the girls and to dear Amma.*
>
> *Love from Hidayat*

Four Missions

Claire Harper: Both Noor and Vilayat spoke French and English fluently. Vilayat had diplomas from both Oxford University and the Sorbonne. Noor had also received her Masters at the Sorbonne in child psychology. They had wanted to complete their studies, but the sad events hampered everyone's plans. During this fierce war, Vilayat and Noor had to make decisions regarding their next course of action amid attacks, dog-fights, the wailing of sirens and blackouts. Defenses were few and training had to be short.

Vilayat joined the Royal Air Force but soon developed a paratyphoid fever. Mother went to visit him but was only able to see him through a glass window. Vilayat had books piled up all around him as he studied plane mechanics and flight manuals. A few weeks later, after recovering from his illness, Vilayat began his pilot's training. Once he completed the course, Vilayat was told that he could not obtain the license as his night vision was insufficient. This deeply upset him as he knew that there was a severe shortage of pilots.

Vilayat's alternative was to join the Royal Navy, though he had never learnt to swim and actually always feared the water. Though he had applied for a commission, the first months of Vilayat's life with the Navy were most disappointing. Picking up cigarette butts from the deck was not his idea of the level on which he wished to offer his service to the cause of freedom. While awaiting his commission, Vilayat studied at Oxford and, at long last, the Royal Navy appointed Vilayat as an officer, a sub-lieutenant, in charge of a mine-sweeping force.

After a couple of years of arduous training with the Navy, Vilayat resumed his studies of comparative religion and philosophy at King Alfred Lancing College near Brighton. In a letter to his mother dated May 8th, 1943, he wrote: "We are surrounded here with the meditative & scholarly atmosphere of an Oxford College. I understand that it is going to entail strenuous study, but opinions vary on that subject & it depends upon the amount of previous training or previous experience that one has had. However strenuous it might be, it certainly is a great relief to return to a more civilized form of existence after the hardships of the lower deck."

Claire Harper: At the military hospital, I was wandering around one day when I stumbled onto a ward where soldiers with burned faces awaited treatment. My heart sank, I turned white and I shied away. I should have stayed and spoken with them, attempting to give them some courage and support. I pinched myself to find courage—these beautiful young men of the future were already crucified. This new experience left me incapable of reaction, unable to help. I was so sad that I became useless as a nurse. My mother told me to look at the brighter side: at least those men were still alive and held a good chance of survival.

A few days later, I received a message from Betty Mitchell to go to the Sir William Dunn School of Pathology. Here I was interviewed by Dr. Heatly regarding a new post in penicillin research. At that point there was only one chemist and one assistant; I accepted the job at once and the next morning I cycled to the research lab.

The silence that reigned in the lab was uncanny. The work that Claire was associated with was classified top-secret and involved lab tests using various strains of the newly discovered miracle drug, penicillin, originally discovered by Sir Alexander Fleming.[9] Since Claire was not the talkative type, the lab's secret proved to be safe. She was extremely grateful for the opportunity to work at the service of Drs. Heatley and Florry, pioneers in penicillin's applications. Claire's duties involved the preparation of penicillin cultures, using Petri dishes and agar-agar. Research was at its very beginnings, in search of developing the medicine to aid human beings and, eventually, to be manufactured on a large scale in the United States. Her direct supervisor, Dr. Norman Heatly, often improvised processes for the development of new ideas in this field. On January 15th, 1941, Claire wrote to her family as follows:

> *Dear Mother & Sister sweet,*
>
> *...these two last days I have been looking through the 'microscope' all afternoon, can you imagine, we test microbes with various strains of which Babli knows, and I know the way to handle a Microscope all by myself, the glass in the 'focus tube' is believed to cost 10 pounds. I have seen so many microbes that I see them 'all over the place' now. I wish I could have a photo of myself look through the microscope.*

Claire Harper: In the winter of 1940–41 Noor lived in Scotland, where she chose to follow a course as a radio operator. She was now a member of the WAAF, the Women's Auxiliary Air Force, a subdivision of the Royal Air Force. The training lasted over six months. Mother occasionally visited Noor in Scotland, which left me quite lonely in my little room in Oxford, keeping alive on breakfast in the early morning and high tea at five o'clock. In the evening I would write letters until the sandman put me to sleep.

No sooner had Noor returned from Scotland to live in London, I thought it might be a good idea to take some courses with the aim of assisting in medical research. My mother spoke highly of Edinburgh and suggested I should study there. For my daily sustenance, I found a job in the blood transfusion service of an Edinburgh hospital. However, money was scarce and biscuits became my staple diet. I even pawned some of my clothes in order to make ends meet. My health was poor, and my mother suggested I join her in London. Having struggled a good half-year in windy, cold Scotland, I followed her suggestion and traveled to the English capital. Jobs were not easy to come by, so in desperation, I joined the Army, asking to be posted in the London area so my mother would not be alone. Based in Woolwich, it only took me half an hour to commute to London, but my low salary was mostly used up in travel costs. My first duty in the Army was as secretary to a captain in the Medical Corps.

In wartime, commodities were scarce; winters were cold to the extreme, meager heat feebly emanating from coal stoves. I developed a chronic sinus condition and suffered badly from chilblains. I would awake at four o'clock in the morning to wash in cold water in a small recess in open air. Had I woken later, queues would have formed and I would have had to wait my turn in the cold with the other girls—so I preferred to get up very early. Marching proved to be painful for my knees and I was subsequently exempted from marching exercises. Within a week, I was able to visit my mother for 48 hours. When I arrived, she was cooking fish over a gas burner on the floor. She had no kitchen and lived in one room with one single bed.

Utterly exhausted, my mother could hardly talk. Her work at the five various hospitals where she had spent long hours of dedicated work, was taking its toll. She seldom had news of either Noor or Vilayat, making her worry, of course. They often missed meals and their military pay hardly covered basic needs. We often had to put money aside for transportation and phone calls; our pockets jingled with only a few pennies.

Though Noor was in the military, she still found time to send a poem on the occasion of her mother's birthday in May 1942:

While passing the well of water
Where all the wishes come true
What wish did we make little Mother
If not for sweet little you?
We wished that our toil would bring riches
That we could hand over to you,
We wished and God grant wishes
To make Mother happy too.

So, dearest, chins up it's your birthday,
And all that we wished shall come true.
We're on duty but it is play-day
And life is just all pink and blue.

A year later, true to her habit, Noor again sent a delightful poem to her mother on her birthday. Little did the family realize then, on May 8th, 1943, that this would be the last poem she would be able to dedicate to her cherished mother:

To Mother Cute

You see it's just the loveliest day,
We all have such a lot to say.
Why is it tell us Mother dear
We long for this all through the year?
Do you remember when quite small,
We peeped behind the garden wall
To watch the birthday man pass by
And pull his bag and ask him why
We wish, and if our dreams come true,
And if the ones we have for you
Were in his knapsack tucked away
To give to Dearest on this day!
He said that he had loads of love
And joy and presents from above.
And off he went but now we're grown
Whenever has the wee man flown?
It's up to us this time to be
The birthday man and try and see
Just how much joy and dreams comes true
We'll manage to make up for you.
Just how much happiness we'll make
Just how much time all this will take
We're apart and far away
But wasting not a single day.
We want to make life a success
And toil and strive for happiness.
And gain it just because there's you
So, tally ho! We'll carry through!

8th May 1943

Claire Harper: One day, as I returned from work, I opened the wardrobe to find a lovely violet taffeta blouse draped on a hanger. As it was my birthday, I realized this was Mother's gift to me! I could hardly believe it—it was wartime, after all, and clothing was hard to come by, especially since we earned so little. To me, the blouse was worth a million and more precious than gold. It was the sweet expression of a mother's love. Its color melted and softened my heart. Turning around, I saw the happiness in Mother's usually sad eyes; she enjoyed my pleasure, and yet my happiness did not belong to the atmosphere of the times.

Though they did not know much about the type of training Noor was involved in, they knew that there was an element of danger. All Noor had intimated to her mother was that she was considering assuming "Special Service duties." Ora Ray tried to dissuade her daughter with the following words of counsel:

> *Dear little Babsy, we think of you every day and all day long. Absentmindedly I wait every night for you to come in the door. I wish you would decide to remain where you are rather than to accept the 'Special Services duties' for I am certain you are less exposed to the trials of life for which you are not strong enough. Do consider my judgment a little bit, won't you Babs?*

Last Words with Noor

Claire Harper: Having met Noor for a minute at 4 Tavington Street where our mother lived in London, she asked me to meet her in the cafeteria at Baker Street Underground (Subway) Station. As arranged, the following day at noon, Noor came running towards me. We were both tense. Noor handed me a letter to pass on to Vilayat. I questioned the sealed contents. Lately, Noor's comings and goings seemed somewhat mysterious. I said, "Babs, where are you going?" "I cannot tell!" she replied. My heart fell to my feet and I insisted, "Don't hide it from me. I shall have to find out some other way!" Noor had told Mother that she was working on a special mission outside London but did not want to elaborate.

Remembering that scrap of information, I asked Noor what she was doing in the yeomanry (British volunteer cavalry force). "When the war is over," she replied, "I shall be wearing the family tartan on horseback." I asked her what color that was. "Lavender," was her reply. "Should the War Office write to you about joining, don't do it. And don't tell Mother," she added. I was puzzled, sad and shocked to learn of Noor's devices. "Bye, bye, I have to rush!" she muttered as she hurried down into the subway. An uncontrollable urge forced me to run after her. Looking back, she warned, "Don't follow me!" "We both run as fast as each other," I retorted. She simply responded, "Be good!" as she often did in lieu of saying goodbye. Forlorn, I stood in the crowded subway hall, lost. The spirit of urgency was well depicted in Noor's behavior. Good thoughts did not come readily to my mind.

A few days later, Noor sent her relatives three farewell notes. Cheerful as always, she knew that she was headed for the lions' den, yet intimated nothing but hope and optimism:

> *Brother dearest,*
>
> *Nothing could have infuriated me more than to have to leave without seeing you, just at the time I was longing to most. How are you, old boy? I am looking out for you. Maybe we will meet someday—somewhere—somehow... what a day it would be... and what a lot we would have to tell each other. How well I can picture you at the front deck in your smart blue, facing the wind with the same frown as in your little MG. And every time the Navy puts up a show, just feel terribly proud of my brother. And duty can pull us apart at different ends of the world but it only strengthens ties and brother is dearer than ever.*
>
> *We'll carry on, old boy. Wish me some luck, the same to you and 'V'* [victory] *very soon. Tally-ho and all the love from*
>
> *Babuli*
>
> *Cutest little Mother,*
>
> *Such a joy to be able to post a letter to you, I'm just dashing for it! So much to tell you in a minute, Mother dear, how can I? How happy I was to hear about you but just to dash home as I used to and see you Mother cute and give you a surprise—nothing I long for more. Still it might be sooner than we think, someday, what a day! Please don't worry girlie, when you don't receive any letters. We're not so far apart after all. I do hope by my next leave you will have a new flat to come to, the one I'm dreaming about. How I long to see Vic and little Claire.*
>
> *Mother cute, I do wish you would give up your Red Cross work for some time. I know you are exhausting yourself and this thought keeps me constantly worried. I feel so helpless over here not being able to look after you. Do excuse my pencil, Mother, I can't help it. I'm sending you some Elizabeth Arden products I found by chance on*

one of my journeys—a friend of mine will bring them over to you. Another friend promised to phone, did he? I really miss you terribly Mother. I talk to you so often in my sleep. Still, next time you see me I will be bonny and beautifully well and shall we celebrate! ... with pink champagne!! And you must be young and bonny too! That's how I'm looking forward to seeing you! Cheers, dearest, a big kiss and all the love in the world.

Little Babu

And to Claire she wrote:

Girlie sweet,

How I miss you! What a celebration when we meet again! How are you girlie? Have you a little crown on your cap yet? Isn't it awful not receiving letters! Just knowing you are well, that's all. Still, girlie, it has taught me that wherever we go in the world and whoever we meet you never can find a substitute for a brother or sister. Perhaps mine are exceptional, maybe. But, gosh, we had a lot of fun together and my little sister makes me laugh more than anyone can!

Girlie, I'm so worried about Mother. Could you do something about her stopping her Red Cross work? It's too much for her I know. Besides she must see a doctor for her throat. ... Still I'll be seeing you and we will have such a lot to tell each other and by that time you will have a wee little crown on the cap and be looking very snob!! In the meanwhile don't forget little Bibou completely and be good. A big big kiss.

(Babuly)

Claire Harper: Once back at my base at Woolwich estuary, I went to the barracks to my little folding bed before the return of the girls from the mess hall. Feeling very listless, I wondered whether I would ever see my sister again. In the silence of the barracks, I heard Noor's beautiful clear voice ringing in my ears. Was she gone forever? Who knows, who knows? My mother in London was already in a state of anxiety. Was one war not enough for her? Vilayat was already in the Navy, and I knew not how to contact him. Noor and he had volunteered for the most dangerous commissions on condition that they were not required to kill anyone.

The War Drags On

Claire Harper: When there was a sense of possibly losing the war, despondency set in. At our low point, we were greatly comforted to hear the famous Irish-American singer, John McCormack, perform on BBC radio. His wish was to console England with Irish songs; he was everybody's favorite singer at the time. We felt uplifted, and this gave us courage to hope and not give up our purposes.

Every now and again, Ora Ray received a note from Noor such as the following, quite carefully worded so that the family would have no clue as to where she was writing from and what she was involved in:

> *Mother dearest,*
>
> *If only I could describe to you the lovely spot I am in—simply marvellous. Of course there is such a lot to do that very little time is left to contemplate the scenery. I feel I would like to bring you round here on a holiday tour after the war—who knows!*
>
> *How is the naughty little girl who never writes—and Vic? Mother please don't worry if sometimes my letters are long reaching you. You see, it is rather difficult at times being in reach of a post. I think there has been some difficulty about your letters reaching me. I am afraid they have been following me round. I'm so longing to receive them! Cheerio and big kiss.*
>
> *Babuli*

Claire Harper: We heard about the details of the German invasion of France and imagined what would happen if the war escalated. Besides the sacrifice of human beings, the beautiful architecture which had made of Paris one of the most gorgeous cities in the world would be no longer. The layout of the Arc de Triomphe, burning its eternal flame, spreads out into avenues to symbolize a star. At the other end, in a straight line several kilometers from the woods and past the Rond-Point des Champs-Elysees, lay Place de la Concorde. In the center stands an obelisk from Egypt towering above fine-looking fountains and statues. The nearby Seine River, the capital's jugular vein, invites strollers to enjoy the city's romantic cityscapes and atmosphere. In fact the Seine River with its artists and cafes, meanders past Notre Dame Cathedral, the official geographical center of Paris. Also, not far from here is the Louvre Museum where the Mona Lisa, as well as thousands of unique masterpieces, is preserved. The trees were the making of the city. For the sake of aesthetics, Napoleon planted trees throughout Paris, the shade and sight of which cannot be replaced. I thought what a crime it would be to see this destroyed.

Yet daily, Mother, Vilayat and I wondered where Noor was. We knew she had answered the call to duty and that she may be working overseas, perhaps in North Africa we had been told, but was she safe?

Beginning on December 17th, 1943, mysterious—yet reassuring—letters were sent to Ora Ray from the War Office. The first read as follows:

> *Dear Mrs. Baker-Inayat,*
>
> *We are glad to be able to let you know that we have just received a message from your daughter. She asks us to forward her dearest greetings to you, Claire and Vic, with lots of love.*

Just weeks before D-Day, Ora Ray again received one of the War Office's regular typewritten reports on Noor. Dated April 25th, 1944, it stated:

> *Dear Mrs. Baker-Inayat,*
>
> *Thank you for your letter of the 21st and for the telegram, contents of which were passed on to your daughter. I am well pleased to tell you that she is very well and sends much love to you, Vic and Claire.*

Despite the government's reassurances regarding Noor's well-being, her mother and siblings could not help but wonder and worry about why they had received no handwritten message directly from Noor for over six months. Noor's last handwritten messages were the following:

> *15th Sept. 1943*
>
> *Dearest little mother*
>
> *Simply too marvellous to receive your wire! I was so happy, mother dear, so happy! Bravo for Vic! I am afraid, Mother, the unexpected leave I was hoping for has not come... Maybe if I don't expect it, some day it might come and I just can't imagine a sweeter dream than to be able to pop home and give you a grand surprise! It's a date! Mother cute, I wish I knew some details about you. Have you been to the doctor? To the dentist? Couldn't you really make a noble effort? Busy as I am, Mother dear, I manage to go to the dentist. Please don't neglect a day longer, you do keep me worried. Had I been sooner, Mother, I could have saved two wisdom teeth—just had to be pulled out. Sheer neglect. And do be good and not worry about me because I'm fine, Mother dear, and looking quite bonnie! And soon I will be right there with you and there will be*

such a lot to talk about, such a lot to celebrate! Isn't the news simply grand! It won't take so long after all, will it! Do send me a wire again soon. A big big kiss and just tonnes of love...

From little Babu

PS a big goodnight kiss goes over to you every night! Mother dear! It's when I miss you most!

She congratulated Vilayat on his receiving his officer's commission:

15th Sept. 1943

Brother dearest,

How grand to hear about you! Bravo! I'm so happy. I guess everything is strenuous right now but very interesting. I miss you terribly but realize now and then that there is a war on. Is your glass of sherry ready? Mine is! Skōll for Italy! Fancy not even being able to chat about all the events with you, Brother dear, it sometimes breaks my enthusiasm!

Till we meet again, old boy, cheers and good luck and all the love in the world.

Babel

Four weeks later, she would fall into the hands of the Gestapo. As soon as SOE suspected her to be captured, they began sending Noor's family the reassuring yet untruthful messages. Little did her relatives know that Noor had agreed to this misleading strategy in order to avoid her mother worrying in the event that she went missing.

Claire Harper: The British fleet polished its buttons; yet it suffered a shortage of planes. The army paraded its tanks, but the enemy was far out of range. The Allies suffered defeat after defeat and were lying low. A miracle appeared to be coming from America, confirmed by the arrival of General Eisenhower. All our hopes lit up like candles which burned with divine fervor, determination and steel courage.

The combined efforts of the British and American armed forces had to be carefully—and secretly—coordinated with the aim of a mass landing on the continent. Where could this take place and how could it be implemented without the Germans knowing where the landing would be? A harbor was needed to land the thousands of war ships and the hundreds of thousands of men and women prepared to crush the enemy. A cunning ploy was put into operation: that of assembling thousands upon thousands of dummy tanks, airplanes and landing craft either made of inflatable rubber or wood and canvas. These were then placed all over the region of Kent in England to make it appear to the Germans that the obvious landing point in France would be at the Pas-de-Calais. The Germans, seeing this large-scale task force accruing in one area, were duped into concentrating their defenses in the Pas-de-Calais region.

Meanwhile, employing a work force of some twenty thousand people, the British secretly constructed all the elements needed to create a makeshift artificial harbor. After D-Day, enormous barges made of concrete would be towed across the channel and, along with floating bridge elements, would be used to create a port comparable to that of Dover. Though a raging storm destroyed much of the installation, one section of these "mulberries" remained in operation for nine months, allowing millions of tons of supplies, fuel, armament and soldiers to land on the continent.

Every single person assumed his post or task with infallible precision. Should anything go amiss, the delicate clockwork of this master plan would malfunction. Throughout England, and in the United States as well, hundreds of thousands of men and women were involved in the preparation of the largest military maneuver in world history. Waves of soldiers arrived daily in England to be briefed and trained further. Under the code name Operation Bolero, over one million young American men traveled to England. Many Canadians, Poles and other citizens joined the ranks of the British and the Americans in anticipation of their chance to change the world. They had only one thought in mind: to succeed.

The Greatest Battle Ever Fought

The collection of ships and boats that was to sail across to France was the largest armada in history. The Germans, though, had placed thousands of floating mines in the channel waters, at the touch of which any ship would spring a fatal hole. Vilayat's mission as an officer on one of the mine-sweeping ships would be to make the waters safe for the upcoming crossing of the massive fleet. This invaluable preparation work of clearing a safe passage for the thousands of vessels that would soon cross the channel waters would be carried out in the dead of night until the break of dawn.

The air was charged with the thought of victory mingled with the fear of danger. No one could imagine as masterful an enterprise as this one. Such a large scale plan had never been made, nor has the like been seen again. Setting a date for the surprise attack was no easy task. The moon had to be waning, the weather had to be calm, and it took weeks for propitious conditions to finally come about.

About forty-eight hours prior to D-Day, Vilayat's mission to make the channel's waters safe finally began. The sea was not only wild with waves but saturated with German floating mines that would spell disaster for the Allied vessels on the big day. The sailors under his orders were as terrified as he whenever a mine needed to be defused. There were many different types of mines bobbing in the English Channel's waters, and each was more dangerous than the next. Nonetheless, time and time again, Vilayat took it into his own hands to carry out the task. On the second foggy night, he accidentally slipped into the glacial water and, had it not been for the compulsory life jacket he was wearing, he would have drowned as no one saw him disappear. Long minutes passed before his shouts for help were heard.

This event took place just before the sailing of the great armada on its way to liberate the continent from German occupation. On that glorious D-Day, that proved to end in untimely death for thousands upon thousands of valiant young men, Vilayat was part of "the greatest armada that ever sailed." The battle was long and vicious; many ships were sunk, but Vilayat was blessed with a safe return to terra firma.

When the weather finally improved, the warships could now storm the enemy with frenzy under a sky black with Allied planes, en route to drop bombs and paratroopers. Anyone watching was stunned to see and hear this omnipotent mass of metal slowly advancing by air and by water towards unsuspecting France at dawn. Within the first few minutes alone, thousands of Allied soldiers were killed or wounded on the Normandy beaches. Safe shelter or the white walls of hospital care were far from reach. With the tragic, yet heroic, battle of D-Day in 1944, began the laborious struggle that ended in victory nearly a full year later: the fall of Adolf Hitler and his heinous plans.

Between June 6th and June 19th, Vilayat and his crew docked four times on the Normandy beaches to deliver men, weapons and equipment while the battle raged on throughout Normandy.

NOOR MISSING

With the end of the war in view, despite the lack of news, the family hoped to see Noor return soon. In the spring of 1945 Vilayat visited the house in Paris and reported that some of the furniture had been found and that he had asked Miss Furnée (Nekbahkt) to take personal belongings to her house for safekeeping. Though it was difficult for the family to hide a growing suspicion that the worst had befallen Noor, Vilayat wrote his mother in March 1945:

> *The war is speeding towards a hasty conclusion today and as you hear over the news broadcasts, camp after camp are being rescued and prisoners retrieved. So it is now just a question of time and this, judging from the general situation is going to be short now... Another month or two should see Germany in full retreat and overrun. Besides, the names of people released are not given for obvious reasons & there is always quite some delay in their coming back. For all we know, it is not impossible that Babsi (Noor) should even be making her way back just now. So just have moment's more patience.*

By May 1945, apart from the agony of not knowing where Noor was, the family breathed a sigh of relief that the War of Wood was over. Yet their newly found joy was not to last. Shortly after the ordeals of battle, Vilayat regularly visited the Mitchell family. Beautiful Myrtle Mitchell was his dream girl, and Vilayat decided to ask for her hand, to which Myrtle's mother agreed.

For him, life couldn't have been more beautiful at this point, the complete opposite of the horrors of combat. Vilayat's mode of transportation at the time was a BMW motorcycle, thanks to which he had plenty of freedom of movement. On one occasion, he asked the Mitchells if they'd allow his fiancée to go for a ride with him. Unfortunately, while in motion, the bike's stand collapsed and caused young Myrtle to fall off. Landing on her back, she suffered a bad concussion and fell into a coma from which she never awoke. Vilayat never found the words to describe the sorrow and remorse he felt over this tragedy for the rest of his life.

Claire Harper: This was a terrible blow to all of us, and in order to regain a sense of normality, Vilayat listened nonstop to J. S. Bach's music for several months. This was the only way he could ever cope with everyday life again and begin assuming the task of his mission.

From D-Day (June 6th, 1945) until the end of April 1946, Vilayat was obliged to complete his commission with the British Navy. On July 5th, 1945 (Viladat Day), Vilayat wrote his mother from Copenhagen regarding Noor:

> *Of course, it is terribly worrying; time is flying by! Surely there must be some information available by now! I can never keep my mind off the subject & it is becoming unbearable. I am writing to the War Office to ask whether we might not at this stage put in for news through the Red Cross. I am afraid, I do not anticipate returning to England for quite a long time—I can tell you now, we are in Copenhagen. It is a wonderful city. I spend my time in the University Library of Psychology.*

On January 6th, 1946, Vilayat became a "fully blown Lieutenant," as he wrote to his mother from his ship. By this time, he was stationed in Chembur, some eighteen miles from Bombay, India, where he spent several months. In March 1946, he took advantage of a ten-day leave to travel to Shrinagar in Kashmir, in search of sages.

Though far from home for nearly a year, Vilayat's letters bear witness to his constant concern for his mother—to whom he regularly sent money—as well as of his worry regarding Noor's whereabouts.

On November 17th, 1945, he wrote from Bombay:

> *Dearest Mother, ... I am studying like hell for a BSc in physiology... They say if you help yourself, God comes in too to lend a hand... Do not worry about a job, but to keep yourself busy, if you feel so inclined, why not do something voluntary? Or take a course in something that might prove useful.*

And later on:

> *Mother Dear, ... I am better off than I have ever been and having paid off all my debts & being decently dressed (at last), do not anticipate putting in for any extensive expenses in the future. In fact, I could easily support you entirely. So, please, do not worry on that issue, we have enough to worry without this! I have written*

to the War Office, insisting again on some news whatsoever, at least more details of the situation. It is so trying!

After the war, Ora Ray was no longer needed at the hospitals but, ignoring her son's offer to support her, she worked afternoons and evenings collecting tickets at a cinema. Meanwhile, Claire worked at an old government office near Victoria Station where, on a most meager salary, she typed numbers on blue stencil paper. "Demobbed," as he termed it—in other words, no longer on active military duty or payroll—Vilayat found a position at an Indian newspaper as a journalist.

Claire Harper: Vilayat's pay was meager and his job unrewarding. Finding work was very difficult at that time and salaries were so low that he couldn't even pay to have his shoes half-soled. Eventually Vilayat went to the Pakistan Office, where over the next few years he worked his way up the ladder of responsibility. After a long time as a conference executive, he became assistant to Liaquat Ali Khan, Pakistan's very first prime minister, a position for which Vilayat won much appreciation.

With Miss Bouman, a Sufi from Holland, Vilayat began holding meetings and creating a Sufi center. We found a flat to live in but had to pay unreasonably high rent. Though shabby, it afforded us a roof over our heads. Noor's name still didn't appear in the newspapers—we all stood on a tightrope of uncertainty. Mother would strain her eyes over the paper until she could no longer. Sorrow was her only staff and she cried bitterly nearly each day.

Such was Ora Ray's sorrowful concern as to her daughter's possible fate that she constantly glanced at the door, expecting Noor to return any moment. In the course of his duties for the Pakistan Office, Vilayat often traveled to the continent: France, Holland and other countries. He took advantage of these trips to find out as much as he could about those missing in action. On August 9th, 1945, Vilayat wrote from France:

Dearest Mother, ...The absence of news is enough to make one go mad, but I have been to quite a few organizations to discover that there are still thousands of prisoners of war—particularly French—mainly in the Russian zone and a lot of work is still being done sorting them. Till soon. Love, Vic

Again, even darker clouds darkened the family's lives when they received a distressing message from the Royal Air Force, dated January 28th, 1946.

It mentioned that they have "learnt with much regret that your daughter is reported missing and I am asked to express our very sincere sympathy."

Even more discouraging was the Air Ministry's letter of March 4th, 1946, to Vilayat, announcing:

> *I am directed to inform you, with regret, that in view of the lapse of time and the absence of any further news regarding your sister, Assistant Section Officer N. Inayat-Khan, action has now been taken to presume her death. As you are aware, no definite date or details of her fate are known.*

Claire Harper: Our despair was beyond description, but we never told Mother of Noor's presumed death. Somehow, we hoped that the military bureaucrats were wrong. So much confusion had come about in this horrid war, and we did not trust the paperwork of the authorities. Any day, we thought, we would hear Noor knocking at the door.

On March 11th, 1947, Major Mott of the War Office informed his personnel to be discrete in divulging information regarding Noor's fate to the Inayat Khan family:

> *Mr. Inayat-Khan informed us that his mother is in a very precarious state of health and in the opinion of her medical advisor any severe shock would be sufficient to cause her death. In view of this Mr. Inayat-Khan and his sister have so far kept the news of the death of A.S.O. Inayat-Khan from their mother, and he informed us that he was seeking to obtain power of attorney which would enable him to deal with all his mother's affairs, and particularly matters arising out of his sister's death, in order that is mother might be spared any further worries. We would suggest, therefore, that at any rate your preliminary approach to Mrs. Inayat-Khan should be made through her son at the address given.*

Claire Harper: Vilayat suggested that I leave my temporary job and join the Pakistan Office where he was working. Heeding his advice, I began working there and was finally able to bring home better earnings. However, there never seemed to be enough for proper food, but I was pleased to work under better conditions.

Living from hour to hour and day to day, life's monotony returned. During that time, my mother thought I should have a new suit for work. Nice clothes were very expensive, but we pooled our money and went out to buy a respectable outfit. When Vilayat and I were working at the Pakistan Office, Vilayat often had to attend conferences abroad.

Mother and I would pack his case so he could find everything easily, all clean and tidy. The contents never came back looking the same, but that didn't matter to us: we were so happy to see Vilayat return! His position nearly took him permanently to Pakistan when his boss, Liaquat Ali Khan, became prime minister there. Vilayat refused the position as it would have meant long separation from Mother. It is lucky that Vilayat did not take the plane that was to fly him to Pakistan as the Prime Minister did: the plane crashed!

Vilayat was promoted to attaché of the Pakistan Delegation to the United Nations Assembly. Because of the numerous conferences he prepared or attended, there were a lot of reports to type. After dinner, Vilayat would dictate them to me, sometimes lasting through the night.

Vilayat was also head of the information department, and I was appointed to assist him. One day, however, a Pakistani lady came along and took his place; I was to remain. She expected me to do all the menial tasks such as opening the mail and tidying up. I abstained from doing anything of the sort for her since this was not included in my duties, so she became very angry with me. One evening after working hours, I was busy doing urgent work for Vilayat; no one was in my office. I was duplicating a report when she walked in and directed her temper at me. I took no notice of what she was saying; after all, she was not my boss, Vilayat was, so I said nothing. She threatened me, screaming, "I'll have you out by tomorrow!" As I left my office, Vilayat and the Minister of Foreign Affairs came towards me. Seeing me, Vilayat felt something was wrong and, after introducing me to the minister, he asked me what had happened. When I related the incident, Vilayat exclaimed, "If that woman throws my sister out, I shall resign!" The minister was horrified, especially since the Pakistan Office respected Vilayat and appreciated the excellent work he did.

The next morning, the angry lady called for a meeting with all the department heads. The resulting conclusions didn't affect me; I remained Vilayat's secretary, and work went on as usual. Soon thereafter, our hot-tempered colleague returned to Pakistan and eventually lost her position. I realized then that divine justice does exist. Vilayat always defied injustice; his brotherly love was such that he would have been prepared to relinquish a promising position.

Throughout the war years we had no direct news from Hidayat, but we heard through Sufis that he and his family were all right. We knew from a telegram received two months after our arrival in Oxford that he had made it as far as Solignac in the Haute Vienne department in France and was staying at Chateau Marbouty. The village was located near Limoges, and he decided to remain there with his wife Iman and daughter Inayat, where they lived off the produce of the land. Meanwhile Uncle Musharaff (Chacha) and his wife continued south to the coast and, later, on to Switzerland. Hidayat reassured us that all the belongings we had packed up and left behind had been recovered by Nekbakht and were safely in her home. We received a telegram from him on September 5th, 1941, giving us his address at Dieulefit near Valence in the Rhônes-Alpes region. We did not often receive news of Hidayat but could only offer up our prayers for his safety. We later learned that he became Professor of Music at the Lycée Musical of Dieulefit.

On September 1st, 1945, Hidayat sent the following message to our mother from Dieulefit, France:

> *Dear Mother,*
>
> *I have not been able to write to you since so many years owing to circumstances. During the first four years of German occupation, correspondence with England was prohibited. Moreover I was not able to correspond by means of Red Cross owing to the difficulties which would eventually arise on account of my British nationality. During the year which preceded liberation I was obliged to hide in the mountains with wife and children but I suppose Vilayat has told you all this. He came to us a month ago and gave me the frightful news about Babuly.... Yours most affectionately, Bhayajan.*

News also arrived of the uncles in Holland. Shortly after the war ended, Ora Ray received a letter from Ekbal Dawlat, the mother of Maheboob's wife, Shadi. Dated September 29th, 1945, she relates:

> *My dear Begum,*
>
> *For many, many years we did not hear from each other, but this does not mean that my thoughts of sympathy and affection did not go very often to you and your children. We were so happy to meet Vilayat and to see him in good health after these terrible years of war and danger. Surely he will have told you that we also suffered much from the war; evacuation, cold, hunger, a bombardment on our house here and 7 weeks of continual danger. But all is nothing in comparison with the agony you are going through about your heroine daughter, our beloved Babuli. I can't tell you how much we are all longing to hear good news about her. There is still hope; Taya*

had a good dream about her; also Shadi saw her once in a dream in the midst of us all. Let us hope and pray. Many have not yet come back, but this does not mean that they don't come back. Murshid's and your eldest child has shown a bravery and a sacrifice which hardly any other person will show… With affection as always:

your Ekbal

On December 13th, 1945, Hidayat gave his mother the following news by telegram regarding Fazal Manzil in Suresnes:

Arrived Suresnes. House partial occupation Red Cross.

Claire Harper: We were happy to know that Hidayat and his family were well. By then, he was father to three children: Inayat, a girl, and two boys, Fazal and Gayan.

In the framework of our jobs for the Pakistan Office, I occasionally accompanied Vilayat on trips abroad. These took us to Geneva and even to Paris where I spent a fair amount of time working for the Paris Office of the General Assembly of the Pakistan Delegation to the United Nations. At that time, my salary was so good that I convinced Mother to come and join me for a while in Paris.

Meanwhile, much work had been undertaken by Noor's former supervisor, Vera Atkins, to investigate her disappearance, as well as the loss of many other SOE woman agents. In the course of her research, Ms. Atkins discovered reasonable evidence that Noor had been killed at Natzweiler-Strutthof Concentration Camp in Alsace, the only German camp on French soil. Rumor had it that she had been given a lethal injection there and, half-dead, had been dragged into the cremation oven while still screaming and clawing her henchmen.

The War Office's official and sanitized announcement, dated April 29th, 1946, read:

Your sister, A/Squadron-Officer N. Inayat-Khan, died at Natzweiler Concentration camp on the 6 Jul 44… Your sister was arrested near Paris in October 43, and remained in various prisons in and near Paris until May 44. On the 12 May 44 a convoy of women left Fresnes Prison near Paris, and in this convoy were eight English girls, who were taken straight to Karlsruhe, where they were put in the City Jail for women. They remained there until the night of the 5/6 Jul 44, when four were taken to Natzweiler, your sister being among them.

> *Our representative has seen the two German women who were in charge of the jail at the time, as well as several former inmates of the prison, and she believes that while conditions were hard they were not intolerable, as was the case in some concentration camps.*
>
> *From a male German political prisoner at Karlsruhe who was employed on various tasks, we have heard the girls were collected between 4/5 a.m. in a large grey car in which were members of the Gestapo and S.S.... The girls arrived at Natzweiler between 1/3 p.m. on 6 Jul 44 and were seen walking down the main camp street... Next morning* [inmates] *made enquiries and heard that the girls had received lethal injection and had been cremated.*
>
> *I hope that the knowledge of the invaluable contribution that your sister made towards final victory in preparing the ground for the invasion of France will comfort you in your great loss.*
>
> *All who came into contact with her during the time of her imprisonment have spoken most highly of her courage and morale.*

The shock to Claire, Vilayat and Hidayat was beyond description, and the thought of Noor's suffering was nearly impossible to bear. Little did they know then that Noor never saw Natzweiler camp. She had been confused with another agent, Sonya Olschanezky, whose physical description was not unlike that of Noor's.

THE SECRET AGENT

Prologue

Agents of the Gestapo were close on her tail, tracing her through the bustling streets of Nazi-occupied Paris. They had received explicit orders from the *Reichsicherheitsdienst* (SD) in Avenue Foch to immediately seize the young woman if sighted. It was said that a large sum would be paid to whoever could help towards the capture of this mysterious person who always seemed to be present, yet could never quite be detected. Now finally, after all this time, the Gestapo was gaining on her. They were at long last only seconds away from having the most wanted and valued secret agent in the whole of France in their grasp.

In the summer of 1943, Paris was teeming with German soldiers, as well as with members of the Gestapo and the SS. There was trouble ahead: rumors of an upcoming Allied landing on the coast of northern France brought ever more soldiers and counterintelligence agents into the country. Paris was also swarming with resistance fighters—French citizens and Allied Forces agents posing as French—who were constantly attempting to counter Germany's plans. They brought about confusion and disorder by sabotaging German war efforts, exploding train lines and communication towers. These people were becoming a real thorn in the side of the German occupation of France.

One of the Gestapo men suddenly slowed: they had been spotted. The young woman, who wore dark glasses and a blue mackintosh, had caught a glimpse of her pursuers by their reflection in a shop window. Though her hair had been bleached, the agents weren't fooled. They knew this was Madeleine, the British spy for whom they had been desperately searching for months without success. She immediately hastened her step and turned a corner. By the time the German Secret State Police arrived at the intersection, there was no sign of Madeleine. She had simply vanished! Again the exotic looking woman who spoke perfect French had eluded them. Next time they had to succeed. Who was this peculiar woman on the run? Why was she on German Military Intelligence's most wanted list?

Joining the war effort

After arriving in England, the Inayat Khan family all did their best to contribute toward the war effort. Having been brought up as Sufis, in the tradition of pacifism and respect of all nations and religions, and rejecting any kind of violence, it was not in their nature to condone killing, even an oppressor or a tyrant. Noor was also of the opinion that she could be of service to the free world without having to shed blood. On the other hand, she never feared for her own life and stated that dangerous missions would not be a problem. The horrors of war had now also reached Great Britain; and Noor, who was desperate to help, joined the Woman's Auxiliary Air Force (WAAF), a group of volunteers assisting the Royal Air Force, on November 19th, 1940. She was registered as 424598 ACW2 (Aircraftswoman 2nd Class) under the name Nora Inayat Khan. Among her qualifications, "Fluent French" was specified; this would prove to change the course of her life forever.

Her training began in Harrogate as a wireless operator, and it soon became clear that Noor was born for the job. She obtained top grades and her report was marked as "V.G" (Very Good). Although the training was hard and also physically challenging, as it involved strenuous exercising and regular drills, Noor continued to blossom and a month later was sent to be trained as a wireless telegraphist in Edinburgh with RAF Balloon Command for six months. Again she completed her signals training with "V.G" and was appointed to HQ No. 6 Group, RAF Bomber Command at Abingdon on 10 June, 1941, an advanced training facility for bombers, where she was even upgraded to Aircraftswoman 1st Class and later to Leading Aircraftswoman.

Despite months of rigid military training and the fact that Britain was under constant bombing by the enemy, Noor's personality remained unchanged. She was very much liked for her endearing, goodhearted nature, as she always was willing to help others and care for them, trying to lift their spirits. Even though she had plenty of training behind her, weeks of additional coaching, prepping and creating a new identity for Noor still lay ahead. Noor's next base was No. 3 Signals School at Compton Basset in Wiltshire on May 11th, 1942, and as before, she mastered her training in an exemplary way, especially the complicated technical and mathematical aspects that were needed for advanced wireless training. She even exceeded many of the men that had been training far longer and, despite the fact that she was often quite clumsy and not especially athletic, she was chosen to join a small private group that would be trained even more intensely.

It is interesting to note that during the course of her extensive and complex radio operator training, Noor wrote a long story in the same notebooks as her technical memos. The story is about Poland's plight—it is said that Noor had a romantic liaison with a Polish officer around that time—and ends with:

> *The flag is now torn down and the Eagle of Poland is wounded, but it can never die: white eagles never die! As soon as its wing is healed it will return to the nest and the nest will be full of knights with lances and spears, and Poland shall live again forevermore.*

The commission

On August 28th, 1942, she at long last had her first interview for a commission that she had been waiting for impatiently, so as to finally play an active role in the war. However when the interview was over, Noor felt she had been too honest, especially because she hadn't lied about her opinion on Indian independence. Her fears were unfounded; in reality her life was now to take a complete different course, one that Noor in her darkest dreams would never have expected.

The Special Operations Executive

It was from now on that Noor was being closely watched by the British secret service in SOE to see if she might become an asset in their operations in France, known as F-section; in other words, to find out if she was suited to become a special forces secret agent. The Special Operations Executive (SOE) was a secret organization developed by British Prime Minister Churchill with the purpose of organizing and supporting an intelligence and resistance network throughout Europe. They trained both British and foreign recruits with the aim of undermining and sabotaging German occupation and troop deployment. On the one side, Britain would channel funds, know-how, weapons and ammunition to British and foreign agents and collaborators; on the other, Allied Intelligence would collect valuable information regarding German military presence. Ultimately, the plan was to create infrastructures in France in preparation for the monumental Allied onslaught: the future D-Day landing.

On July 19th, 1940, former Prime Minister Neville Chamberlain, Lord President of the Privy Council, signed the secret paper which served as the basis for the founding of SOE. It was the Prime Minister's last major act, as he died shortly after, to be replaced by Winston Churchill, who called it the "Ministry of Ungentlemanly Warfare."[(D)] Throughout the years, SOE became more and more organized, trying to create an infrastructure in France and gain supporters and as much knowledge as possible. They provided explosive material and devices in large quantities for sabotage missions, donated vast sums of money to opposition parties and set up communications networks that included wireless sets, "mail boxes" and airplane drops. The success of their work depended greatly on the support of those French who weren't in favor of the new regime and who risked their lives trying to aid SOE agents. F-section was led by Maurice Buckmaster, who worked with the French RF-section under De Gaulle, leader of the Free French movement. To find a suitable candidate for F-section was extremely difficult, as the agent was required not only to speak fluent French, but wasn't allowed to have the faintest hint of an accent. The agent's character was very important as well: honesty, courage and steady nerves were a necessity. The candidates were studied by psychologists in order to evaluate their suitability and motivation.

The following observation regarding Noor was logged by Jepson at SOE's Personnel Office on Jan 25, 1943:

> *If satisfactory after training, will be used in important operational role for which she has special linguistic and geographical qualifications. (F Section)*

By 1944, SOE had 15,000 members working all around the world, 1,500 of them wireless operators and cipher clerks who carried on working day and night, constantly sending, receiving and deciphering messages from the numerous agents behind enemy lines. However, the number of SOE's male agents was slowly dwindling, so Prime Minister Winston Churchill decided to send women instead, something that had never been done in any war. Thus it came to be that Noor-un-nisa Inayat Khan, "WAAF No. 424598, was called for an interview at 1600 hours on 10/11/42 at Room 238, Hotel Victoria" [D] with the so-called "Inter Services Research Bureau": in reality a cover name for SOE headquarters located in London's Baker Street. "The brief entry simply said: 'Has interesting linguistic qualifications which might make her of value for operational purposes.'" [D]

Enlisted to SOE

Noor didn't know what to expect when she entered the shabby hotel and hoped she might finally be of real help to the war. A man called Selwyn Jepson, who was the chief recruitment officer for SOE and was known for his surprisingly exact judgment of a person's character at first sight, received her and felt he could immediately trust her and come right to the point. "He had never felt this way with other potential recruits. He recalled later that 'in spite of a great gentleness of manner' she seemed to have 'an intuitive sense of what might be in my mind for her to do.'" [D] Due to Noor's gentle soul, whose passions were storytelling and music, she came across as a most unlikely candidate to be involved in a perilous, international, undercover spy game. However it only took one interview for Jepson to gain trust in Noor and recruit her, for he "felt that Noor was almost perfect for the job of a wireless operator. He felt she was careful, tidy and painstaking by nature and 'would have all the patience in the world'—an essential characteristic for a wireless operator." [D] Noor had clearly impressed Jepson, as he later remembers: "I see her very clearly as she was that first afternoon, sitting in front of me in that dingy little room, in a hard kitchen chair on the other side of a bare wooden table. Indeed of them all, and there were many, who did not return, I find myself constantly remembering her with a curious and very personal vividness which outshines the rest … the small, still features, the dark quiet eyes, the soft voice, and the fine spirit glowing in her."(D)

Noor realized her new job would be extremely dangerous; however she agreed to become part of SOE and at long last felt worthwhile. A few months passed before Noor finally signed the Official Secrets Act on 15th February, 1943; she was now part of Special Operations Executive and was to become one of Churchill's most valued secret agents. Her friends realized one day that Noor had simply disappeared!

Secret Training

Noor's new identity was Nora Baker, so as not to link her to her Indian heritage. She was put into the First Aid and Nursing Yeomanry (FANY) that had been created prior to the First World War as a link organization between frontline fighting units and field hospitals. Basically, her membership in FANY would serve as a cover in case of questioning by the enemy.

Later Noor was also placed in the Air Ministry Unit for service under Air Intelligence (A.I 10) as a cover for SOE. Additionally, she was made an officer to provide her some security in the event of capture. By the time Noor began her training with SOE, the organization had developed a whole range of imaginative gadgets and devices, such as "dead rats fitted with explosives, secret wireless transmitters concealed in bundles of logs and sticks or petrol cans, exploding animal droppings (horse droppings were collected from Hyde Park), TNT painted to look like coal lumps, exploding nuts and bolts, exploding fountain pens and milk bottles and improved plastic explosives. The tiniest of spy devices too were produced: microfilm dots on spectacles, button compasses, miniature escape saws, silk-scarf maps, forged papers, clandestine radios, invisible ink and much more."(D)

Noor felt positive that she was strong enough to handle her new job and boarded the train to Surrey, where she would attend one of the Special Training Schools (STS) for F-section agents located on Hog's Back. It was a stately mansion that went by the name of Wanborough Manor and offered a lot of space for secret training. Her commanders and most important trainers were Major Roger de Wesselow and Joan Sanderson.

The extreme and intense training began right away and, besides extensive wireless and Morse code training, it involved a demanding physical fitness program, along with a series of classes in handling a wide range of weapons and explosives and psychological tests. Noor was also taught how to read maps and sketch fields, as well as more gruesome tasks like dealing with being tortured, sabotage and gaining knowledge in capture and escape. At all times the agents were closely observed to evaluate their character and loyalty, especially when they were drunk, which they were sometimes encouraged to be, or in the night, to monitor if they spoke in their sleep, and if so, in what language. This was important, because they had to be taken for a French person through and through. Noor did not do well in some of the disciplines and was frightened of the weapons.

On the other hand, she mastered the complicated world of the wireless, not only perfecting the reading and sending of coded messages but learning the workings and the repair of the complicated devices. She was very motivated and tried to put as much effort as possible into everything she did. Even so, not everyone had faith in Noor: one of her trainers felt that "it was doubtful whether Noor was suited to work in the field" and others said she was "clumsy" or "studious rather than clever."[D]

An SOE report on Noor in April 1943 read as follows:

> *This student, like her two F.A.N.Y. companions, has thrown herself heart and soul into the life of the school. She has any amount of energy, and spends a lot of it on voluntary P.T. with the object of overcoming as far as possible feminine disabilities in the physical sense.*
>
> *She is, also, very feminine in character, very eager to please, very ready to adapt herself to the mood of the company or the tone of the conversation, interested in personalities, capable of strong attachments, kind-hearted, emotional and imaginative. She is very fond of her family… The motive for her accepting the present task is, apparently, idealism. She felt that she had come to a dead end as a W.A.A.F, and was longing to do something more active in the prosecution of the war, something which would make more call on her capabilities and, perhaps, demand more sacrifice… It is the emotional side of her character, coupled with a vivid imagination, which will most test her steadfastness of purpose in the later stages of her training.*

However, nothing would stop Noor's determination and her avid, positive outlook in life. This wasn't missed, and despite some negative comments, she was praised and often received great remarks from her trainers. One of them, Lance Corporal Gordon reported: "She is a person for whom I have the greatest admiration. Completely self-effacing and un-selfish. The last person whose absence was noticed, extremely modest, even humble and shy, always thought everyone better than herself, very polite." Yet the most significant report was Major Roger de Wesselow's, as it was sent straight to Maurice Buckmaster, head of F-section. He sensed Noor's strength and developed faith in her. Noor was now ready to move on and was the first woman agent to attend the challenging Special Training School 52 (STS 52) for specialist signals training in Oxfordshire on 29 March, 1943.

She was now immersed deeper into the complicated and extremely technical world of codes and ciphers, and she learned how to create her own style of transmitting so that others would recognize who was sending messages. Further knowledge included wavelengths, atmospherics, blocking messages, putting up and using aerials, hiding and repairing radio sets. She was doing extremely well and was ahead of all the others as a result of all her previous training with WAAF. Later she studied new technologies like double transposition and the Playfair code, to increase the safety of the code, making it therefore nearly impossible for the Germans to crack. Furthermore, each agent was taught to use two security checks that were personal to him or her which would help to alarm the others if he or she was caught by the enemy. One was the bluff check which could be given to the enemy, if forced, and the other the true check. Both checks had to be integrated in each message the agent sent. If the true check was missing and only the bluff check transmitted, then the head of office would know that the agent had been captured and was in enemy hands.

When Noor's Morse speed was the fastest it could get, she was moved on and, though her next steps weren't all exactly clear, her final school was the famous Beaulieu in Hampshire, a grand luxurious estate buried in the depths of the New Forest. Here she learned in very great detail how to survive behind enemy lines, training alongside very important people and organizations, working under cover for extremely crucial and dangerous missions. Noor apprenticed all the elements of survival and how to become an active secret agent in the field. She learned every single aspect there was to know concerning the modern French and German lifestyles, the

German police, such as the Gestapo or the Sicherheitsdienst, and the Nazi regime and where their headquarters were located.

Any minor mistake or lack of knowledge could lead to the agent's sure death and risk the lives of many others as well. For example, if an agent appeared to be fluent in French but used an inappropriate turn of phrase or expression, even though it may have been grammatically correct, it could prove to be fatal. Additionally, Noor had to painstakingly commit important faces to her memory, master microphotography and study forgery. There were amazingly numerous facets that agents at this stage of training had to be skilled in, but probably the most severe was the harsh, Gestapo-style interrogation practice that often was carried out at night and was used to harden trainees mentally and prepare them in the event of capture. Sometimes these interrogations lasted for hours, and it was difficult not to break. Noor was utterly frightened of the real Gestapo and especially terrified of torture. Small in stature, this delicate young woman did not look cut out to endure Gestapo brutality. Even though Noor was repelled by these drills that completely wiped her out, she learned how to work under pressure and gained confidence as a real spy. Once all her training was completed, Noor would be a valuable communications agent within the British resistance effort on French soil. As time passed, Noor returned home more and more seldom. She wouldn't talk about her work with her family or colleagues and, when asked, remained vague. Little did we know that Noor would soon be embarking upon a perilous mission from which she would never return.

The following report was drafted several weeks after Noor was pulled out of training as she was urgently needed in the field:

> *Signal Training Major* *June 30th 1943*
>
> *This student was withdrawn during the month at the request of her Country Section. While she cannot be considered a fully trained operator because of her shortened course, she is quite capable of handling her set, and of messages. She should, however, gain more confidence in time...*

Preparations for F-section

Finally, in the spring of 1943, the day came when Noor's supervisor, Vera Atkins (Maurice Buckmaster's assistant), called her into her office. She explained that she would be needed for a special mission in France and was to fly by Lysander on the next full moon the coming June.

The decision had not come easily, as the highest-ranking British intelligence officers had only entertained the fantasy of employing women agents behind enemy lines. They believed war was to be fought by men. However, more and more SOE networks were being infiltrated by German intelligence, and male agents were being arrested by the score. The successful outcome of the D-Day operations greatly depended on the valuable information sent by the Allies' spy operations in France. Only as a last resort would women's lives be risked in this way. Being a wireless operator was the most dangerous and also the most valuable job, as all other operations depended on it. The dangers of transmitting wireless messages from behind enemy lines were extremely high, because they could easily be intercepted by German technology and their physical source traced within minutes, therefore revealing the wireless operator's hideout.

Even though Noor hadn't quite completed all her training, both Vera Atkins and her superior, Maurice Buckmaster, were in agreement that she was the best candidate and put all their faith in her. Noor jumped at the opportunity to finally serve the cause of freedom and after a 96-hour course in Bristol, a last vital stage that prepared agents for the real work in the field, the moment came when she had to say goodbye to her family. This was the hardest part for Noor, since she was very attached to them. She told them she would be out of town for a while. The last words she said to her little sister were: "Be good!"

Noor was vowed to absolute secrecy as to the nature and location of her mission. For this reason, she had to again remain quiet and lie as she had done during her training and her work, something that she found excruciatingly hard to do to her loved ones.

She was now to wait in a house full of fellow agents awaiting their missions in Chalfont St Giles in Buckinghamshire (nicknamed Chorleywood). At this point, there was a lot of controversial talk regarding Noor. Many thought she wasn't ready to be an agent yet and should complete her training. Others had complete faith in her. However, Noor was urgently needed; and after a meeting with Leo Marks, master code-maker and head of communications at SOE, she spent her last days in England at the legendary Orchard Court, where agents could prepare themselves mentally and practically in safety and comfort before they set out onto their often perilous or fatal missions.

Here all her clothes were tailored in the French style, and every single aspect and detail of her belongings and cover story was repeatedly scrutinized and rechecked. SOE was extremely precise when it came to perfecting an agent, as these measures were crucial not only for his or her safety, but for the safety of many others. Cover stories were often quite involved, including Noor's. The following identity, fabricated by the SOE, is what Noor would have to adopt:

> *Identity Card: Bordeaux 24/2/43.*
> *Ration Card: Paris XVIe 30/12/41.*
> *Textile Card: Paris.*
>
> *Jeanne Marie Renier was born in Blois on the 25th April 1918. Her father Auguste was Professor of Philosophy in Princeton and her mother, Ray Baker, was American by birth and French by marriage. Her mother, who lived in Paris, had moved to Blois when the Germans advanced on the capital. Her father was killed in the Marne in the Great War in the 1918 retreat. Her mother returned to Paris after the Armistice.*
>
> *Jeanne went to school in St. Cloud, and passed her Bacchot at the Lycée de St. Cloud, then went to the Sorbonne till 1935. She studied there till 1938, specialising in Child Psychology.*
>
> *During the second Great War in France, Jeanne worked as a Nurse in Paris. Her mother went back to America just before the collapse of France.*
>
> *When the Germans broke through, Jeanne went south and stayed for a while in the Bordeaux area. She became employed as a Governess in a family named Jourden in Royan.*
>
> *In the winter of 1941 she spent Christmas in Paris and obtained there her new Ration Card on 30/12/41.*
>
> *A new Identity Card she obtained early this year when she was in Bordeaux looking for a family who would need her services as a governess. Her Textile Card she obtained whilst she was in Paris…*

In addition, her code name would be "Madeleine," and "nurse" was the radio code she would use to identify herself when communicating with headquarters. Noor was also issued four pills; one was a sleeping pill to slip into an opponent's drink, another would make one feel sick to feign an illness. The third was filled with Benzedrine, a stimulant to keep an agent alert and energized in case of over exhaustion in moments of danger. The last pill contained cyanide poison and was to be used if all hope vanished and the agent chose to commit suicide to possibly avoid a gruesome and slow death while being tortured.

Life expectancy: six weeks

Noor's mission consisted of being dropped into Nazi-occupied France and, as a wireless operator, to ensure regular communication between the circuit—a group of couriers, spies, informants and saboteurs—and the intelligence departments in London. She would send and receive coded messages containing valuable information or orders relating to sabotaging enemy plans or providing resistance fighters with equipment, arms, supplies and funds. In particular, her job involved assisting agent Francis Suttil in Paris. His network, code-named "Prosper," was extremely successful in recruiting followers, sabotaging railway lines and receiving arms drops. The circuit had grown so large that he needed all the communications backup he could get. This was a most risky assignment, since a wireless operator's life expectancy in 1943 was only six weeks. Usually a radio agent remained on enemy soil for four weeks maximum before being flown back to safety on the next night of the full moon.

However, Noor felt ready and spent her last afternoon on English soil with supervisor Vera Atkins, who infused her with courage and assured her that the Inayat Khan family would receive regular "good news" reports of Noor. Her loved ones shouldn't ever suspect she was behind enemy lines. She also allowed Noor one last chance to bow out of the commitment gracefully, if she did not feel up to it. "'You know that if you have any doubts, it is not too late to turn back,' Vera said. 'If you don't feel you're the type—if for any reason whatever you don't want to go—you only have to tell me now. I'll arrange everything so that you have no embarrassment. You will be transferred to another branch of the service with no adverse mark on your file.' She ended by adding: 'For us there is only one crime: to go out there and let your comrades down.'"[F]

But Noor remained immovable in her resolve and insisted she was ready for the mission. She couldn't turn back now. Darkness slowly emerged as Noor, alone with a hundred thoughts in her mind, anticipated with a mixture of fear and suspense her dangerous mission, now just a few hours away. The air was tense as the minutes slowly crept by, however, one development would soon change the importance of her role. Neither Noor nor SOE knew that the highly successful Prosper circuit, their most important network in France and the one to which Noor was assigned, would be completely rounded up by the German Intelligence Police shortly after her arrival. This would leave Noor in a position as the sole secret service and resistance support link between Paris and England. Her post would become the principal and most dangerous one in the whole of France.

Finally the two Lysander planes arrived, and Noor boarded one of them accompanied by Cecily Lefort, who was being sent to France as a courier. The full moon cast its light into the darkness when the planes, at long last, departed on June 16th, 1943, from Tangmere—just under one year before D-Day. Headed for unknown perils, Noor did not realize that her peers had kept something from her: she was the first woman wireless operator ever to be sent to France by the Special Operations Executive. Madeleine, as she was now known, was about to engage in the most perilous work of all.

Noor returns to Paris

After a flight full of suspense, Noor's plane landed in a dark field near Angers, some 200 miles southwest of Paris, the most risky place to be at that time. Agents, of course, wore no uniform when they arrived in France, and as a civilian Noor knew that if captured, she would not enjoy the protections guaranteed by the Geneva Convention. The planes left almost immediately after the agents had disembarked and were replaced by five new passengers that had completed their missions and were being flown back to safety. Already waiting for Noor and her colleagues was a Frenchman, known as Henri Déricourt, assisted by Rémy Clément. He was in charge of the arrivals and departures of agents; yet unknown to SOE at the time, Déricourt was a double agent who informed the Gestapo of the names and details of every traveller arriving or departing by Lysander plane. It was part of Déricourt's dangerous game between the fronts to decide what information he would reveal to each of his "employers." He made copies or retrieved information from the presumably secret messages contained in the mail bag that was flown back and forth between headquarters in Great Britain and various SOE agent circuits in France or beyond. For some reason, Déricourt decided not to report Noor's arrival, omitting her name from his notebook.

Noor was now on her own as she quickly buried her gun, which might have been needed in case of an ambush while getting off the plane. From the tiny, improvised landing strip amid wheat fields, vineyards and forests, Noor had to find her way to Paris by herself. She had been told to head to 40, rue

Erlanger, where she would receive help and further instructions. However, her radio set had not yet arrived, so for the time being she had no way of communicating with headquarters for additional information or assistance. From now on, her struggle for survival would not only be for her safety and anonymity but would also be a great financial one. Money trickled in to the agents in enemy territory only very slowly and with great difficulty and long delays. The only possessions Noor carried with her were numerous meticulous codes for different occasions, emergency addresses and escape routes through Spain which she was to dispose of as soon as possible.

Once arrived in the occupied French capital, she headed straight for 40, rue Erlanger to report to her local superior, who—she was told—was an elderly lady. Accordingly, Noor bought her some flowers, yet when she arrived, the door was opened by a man, which completely shocked her. Awkwardly exchanging pleasantries, neither wanted to reveal a password, just in case there was a mistake or this was a trap. Noor hesitated to disclose her secret phrase, especially because a third party was present: a young lady who introduced herself as the man's fiancée. When she eventually left the room, Noor, not knowing what else to do, finally uttered her password: "Je viens de la part de votre ami Antoine pour des nouvelles au sujet de la Société en Bâtiment." ("I have come on behalf of your friend Antoine for news on the building society.")

The man proved indeed to be the SOE contact and replied: "L'affaire est en cours." ("The business is underway.") He affirmed to be Lieutenant Emile Henri Garry, and as soon as things were cleared up, there was much laughter and rejoicing. However, these high spirits were not to last long. In the next days—despite the fact that Noor wasn't exactly supposed to be in much contact with anyone in the field—she met many important SOE agents and heads of Prosper's sub-circuits, such as France Antelme, Gilbert Norman and the famous Francis Suttil himself, head of the leading Prosper circuit. In the meantime, Noor used other radio sets. These were usually A Mark II radios, devices that could both receive and transmit messages and whose frequency was determined by removable crystals.

Working with the radio was extremely dangerous, so agents had to be very quick and alert while sending messages and not exceed 15 minutes. German Intelligence developed expert techniques in locating the source of clandestine radio transmissions. The direction-finding (D/F) teams used unmarked delivery vans to surprise their targets. Their agents were dressed as civilians and were often not suspected until it was too late.

In the next few days, Noor stayed at the Agricultural School at Grignon that was used as the Prosper circuit's secret headquarters. Several agents worked here, among them Professeur Eugène Vandervynckt who was the school's director. It was with the professor and his family that Noor was to live during her mission in France; however the comfort of this castle-like home would not be enjoyed for long. It wasn't until almost a week after she had landed, that Noor's belongings and radio set finally arrived in the night of June 21st/22nd; however, the suitcase that was parachuted down broke in the tree tops, spilling all her belongings. A long search followed, trying desperately to remove all the evidence, before watchful German eyes would notice. Luckily the quest could be undertaken in secret. Little did they know that German intelligence infiltration had already begun, and the Prosper circuit was about to be exposed. Noor set up her wireless in a greenhouse close to Professeur Vandervynckt's house. During the day, she attended some classes and was introduced to the students as a new special student of agriculture. Here at the heart of Prosper's network, some twenty miles outside of Paris, Noor and her French resistance colleagues felt far from possible danger.

The collapse of Prosper

The largest and most powerful of SOE's French-based networks, Prosper was becoming more and more successful, thanks to Francis Sutill's expertise and the skilled work his agents carried out. However, the network eventually grew too vast, its range of activities reaching throughout Paris and the Loire Valley regions. It was just a matter of time until the enemy would succeed in infiltrating its ranks, as it was becoming too large to be easily kept secret. German counterintelligence efforts in the so-called *Funkkrieg* (radio war) were already being made very early on in the war by the SD or Sicherheitsdienst (the Reich's Security Service). Not only did the SS and SD painstakingly train their best radio operators to copy the styles and codes of Britain's military wireless system, but also set in motion an enormous code-cracking operation. Moreover, the SD managed to slip their own agents into the system or simply bribe some Allied agents into leaking sensitive information back to Germany. Additionally, assistance from double agents like Henri Déricourt played a considerable role in exposing the circuit. The larger and the more important the Prosper network became, the more vulnerable it was to enemy infiltration. Several events and leaks led to the disastrous rounding up of the organization.

One of the weak links was the fact that one of Prosper's radio operators, Jacques Agazarian, was so badly needed to transmit messages that he agreed to broadcast for as many as twenty-four different agents, some of whom did not even belong to the Prosper organization. These favors created trails to Prosper's radio set that could be all the more easily detected by German counterintelligence. The arrests began towards the middle of June 1943. First two Canadian agents, John Macalister and Frank Pickersgill, were arrested at Gestapo roadblocks shortly after arriving on French soil. Soon after the de Gaulle resistance group headed by the charismatic Jean Moulin was rounded up. Jean Moulin died as a result of the brutal treatment he received at the hands of the Gestapo. A few days later, on June 24th, head of Prosper Francis Suttill himself, his courier Andrée Borrel and some fifteen others were arrested by the Gestapo. At the same time Prosper's principal radio operator, Gilbert Norman, who had taken Noor under his wing during the first days of her time in Paris and who helped her perfect her transmitting skills, was arrested at his apartment in the middle of the night.

At the Agricultural School of Grignon, Professeur Vandervynckt and three other agents were arrested. Fortunately for Noor, she was absent when the roundup took place, and the four men did not reveal her existence to the interrogating officers. Sadly, Professeur Vandervynckt died as a result of maltreatment at Dachau concentration camp on May 1st, 1945, three days after the US Armed Forces liberated the camp.

These arrests were just the tip of the iceberg; and one arrest led to the next, as the agents often carried valuable information endangering their colleagues. Reports and evaluations vary concerning the number of arrests that took place throughout Paris, the Loire Valley and Brittany as a result of the German infiltration of SOE's Prosper network. The conservative figure estimates 400 and some claim that as many as 1500 suspects were arrested from June through August 1943. Within days of Noor's arrival behind enemy lines, the group of agents whom she was to assist was already in German hands, leaving her as the only radio operator in Paris and all its outskirts.

She immediately contacted Maurice Buckmaster and informed him of the devastating fiasco that had taken place in the past days. Buckmaster was utterly shocked and advised Noor to fly straight back to England, for he knew she was in extreme danger and was most likely to be caught any moment. However Noor willingly refused, as it was clear that she was the only hope left to help reorganize a network as a wireless operator. Her messages would now represent the only connection between Allied intelligence in London and underground operations in Paris. Suddenly everything depended solely on her, as her secret mission had just taken a crucial and perilous turn.

Poste Madeleine

Noor started working very closely with three French agents—Robert Gieules, Charles Vaudevire and Paul Arrighi, and chose "Raymonde" as her new secret code name. Even double agent Henri Déricourt depended on her. Noor was now needed for all radio transmissions and she organized meetings between the few agents still left, prepared flights back to London and had to handle important sums of money. Additionally Noor arranged escape routes for agents and tried her best to rebuild the Prosper circuit by helping to recruit new agents chosen among members of the French resistance.

She played a dangerous game, always on the move, traveling between locations and narrowly escaping the Gestapo on a regular basis. Unknown to her, one of the apartment houses she stayed at for some time near the Bois de Boulogne was mostly inhabited by SS officers. However, she managed to remain undercover and handled the great amount of work that was laid heavily on her shoulders. "Single-handedly she did the work of six radio operators. She went on air and exchanged messages with Antelme (now in London), who wanted her to keep in touch with Octave Simon and send him information about the financing of troops during the invasion."[(D)]

However, as time passed, the Gestapo learned of Noor's existence and how valuable she was to England. They set everything in motion to put an end to her activities. Unfortunately, due to captured fellow agents, the Germans gained a very accurate description of Noor, and so she often found herself being secretly pursued. Yet she always managed to escape in the nick of time, outrunning the Gestapo on various occasions. She was forced to change her hair color and her general appearance every few days, in true international spy fashion, and finally contacted old friends she knew from the time she lived in Paris, in order to find a safe place to stay. They were surprised and delighted to see Noor, but at the same time were shocked to hear what a fatal mission she was on and tried to convince her to give it up and fly back to safety. However, as always, determined to pull through, Noor would rather risk her life than fail all those now depending on her.

For Maurice Buckmaster, Noor had become one of his foremost agents in France, and she knew that to him her continued presence in Paris was vital. To avoid detection, Noor moved around as much as possible, often circulating through Paris on bicycle and always on the lookout for secure places to transmit clandestine information. She sent as many messages as possible, feeding London with the latest news; however, in order to use her radio set, she had to attach the aerial line outdoors. This was extremely risky, as the aerial measured 70 feet and could easily be spotted by suspicious eyes. Furthermore, her transmissions were continuously being picked up by German intelligence, which left her constantly escaping just in time.

There was one incident where Noor attempted to attach the line from her window to a tree to report urgent news back to England. In the midst of this revealing process, a German officer happened by and spotted her. Instead of hiding her actions, Noor asked the soldier if he would give her a hand to string up her "clothesline." Luckily he didn't realize that he was unwittingly helping to set up an aerial for his enemies. Another day, while Noor was traveling in the metro, a couple of German guards suspected Noor's case of appearing heavier than one of its size should weigh. Though concealed in a small leather suitcase, a wireless transmitter weighed some thirty pounds, and it was obvious that it burdened Noor's slight frame. "One of them asked her gruffly: 'What have you in that case, Mademoiselle?' She replied, 'A cinematographic apparatus.' They ordered her to open her case and Noor complied. 'Well, you can see what it is. You can see all the little bulbs.'"[E] Amazingly, as if by a miracle, the Germans let her go. However, mistakes were not only made by the Germans. Unfortunately for Noor and her comrades behind enemy lines, SOE wireless operators at the transmission room in London—as well as their high-ranking decision-making superiors—often made unpardonable blunders that led to some of their agents' capture, torture or even death.

After having spent several sleepless nights on the run, Noor decided to go to Suresnes, the suburb she had grown up in, to have a look at her beloved Fazal Manzil. When she arrived, she was dismayed to find that her family's home had now become Gestapo Headquarters. Continuing on through the neighborhood, Noor went to the home of one of her best friends, Raymonde Prénat. Extremely surprised to see her back from England, Raymonde took her in and allowed her to make regular radio transmissions from her house. "Madame Prénat liked to see her eat a good lunch and dinner on those occasions, as she suspected that she did not fee herself very well… Raymonde and her mother both used to feel that Noor ran a big risk in coming to Suresnes, where everybody knew her."(E) But Noor felt safe in Suresnes.

Noor often visited the family of Dr. Pierre Jourdan, the family's physician. During the years preceding the war, a close friendship developed between the two families. On December 30th, 1945, Dr. Jourdan wrote to Ora Ray explaining that he believed his family to be the last friends to see Noor prior to her disappearance. They often invited her to stay with them in Paris at Faubourg Poissonnière and they helped her with her work from June to September 1943.

The dragnet closes in

After much moving around and transmitting from different places, including a room in the Rue de la Faisanderie, strangely, just blocks away from the much feared SD/Gestapo headquarters in Avenue Foch, Noor was ordered to liaison with the two Canadian agents, Pickersgill and Macalister, at a café on the Champs-Elysées. Tragically, neither SOE's F-Section—nor Noor—had yet realized that the Canadian agents, who had landed through SOE's services many weeks before had already been arrested. When Noor arrived at the café, however, there were indeed two men already waiting for her whom she suspected to be her contacts. In reality they were two German agents, Karl-Horst Holdorf and Joseph Placke, posing as the Canadians. German counterintelligence had used the real Canadian agents' wireless set to continue making Allied headquarters believe they were still free. This was also how the meeting with Noor had been organized.

Everything went according to plan, and the agents informed Noor that they wanted to set up a new network in the north of France but needed to contact a certain Desprez, an agent who was known by Noor's French colleague, Robert Gieules. She introduced them to Gieules, believing that everything was under control and not suspecting the slightest scam. Needless to say, Robert Gieules did not return home that night, yet Noor remained unaware of his capture.

Shortly after arresting Gieules, with whom Noor had worked regularly for weeks, German counterintelligence aimed to set up a sly trap. Forcing Gieules to contact Noor, he was obliged to organize a meeting with her on October 1st near the Arc de Triomphe. Trying to sound as vague as possible, he was successful in warning Noor that something wasn't right, and it dawned on her that he must have been arrested. So Noor bid a fellow agent reassure her suspicions by observing the scheduled meeting place from a distance. Sure enough, Gieules stood there waiting for her, looking nervous, as six dominantly positioned men watched his every move from nearby. Noor, luckily, had sensed the trap and used her sixth sense to avoid capture yet again.

Nonetheless, she knew that her good fortune wouldn't last forever while she remained in Paris, especially now that the Gestapo had already seen her in person and would do their utmost to capture her. This threat caused her to change her appearance anew; yet slowly, Noor was becoming weary of the dangerous spy life she had been leading for three months, instead of the originally planned four weeks.

Throughout September and early October, Noor's life resembled a game of cat-and-mouse. She constantly changed location for transmissions, sent only short messages as an additional precaution and changed lodgings even more frequently. The German *Funkkrieg* experts were close on her tail, almost detecting the exact whereabouts of her signal source, yet never quite finding her.

Nevertheless, they were gaining on Noor and almost captured her again by a hair on two further nerve-racking occasions. Always relying on her instincts, she managed to see through the clever traps set up by the SD, but knew her escapes couldn't get much narrower. She shared her fears with her few other colleagues who already had constantly been advising her to lie low in the countryside of Normandy or to return to England. Buckmaster had been urging his most valued agent back as well, as it was just a question of hours until Noor's mission would tragically end, considering the increasingly dangerous situation she was now in.

At long last, she actually strongly considered the possibility of returning to London, on condition that she would first be replaced by another agent. Relieved by her decision, Buckmaster organized a flight back to England for her on October 14th, knowing with somewhat regret that the most important post in France—Poste Madeleine, as it had become to be known—would soon be occupied by a new British secret agent. Noor began saying her farewells to colleagues and friends, joyful that she would soon be leaving for England and see her dear family again. Sadly, this was not to be. After three months of excellent work carried out in the most dangerous of situations, Noor's luck would turn.

In "protective custody" of the SD

In the end it was not German counterintelligence that proved to be Noor's downfall, but rather an envious acquaintance. A young woman called Renée Garry, who was in fact the sister of Noor's former network superior Emile Henri Garry, was in love with France Antelme, an agent Noor had worked with and with whom she had developed a close friendship. However Antelme seemed to have considerably more affection—possibly romantic notions—towards Noor. Renée, bubbling with jealousy, thus couldn't stand Noor and decided to march off to SD/Gestapo Headquarters in Avenue Foch and in retribution betray the British spy, telling the German officers Noor's whereabouts in return for money. She knew Noor was staying in the Rue de la Faisanderie at the time and asked for 100,000 francs in return for her information (one-tenth of the sum the Germans usually would have paid for a British spy).

Head of SD, Hans Josef Kieffer, was absolutely thrilled about the valuable knowledge he had gained and ordered his men to keep a close watch on Noor's house. Eventually Noor stepped out of the building, and the German officers emerged from their hiding and started pursuing her, attempting to finally arrest the agent they had been tracing for so long. However, Noor suddenly was aware of being tailed and cunningly managed to slip out of sight of her trackers one last time. Eventually Noor returned to her apartment, not realizing that the Germans had her exact address, and was utterly shocked to find a man standing behind her door who immediately grabbed at her. Fuelled with fury, Noor viciously tried to free herself from his grip, using all her defenses until he was a bloody mess and had no choice but to withdraw. She was blazing with rage and so ferocious that the man had no chance against her and was forced to pull out his gun. He instantly called for reinforcements; and Noor, now largely outnumbered, watched helplessly as five men cuffed her and forced her into their car.

It was a quiet afternoon when she was arrested on October 13th, 1943, just a few hours before she would have been flown back to England, to her family and to safety. The person who had captured her was Pierre Cartaud, a Frenchman working for the Germans. Victoriously, Noor was driven to one of the grand apartment buildings on Avenue Foch and finally stood face-to-face with the German head of counterintelligence in Paris, SS Sturmbannführer Hans Josef Kieffer, who was delighted to contemplate his prize catch. Inwardly he smiled at how little he had had to pay the French woman who betrayed Noor—he would have willingly given ten times the amount or more in order to finally hold "Madeleine" in his grasp. And, as if this weren't glorious enough, Noor's radio set and notebook, with all her codes and the messages she had sent, had been found as well. She never should have kept these important documents; however in London, someone had explained that she should carefully "file" all her messages. Noor misinterpreted this and had kept everything closely with her at all times. This crucial mistake could easily have been avoided with clearer communication on the part of her trainers.

Finally Noor was led to a cell on the fifth floor and, still livid with anger, wouldn't answer to anything she was asked. After a while her guards gave up; and she then demanded a little privacy for a bath, so that a lady could wash herself and have some time on her own in such a dreadful situation. Surprised by her sudden request, they eventually allowed her the favor, not wanting to upset her even more, and so she was led to the bathroom. Immediately, Noor clambered out the window and risked a dangerous escape from the high towering roof. Any little slip would have been fatal; however, she didn't manage to go far, because one of her main guards and interrogator, Ernest Vogt, spotted her and carefully reached for her hand from the next window. She took it, knowing she wouldn't stand a chance; and, acknowledging that she was defeated, let herself be accompanied back into the cell.

In the next few hours she was treated surprisingly kindly, as food was regularly brought to her and pleasantries such as cigarettes were offered. She didn't touch a thing, however, and realized her captors were going to try a psychological technique to soften her up. Later, Noor was interrogated for hours by Vogt, who was extremely skilled at his job, managing nearly always to persuade his prisoners to tell him what he wanted to hear. He would make the agents think he already knew everything by providing them with astonishing facts and knowledge that he wasn't supposed to know, letting them feel it was worthless keeping their mouths shut. In Noor's case, he also showed her all the copies of the letters she had sent to England and to her mother; these had been passed on by double agent Déricourt. In addition, he demonstrated how he had cracked all her codes. Moreover, Vogt tried posing as a "friend" in many ways, but Noor never fell for his tricks. She showed astonishing willpower, and it was impossible to break her stubbornness.

A few days later, London received a message from "Madeleine." The true security check had been sent, but the bluff check was missing. This unmistakably implied that Noor had been infiltrated or captured, yet no one at headquarters in Baker Street seemed to pay attention, not even to the fact that she hadn't yet returned to England. The only person alarmed was the code-maker Leo Marks, who was fond of Noor and had carefully been following her wireless messages. Her transmissions were always perfect, and she never had forgotten any security check in a message. But when he frantically reported this to F-section head Maurice Buckmaster, the latter dismissed the thought right away, assuring Marks that Noor was fine. Additionally, the fact that no written messages had come in—only wireless messages—Buckmaster understood as proof that Noor was attempting to lie low and had increased her concern for security. This wasn't the only time that Buckmaster refused to acknowledge the obvious signs that his agents' wireless sets were being used by the enemy, thus bringing other agents' lives in danger. In truth, Noor's wireless set was now in the hands of German radio expert, Josef Goetz, who played his little game with SOE headquarters in London. He cunningly mastered his job and successfully used the captured agents' radio sets in order to thwart Allied plans. These little tricks and SOE's ignorance led to hundreds of arrests and helped German counterintelligence gain supplies and equipment.

Meanwhile, Noor calmed down and even started talking to Vogt during his regular interrogations; however, he knew he would never get anything valuable out of her. The only thing she revealed was her supposed real name, calling herself Nora Baker. Ever since she had joined SOE she had gone under this pseudonym; and nobody, not even her closest colleagues, knew her real name. She was scared they might find her brother Hidayat and his family still living in France and use them in order to blackmail her. "Vogt later told Jean Overton Fuller (one of Noor's good friends) that he had never met anyone like Noor and he admired her courage, bravery and kindness. He once asked her whether she sometimes felt that she had wasted her life by joining the service and that her sacrifice had been in vain since they mopped up three-quarters of the French section. But she replied that it did not matter. She had served her country and that was her recompense."[(D)]

It is likely that, despite her captivity, Noor received the best treatment possible at Avenue Foch SD/Gestapo headquarters. Kieffer was known to shout and threaten at times but it appears that he practiced diplomacy, as well as mutual admiration and respect whenever possible. Small gestures of kindness and warmth towards his prisoners locked in their cells on the building's fifth floor were commonplace. He seemed to know a lot about England and frequently showed admiration for the British and their ways. Perhaps this was the game that the head of German intelligence in France used to his best advantage. Noor was even brought clean clothes and a few other things from her apartment when she had asked for them.

Plans of escape

The Germans had done her the favor of not realizing that, in her mind, Noor was already forging a brilliant plan: one night, Noor lightly started tapping a message in Morse code against her prison wall and suddenly received an answer. Restlessly, the two began tapping back and forth, and later Noor even succeeded contacting a second prisoner. The two secret agents captured in the adjoining and opposite cells were Colonel Léon Faye, a Frenchman working closely with MI6 who had led an important resistance network, and Captain John A. R. Starr, an F-section agent who had been active in the east of France. Together, the three started plotting a clandestine escape plan, which was not only extremely risky, but magnificently ingenious.

Starr was allowed to move around more freely, as he proved to be a talented artist, and the Germans needed him to do special work for them. One day, as he was let out of his cell, he managed to secretly push a note under Noor's prison door that told her to use the lavatory, which all of the prisoners shared, to hide secret messages. This is how the three attempted a bold interchange (as Starr was too far away to hear Noor's Morse code) and started communicating by leaving little notes under the basin in the lavatory whenever they were let out to use it. Starr announced that the bars in his window could easily be unscrewed, as the frame they were attached to was made out of wood. Noor's and Faye's thick bars were screwed right into the rock wall, so it would require quite some effort to loosen them; nevertheless, it could be accomplished. But how on earth would they manage to retrieve a screwdriver?

Surprisingly, the answer came a few days later when the cleaning maid fussed about her Hoover being broken. Starr immediately offered to help and requested tools so that he could fix it. The German guards knew he was good at handiwork and they allowed him to carry out the task, while keeping a close eye on every single move he made. Thus Starr was forced to repair the Hoover badly, so that it would break again and he could once more attempt to secretly acquire a tool. The second chance came soon enough, and this time he was in luck and actually managed to slip a screwdriver into his clothes. He immediately hid it in the lavatory; and, together with Faye, Noor set straight to work. The screwdriver was passed between them, and every night they diligently worked on the bars, hardly getting any sleep. It was exhausting work and very risky, as the windows were so high up that they needed to change the position of their beds in order to reach them. So as not to arouse suspicion, they had to start moving their beds around a few days earlier, saying they needed change and a different atmosphere. The guards weren't exactly delighted about this, but after a while they didn't pay attention to the constant shifting around.

Still, Noor could hardly reach her window, and one night she even came crashing onto the hard floor because she couldn't hold herself up on the window sill anymore, causing much noise. Immediately the guards came running, and she had to make them believe that she had been trying to commit suicide. Luckily, they let the answer pass and didn't notice the bars almost falling out of the window.

When the bars were almost loose enough to be removed, Noor used the face powder and cream that she had demanded be brought from her apartment to fill the holes and thus secure the bars. She then left the cosmetics in the lavatory for Faye. She also insisted that all her clothes be brought to her, because she couldn't stand wearing the same things over and over again. In reality, she remembered having Metro tickets in her pockets; and, the guards not realizing this, she managed to secure them.

Starr was now given the screwdriver, and after many sleepless nights the significant hour finally came on November 25th to find out if all their work had been in vain. They were ready to escape. When darkness fell, Starr started whistling loudly and making noise, as he knew that Noor's and Faye's bars would cause suspicious sounds when being completely removed from the holes. Finally the guards locked him in his cell for the night; and Starr took off his shoes, removed his bars, and clambered onto the roof. Faye did the same, but Noor still had problems removing her bars. Panic arose, and all three of them desperately wrestled with the bars, trying to pull them out without making too much noise, which was impossible to do. They knew that time was slipping away, and the guards could come at any second. Their hearts beating heavily in their chests, they finally managed to free Noor after two hours of strenuous work and, in true spy story fashion, quietly scampered along the rooftops to make their way to neighboring houses where they hoped to find a safe and low place to jump.

To this end, they had brought their prison blankets and began knotting them together to make a rope. Any minute now, they would be in safety! Escaping the Germans would have been accomplished gloriously and the agents' cunning plan much celebrated, if the following event hadn't happened at that precise moment in that exact place. They had gingerly climbed down several stories towards the safety of the street and were just about to jump, when suddenly, to their great dismay, air raid sirens started wailing loudly throughout the neighborhood: RAF planes had come to attack the Germans! Quickly the agents struggled to get off the roof, but it was too late.

During a bomb scare or attack, prison cells were routinely checked, and the guards had already realized they were gone. Kieffer was alarmed and he sent all his men to surround the building, while the three fugitives broke into one of the houses. They meant to escape from the other side of the building and, dashing out of the door, they made a run for it. Sadly, the Germans were too numerous and had already secured the whole area. The agents were trapped! It was quite impossible to escape the Gestapo, and it only took a few seconds until they were spotted and recaptured.

After they had been beaten blue and bloody, they were hauled back to their cells, utterly disappointed and cursing their extremely bad luck. If it hadn't been for the unfortunate timing of a British air raid on Paris, Noor and her accomplices would now be free. Kieffer was shaking with rage and gave the impression that he was terribly disappointed by his prisoners' behavior. How could they have betrayed his trust in them? First threatening to shoot them on the spot, Kieffer finally decided to give the agents another chance. He advised them to sign a declaration that they would stay in their cells and never attempt to escape again. Starr cooperated; however, Faye and Noor remained honest and refused, knowing they would always flee to freedom if the chance allowed it. They wouldn't promise anything. Visibly disappointed, Kieffer felt he had no other choice but to send Noor to a German prison.

Prisoner in Pforzheim

So it happened that Noor was sent to Pforzheim prison that same day and became the first female Allied agent to be put behind bars on German soil. It must be said in Kieffer's defence that, despite his position as head of SD, he behaved towards Noor in as fair a manner as he felt permissible; any other SS Sturmbannführer in his position would undoubtedly have sent his rebellious captive to a concentration camp or have her shot.

On her way to Pforzheim, Noor miraculously managed to escape a second time. How she did remains unclear, but her friend Raymonde Prénat remembers meeting Noor some time in November and noticing she was out of breath and on the run. Telling Raymonde she would be back, Noor disappeared again and obviously had been recaptured, as she never did return.

When Noor was delivered to Pforzheim's civilian prison on November 27th, 1943, authorities in Berlin had labelled Noor as "extremely dangerous," in the sense that she would probably attempt to escape and that she should be treated as a *Nacht und Nebel—Rückkehr unerwünscht* prisoner, meaning "Night and Fog—Return undesired." As the name suggests, this meant that those targeted were removed in total secrecy and no records made of their fate.

According to a fellow prisoner she was put into "solitary confinement and had to be chained hand and foot. A third chain connected her hands to her feet. No one was allowed to talk to her. She was kept in a cell on the ground floor, separated from the other cells by two wire fences with heavily locked gates."[(D)] A woman came to wash and feed her, as she wasn't able to move by herself. Noor was treated deplorably and, totally isolated from the outside world, she had nothing with which to pass her time.

Although the prison director, Wilhelm Krauss, was protective and reasonably kind to Noor, even having her manacles removed, he was subsequently scolded by the local Gestapo and forced to keep Noor in chains for the duration of her ten-month stay. Noor only received poor meals consisting of potato peel or cabbage soup and was never let out of her cell. She spent months like this, completely alone and starved in darkness, not being able to communicate with anyone and not knowing how long she would remain in isolation.

One day Noor unexpectedly noticed that a message had been scratched underneath her plate: "There are three French girls here." The three girls were Yolande Lagrave, Rosy Storcke and Suzy Chireiz, political prisoners who had been sent to Pforzheim in January 1944. They had noticed that the captive in cell number 1 was never let out and was treated quite harshly. So they forged a plan to try to contact the mysterious person by etching secret messages into their food platters. Their strategy had certainly succeeded, for Noor had received their plate one day and replied: "You are not alone; you have a friend in Cell 1." This is how the four women communicated from then on, always learning more from each other and eagerly waiting for the platter to make its rounds.

After four horrible months had slowly passed, Noor was at last allowed outside her cell for the very first time. Naturally she was closely guarded and was only let out for a short time; however she must have felt extremely relieved to finally be able to see bright daylight again and move her stiff limbs that hadn't been exercised for ages. Strangely, Noor never held a grudge against her captors; and Yolande later remarked that "She spoke good German and was polite to the officer who let her out." Her sister Claire remembered that Noor never disliked Germans, even her captors, whose job it was to guard her; but she did not tolerate Nazi ideology.

Meanwhile, the operations officer at SOE voiced concern that Madeleine's messages were peculiar: her "fist," or tapping style, was different. Vera Atkins suggested they query the sender for information of a personal nature that only Noor would be able to answer. The answers were deemed acceptable and all were reassured that Noor was still operating freely.

As agreed in June 1943, before Noor's flight to France, SOE continued to send their reassuring notes to the family. While Noor had already been languishing in the enemy's hands for nine months, a note from the War Office was sent to her mother on June 30th, 1944:

> *Dear Mrs. Baker-Inayat,*
>
> *Thank you for your kind letter of June 20th, enclosing a note for your daughter, which we were pleased to forward to her.*
>
> *I am happy to tell you that she is perfectly well, and, as always, sends her love to you and to Claire and Vic.*

In reality, Noor was growing frailer by the day, her strength and energy clearly abandoning her. The abominable conditions she was in were almost unbearable, as she was hardly fed and was regularly beaten up and badly violated by her guards. Even under these horrible circumstances, Noor remained sovereign and sought power through meditating in her prison. The three women who had managed to contact Noor knew about her dreadful state: "'That day again all of us felt deeply for Nora,' said Yolande, who had become very attached to the frail and gentle young woman who bore all her torture and abuse with tremendous spirit."[(D)] One day in September 1944, Yolande remembered Noor being stripped of her clothes and taken away to an unknown destination.

Death at Dachau

In the aftermath of D-Day, as Allied troops advanced ever closer to Germany, Adolf Hitler sought revenge on those who had in any way participated in trying to crush his Third Reich and fanatic ideologies. Many of these people—especially secret agents such as Noor—were already held in German custody. Orders were given by Hitler's Obergruppenführer Ernst Kaltenbrunner, head of the RSHA (Reich's Main Security Office) that such offenders be disposed of under the provisions of *Nacht und Nebel* operations.

Noor fell in this doomed category and she was picked up from Pforzheim prison on September 11th, 1944, and was taken to the train station with three other female agents, Eliane Plewman, Madeleine Damerment and Yolande Beekman. Yolande recognized Noor, as they had trained together at Wanborough Manor. Unknown to all of the women, they were about to board a train that would take them straight to one of the most feared places in Germany—they were leaving for Dachau concentration camp. Kaltenbrunner's direct orders sent by telegram indicated that these four women were to be "executed at Dachau." As Kaltenbrunner received orders directly from Hitler, we can deduct that Noor, along with her three comrades, were most likely executed on the orders of Hitler himself.

They reached the camp, which was normally a men's facility, at midnight; and the four women were immediately beaten and thrown into cells. In the early hours of the morning, Plewman, Damerment and Beekman were hauled out of their cells, shot in the head, and transferred straight to the crematorium. For Noor it wasn't over yet: because of her darker skin and the fact that she had been labeled as "extremely dangerous," she was going to receive the "full treatment."

Hours of gruesome torture still lay ahead of her, during which she would suffer greatly. Numerous testimonies were given by inmates several years after the end of the war, and they all confirm that Noor's end was a brutal one; some thought she had been raped. Even though the versions differ, the most likely one is that Noor became the victim of the assistant camp director's sadism and brutality. His name was Wilhelm Ruppert. According to an eyewitness, a Dutch prisoner called Joop:

It was terrible what happened. The SS undressed the girl and she was terribly beaten by Ruppert all over her body. She did not cry, neither said anything. When Ruppert got tired and the girl was a bloody mess, he told her that he would shoot her. She had to kneel and the only word she said, before Ruppert shot her from behind through the head was, "Liberté!"

Posthumous Awards

Thanks to Noor's supervisor, Vera Atkins, her deeds were not forgotten. Atkins spent long years traveling to former concentration camps and worked closely with the international Red Cross, in order to find clues as to the fates of Noor and other missing female agents. Atkins' tireless investigations and interrogation of key witnesses, such as Kieffer, allowed various authors to learn the full story of Noor's tragic destiny.

When Noor's heroism was discovered by the governments of Britain and France, she was posthumously awarded foremost distinctions.

On October 4th, 1945, the War Office wrote a detailed report of Noor's services of which the last lines read:

Her companion, since returned, stated that 'she was magnificent, and everyone at the Gestapo H.Q. admired her.' This officer is worthy of high recognition for her outstanding bravery and devotion to duty in carrying on after the arrest of most of her colleagues. It is strongly recommended that she be appointed a Member of the Order of the British Empire.

Sir C. Gubbins at SOE drafted a moving report of Noor's merits ending with the request:

It is recommended that, in recognition of her outstanding courage, both moral and physical, she be awarded posthumously the George Cross.

The King of England, George VI, personally handed the George Cross to Vilayat and Claire in memory of Noor. This decoration was awarded "for acts of the greatest heroism or of the most conspicuous courage in circumstances of extreme danger" and was awarded to only three women, one of whom was Noor.

The king's official note from Buckingham Palace read:

The Queen and I offer you our heartfelt sympathy in your great sorrow. We pray that the Empire's gratitude for a life so nobly given in its service may bring you some measure of consolation.

(signed George R.I)

In France, Noor received the highest civilian award, the Croix de Guerre with Gold Star.

Memorials to Noor

In England there is a memorial to members of FANY at Runymede.

At the Dachau Concentration Camp Memorial Site, apart from the memorial plaque in the crematorium, there is a write-up in the museum and a copy of the marble plaque that was placed in front of Fazal Manzil.

Each year, towards the end of April, the town of Suresnes honors the memory of Noor at a ceremony in front of the memorial plaque placed on the wall outside Fazal Manzil.

In the lower part of Suresnes near the Seine River, a square was named after Noor: Cours Madeleine.

In Valençay, France, a monument was erected in 1991 to SOE's French Section heroes of World War II, among whom Noor was remembered. The ceremony was presided over by England's Queen Mother, as well.

Other memorials to Noor's memory include:

- A plaque in front of the family home, Fazal Manzil
- A plaque in Dachau camp's crematorium
- Her name is engraved at Blois. The ceremony was presided over by the British Queen Mother.
- A memorial in England in 1953
- Mention at the war memorial of Runymede

Books

Numerous biographies of Noor have been published since the 1950s, and her unusual story has been featured in many books on World War II. Newspaper articles in both English and French have helped immortalize her memory, as well as three films and documentaries. In addition, Noor has inspired two novels. The main publications include:

Born for Sacrifice—Jean Overton Fuller
Madeleine—Jean Overton Fuller
Noor-un-nisa Inayat Khan—Jean Overton Fuller
The Penetration of SOE—Jean Overton Fuller
The SOE—M.R.D. Foot
A Life in Secrets—Sarah Helm

Spy Princess—Shrabani Basu
Flames in the Field—Rita Kramer
The Women who lived for Danger—Marcus Binney
Between Silk and Cyanide—Leo Marks
A Man called Intrepid—William Stevenson
All That I Have—Laurent Joffrin
The Tiger's Claw—Shauna Singh Baldwin

Magazine and newspaper coverage

From 1947 till the present day, literally thousands of articles have either featured or mentioned Noor's heroic role in WWII victory. They have appeared mainly in English, as well as in several other languages including French and German.

Film coverage

In 1979, a full-feature Hollywood-style film starring David Niven and Barbara Hershey, *A Man Called Intrepid*, featured a romanticized and not altogether accurate account of Noor.

In the 1990s, a series came out in India with, again, a rendering of Noor's merits that left much to be desired.

In 2006, Britain's BBC television produced an excellent in-depth and historically accurate account of Noor's life and war mission. Shown as a fifty-minute documentary, it was watched by over four million viewers, breaking all the records for that particular series known as *Time Watch*. Claire and Hidayat were interviewed for the film, and David played a major investigative role in the production. Much of the new material and factual evidence released in the documentary was the result of Claire's preciously kept letters, photographs and documents on the one hand, and the British government's recently declassified file on Noor on the other.

Homage

Noor will always be remembered, like so many other courageous men and women who, answering the call of war, left their homes, their comforts and belongings, their cherished families, their plans for future conjugal happiness and their sweetest hopes behind them—perhaps never to return again. Noor's courage nourished by hope, and her body strengthened by willpower, she spent many a weary dark night in fear, hunger and pain in the cause of justice and freedom.

Claire Harper: She rose above the prison bars, overcoming cruelty and torture. Her whole being was courage. In her dying moment she personified the heart of humanity, making herself immortal.

Tribute to Noor

PRINCESS SPY

song by David Harper

Noor was a dreamer, a weaver of tales.
A friend of the fairies—tender and frail.
Noor was an angel when playing the harp;
But good at her studies, her thinking was sharp.
Noor was a writer, a poet as well:
In English and French her stories she'd tell.
"Noor" means the Light: a star in the West.
Her aim was devotion; her life was a quest.

TO FREE THE LAND, NO MATTER THE COST
EVEN IF HER LIFE BE LOST.
SHE CHOSE TO FIGHT WHEN RISKS WERE HIGH
SUCH WAS OUR GIFT FROM THE PRINCESS SPY.

Noor was exotic: a most "foreign" blend.
Yet the freedom of England and France she'd defend.
Noor was a tiger when faced with her foe
And none of the secrets were ever let go.
Noor was an agent who trained for the day
When she might become useful preparing the way
For the great D-Day landings to strike with surprise
This was the task of the SOE spies.

TO FREE THE LAND, NO MATTER THE COST
EVEN IF HER LIFE BE LOST.
SHE CHOSE TO FIGHT WHEN RISKS WERE HIGH
SUCH WAS OUR GIFT FROM THE PRINCESS SPY.

Among all the heroes, Noor loved Joan of Arc
And thus did she battle, leaving her mark.
Like Joan she was captured, ere she returned.
Just like her heroine, in the end she was burned.

TO FREE THE LAND, NO MATTER THE COST
EVEN IF HER LIFE BE LOST.
SHE CHOSE TO FIGHT WHEN RISKS WERE HIGH
SUCH WAS OUR GIFT FROM THE PRINCESS SPY.

Part Five: Rubies Three, 1947–2010

MOTHER'S PASSING

Claire Harper: In 1947, Mother had grown weary but she stubbornly continued to work for next to no pay. Since Vilayat and I earned enough for us to meet our needs, we decided that she should stop working. One day, we cleaned the apartment thoroughly, and Vilayat went to fetch Mother from work for the last time. She had been showing signs of great anxiety; we tried to help and comfort her all we could.

One day when I returned from work at the Pakistan Office, Mother was resting. When she awoke, she told me she had experienced dying and that she knew what it was like. It was hard to ward away the thoughts she was fostering. Alone with mother, I faced a dilemma. The first thought was to change her mood and to help her out of bed. After drinking some tea, she appeared to feel better and became more communicative. I avoided the subject of death during our conversation.

Once ready for the evening activities, I did my best. Vilayat usually returned with his thoughts full of business. The dinner we could offer up depended on our payday. That evening mother was very tired; I helped her to retire to bed. There were not enough blankets and no means to buy any; after the war everything was overpriced. Vilayat had not returned and was probably with his Sufi group. Mother was still awake but her feet were frozen so we piled the bed with coats. Mother began talking about cremation, a subject that horrified me. She then proceeded to tell me much of her life story in detail. As her story was drawing to a close she stated, "When I die I want to be cremated."

At the time, doctors were neither very knowledgable nor of great help; but Mother never complained, and we were more than happy to have her close. She tried to get as much rest as possible but insisted on going out to do our shopping every day. Her health diminished visibly and she seemed barely strong enough to carry out normal tasks, swaying to and fro by some unseen longing.

Vilayat suggested that Mother and I should go to America to start a new life there. This idea brought hope to our hearts, yet it all seemed so impossible: where would the journey money come from? Where would we stay? Would I find work to support us both?

One day in 1948 the War Office informed Vilayat that a commemorative report on Noor's heroic war story would be printed in the British newspapers the next day. Knowing that Mother would read it, we realized then that seeing a nationwide newspaper coverage of Noor's deeds and sacrifice in the papers would be disastrous. Mother was in the habit of buying the newspapers each day in search of reports on Noor. In order to spare her this added ordeal of seeing her daughter's photo and tragic story written up in the papers, we decided to leave for Suresnes that very night.

We packed her off to Suresnes, and I left my job at the Pakistan Office, keeping my mother company in Fazal Manzil. Shortly after, Sirkar and Saida van Tuyll very kindly invited us to Holland, where they provided us with an apartment in the Hague to help us recover from the war trauma and loss. After some weeks, however, my mother felt that she could not spend the rest of her life in Holland but for moral reasons should return to Fazal Manzil, despite the memories the house would bring back to her. It was around this time that I occasionally traveled to Switzerland and Italy on invitation of a former mureed of our father's, Baroness Farinola-de Tanfani (Zeb-un-nisa), who offered to introduce me to Europe's high society.

In early May I returned home to find my mother in great pain. I asked Dr. Guillaume, who was renting the top floor in the house, to come see her. He said she needed an operation, but Mother did not believe him. She lay awake all night in pain. The next morning I went to see our family doctor, who lived in another town. Though it was Sunday, I pleaded with him to come. He said that if it was only the intestines, the disorder would soon improve but that he would come to check on her the next day. All that Sunday, Mother was in a great deal of pain. I should have thought of taking her to the American hospital but, not having money, I waited for Vilayat to come home. That night, Vilayat missed the last plane from London to Paris, so he did not arrive till the next morning.

During the night Mother developed an intestinal occlusion, and we rushed her to a hospital where Noor had had an operation years before—Mother felt she might have a better rapport with the surgeon. However, waiting the night had done too much damage, and it now proved to be too late to save her. The attending nurse was a nun dressed in black; Mother was horrified by this sight and was sure that this was the end. She was right: our mother did not survive the operation.

Ora Ray, Pirani Ameena Begum Inayat Khan, left this planet long before her time. Though her face was thin, she still wore the glow of youth. Perhaps Mother could not visualize herself under the ground in the neighborhood. She wished to be with her Thea in the skies and the stars. Vilayat and I went to the crematorium to make arrangements. I intended to take Mother's ashes to the family grave in America.

For several nights I slept in Mother's bed, attempting to fill the void she had left. One night I had a vivid dream. It was daylight, and I opened the front door to find Noor at the top of the steps. She looked smart, wearing a heavy jacket, a Russian fur hat and high leather boots. With a stern look on her face she asked, "Where is Mother?" I was shocked that she appeared not to recognize me. She seemed curt and in a hurry. I replied, "She is no longer here." Noor made no reply nor did she show any sign of emotion. She ran down to the gate as if searching for Mother, whose birthday was the next day.

Hidayat occasionally visited the cemetery in Paris and, one day, he saw that the urn was missing: the management had thrown it out because, unknown to us, we should have paid an annual fee. I was relieved, thinking that Mother's ashes were free in the light and the air to blow away into the blue sky of the Great Lord's palace.

THE PIR

Claire Harper: There was no appropriate work to be found for me in Paris, so I returned to London to resume my job for the Pakistan Office. With Mother gone, our flat was sadly large—large enough to house more renters. Two sisters, Mary and Barbara Walls, helped share the rent with Vilayat and me.

Mary was young and beautiful. She had lost her father when just a baby, and her mother remarried. She and her sisters spent their entire school age years at a strict Catholic boarding school for the wealthy (generously provided for by her grandmother). Barbara was doing secretarial work at the Pakistan Office, and Mary soon found employment there as well. Vilayat was set on winning Mary's heart, however his courting attempts were not noticed for several months. By and by, the romance shared by Mary and Vilayat became larger-than-life.

On vacation, they visited Uncle Mohammad Ali in Switzerland, where Vilayat wanted to introduce Mary. For several weeks Mary had been suffering from shortness of breath. Mohammad Ali, upon meeting Mary, told her she had tuberculosis. Back in London, the diagnosis was confirmed, and she was given six months to live. Mary underwent lengthy and unpleasant treatment that included injections of air into the lungs to puff them out again. It was Mary's strength of will and the power of prayer that helped her recover from the killer disease.

By and by, they were married at a Catholic church in Streatham, London, as Mary hailed from a Roman Catholic family. Though he could have achieved power and recognition as a diplomat, Vilayat felt he was wasting time working for the Pakistan Office. He harkened to the deep calling to carry on the mission that—he felt—his father had entrusted him with at the age of ten. This charge must be initiated in Suresnes, he said; so Vilayat and his young bride left London for a new life in France.

Getting through the winter would not be easy for the young newlyweds, with no heating except a few branches in the fireplace. Great would be the young couple's struggle in those early years, as Vilayat set out to restore Fazal Manzil to the Khankah that our father had established there.

Hardly a romantic destination, Fazal Manzil had been ruined during the war and the years thereafter. Hidayat and his family occupied the ground floor and ran a ceramic workshop (La Céramique de Suresnes) located in the basement. Their son Fazal occupied a couple of rooms on the top floor, and two more rooms on that same level were lent out as a medical practice to Dr. Michel Guillaume. Patients trod up and down the central wooden stairs, day in and day out, right through the privacy of Vilayat and Mary's living quarters. Many of the rooms were bare; the walls were moldy and damp. Money was scarce, but Vilayat's faith was strong. He held regular meetings in French for the few Sufis still around after the war. It is an ungrateful task to wear the shoes of the Master. Vilayat knew he should build a new structure on the foundations laid down by his father. Unfortunately, he received little support from his uncles, save for Maheboob. A yearlong struggle to legally assume leadership of his father's Sufi Movement led Vilayat to step out of the line of fire and to create his own organization: the Sufi Order. The name itself was in harmony with the line of the Sufi Chishti Order to which he continuously adhered.

While respecting and carrying on the traditional teachings and practices of Pir-o-Murshid Inayat Khan, Vilayat managed to explore new dimensions of Sufi awareness and teaching. Meditation on light, the study of the Sufi mystics, the interplay of mysticism and science, as well as spirituality in psychology were just some of the realms into which Vilayat extended his students' experience. Over the years his vision broadened, his thinking became genial. Public discussion of religious and philosophical themes by a panel of respected representatives of varying religions was one of his innovative ideas. In addition to carrying on his father's tradition of the Summer School, Vilayat took it a step further by organizing summer camps where hundreds of people could learn meditation, take retreats and be initiated to higher level practices in an alpine environment of inspiring beauty.

Vilayat's musical mission was not the vina, but rather a selection of eclectic music, some Eastern, but mostly Western, with a predilection for J.S. Bach. He never lost the opportunity to include music in every lecture or gathering, thus tuning participants through music in the true Sufi way. At every summer camp, Vilayat formed a choir which he loved to conduct; here he resembled a creator, sparking galaxies and constellations from his fingertips. Sometimes he played the cello or even sang with the deep emotion of spiritual experience. Vilayat did not clothe himself with the title that was his right but, rather, contented himself with being known as Pir (head of a Sufi order).

THE NEW WORLD

Claire Harper: The 1950s brought a time of great change. No Mother. No Noor. Before leaving London with his wife Mary for Suresnes, Vilayat advised me to go to America. I followed his advice and left for the New World on the Queen Elizabeth's maiden voyage. It was a boon, but my heart felt for Mother. We had planned to make this trip together. From the deck I waved farewell to Vilayat and Mary, who appeared very small, so huge was the crowded ship. The ship was grand and it featured a gorgeously decorated Christmas tree in one of the halls.

Feeling lonely, I missed Mother. I was going to her land alone and forlorn. Mother was painfully missing in my life. My calls to her remained unanswered. A traveler said to me "A mother is sacred; there are never two of them." I bought a scarf; it felt strange to make a purchase on a ship. Five days later I came face-to-face with the Statue of Liberty, and Mother's descriptions of it rang in my ears.

Gift of God

Claire Harper: Arriving and stepping on American soil for the first time gave me the feeling I had come home. I never suspected I would have this experience. I stayed at Hotel Lloyds where a room had been reserved for me. A childhood friend, the daughter of Zeb-un-Nissa, Marquise Farinola, or José, happened to be in Manhattan for a few days before returning to her home in Rome. She introduced me to her aunt Lina, who was looking for a lodger. All seemed to work out perfectly. I found work at UNICEF and was looking for a job in the newspaper field. Lina referred me to a certain John Sanford Harper who held the position of managing editor at the New York Post. Every now and then I called him to find out if there was a job vacancy for me. Repeatedly there was nothing, but one day, John invited me for a drink on Madison Avenue. There I was served my first cocktail, quite a contrast to my simple and shy way of living. As he appeared in the soft light of the entrance, unspoken words came to me such as "the father of my children." Gentleman friend, yet married, none of this came to mind. I was fascinated to meet such a handsome, well-dressed and soft-spoken person. Descended from a family of achievers, his forebears fought in all the wars in which the United States had been engaged. John had served in the Navy in the Pacific during WWII and was a commander in the Naval Reserve.

He spoke of his ruined marriage—"On the rocks," he said. His only loyalty was to his little boy, Jim. He sounded like a very good father. Jim was ten years old and well-loved. We parted, not having spoken about work. As I walked down the street, I felt I was walking on air. I was exhilarated; life seemed very pink. My cheeks felt pink, my heart felt pink. Everything was pink! I asked myself why I was feeling so elated. The poles in my world had switched places and I could feel nothing but wonder. Impressions turned to dreams; dreams to emotions and, fired by promises of marriage, emotions turned to love.

A child of love was soon to be born, and I felt alone and terrified. Vilayat suggested that Mary come to New York to be with me. Very kindly, she traveled to New York and was able to find a job and a place to stay, looking after two small children to make a living. Mary often visited me at the home where I was staying, which meant that she had to cross through Central Park, a dangerous place. But Mary's faith and courage were enormous. In one way, I wished she would return home to France as she was so young and frail and had recently suffered from tuberculosis. On the other hand I was comforted that Mary was with me.

Standing on a bus late at night, my water burst. At Lexington Hospital they told me that I had a breeched baby; I remained in labor for twenty hours. Then I remember being given a sleeping pill. On awakening, I asked the nurse for my baby and whether it was a boy or a girl. "A boy!" came the reply. It was a boy with a dimple on his left cheek and long fine fingers. "David," meaning "Gift of God," was his name, after King David who sang and danced, worshipping the Great Lord. He tended the sheep and built a slingshot for the protection of his flock against wild animals and, later, he defended his nation against the enemy.

David was born on Christmas Day and was the cherub of my youthful dream; the greatest thrill was when this tiny boy looked at me for the first time. Mary had already seen and held baby David, but I had been asleep for a long time. When I held my son for the first time, a great emotion arose, giving peace to the entire universe.

Ravaging itch

Claire Harper: When my darling baby was but a few months old, he began to itch and scratch and wiggle. At the home where we were still staying, the director suggested leaving his diaper off, but this provided no improvement and his nights must have been unbearable. I was looking for a job, and there was no nurse present at the home. Though I looked in on David whenever possible, my time was taken up by the job hunt. At the home, the director told me that David had been crying continuously and would throw up after each feed. Since he was not getting enough nourishment, I took him by bus to the hospital—his eyelids were puffy and swollen.

I left David in the hospital's care. Whenever I visited David, I was allowed to see him only through a pane of glass. He lay without clothes on a plastic sheet and his arms were pinned by bandages to the bed to prevent him from scratching. His whole body was covered in eczema and he was very distressed. I had brought a fluffy bear as a gift for him but was not allowed to give it to him. I left with a heavy heart.

After a few months, I finally received a telegram from the hospital telling me I could fetch my little boy. He was, very simply, allergic to milk and was put on a soy substitute. He could not be washed with water but with corn oil. I continued this treatment and he was fine.

Always On the Move

Claire Harper: During the time that David was in hospital, I had been looking after three young girls in Long Island but with a baby in arms now, I was asked to leave and look for another job. I was quite happy to move on as it was not appropriate to look after three other children when I had my own baby to care for.

One morning a friend of a friend, Peter Peterson, came to fetch us. He helped pack all our things into his van, and within an hour we were off. Peter had found a place for us, he said, and drove us to a nice area, Manhasset on Long Island, where I was to cook and look after the house. A lame father and two teenaged girls lived there. They made dinner, and everyone was quite happy. Before doing the dishes, I put David in his cot and he quickly fell asleep. His room was very small but could accommodate a small bed for me. Before I knew it, the girls had gone out for the evening.

While I was tidying the small room, I heard someone shout my name from next door. The door was open, and the light was on. The mister was in bed and said "Come on in here, will ya?" I was shocked and said: "Just a minute, sir." I rushed into my room, put on my coat, snatched up my bag and little David from his bed with his blanket around him and went downstairs as silently as possible. Sitting on the chair close to the door, I checked on the lock. I kept the key, leaving the door unlocked. If that man intended to come for me, I could go out the door and go to the neighbor's. I was very tired. Two hours later, one of the daughters returned and, surprised to see me, asked what happened.

"Not again," she exclaimed when I related the events. I told her we would be leaving in the morning, once I had made a phone call.

Next morning Peter arrived and packed us and our belongings into his car again. David was happy to see Peter. We went to the trailer where he and his wife Dagne lived while waiting to move. Dagne was taking care of her very young girl who was suffering from a bad case of whooping cough.

As I sat, I wondered where to go next. I thought of a young woman who lived in Brooklyn, so Peter dropped us off there. For the next two years, I moved several times, working at Macy's Department Store, at the Commodore Hotel, at a coffee shop, as well as at people's homes sitting their children.

Alone with David, we celebrated his second birthday. Vilayat arrived—it was a great surprise—and he gave me money to make a Christmas/ birthday dinner. I spent all this wealth on food at the supermarket. It was only a short walk back to the building and then three flights up to the apartment. Vilayat was delighted and put the chicken in the oven. While waiting for dinner to cook, we made a little Christmas corner.

A few days later, Vilayat and I visited the home of our mother's half-brother, Pierre Bernard, and his wife, Blanche de Vries. "Uncle Pierre" gave us a cold reception, and during the course of the conversation the theme of our mother's escape to Europe arose. Sitting at his desk, he opened a drawer and showed us a gun. "If I had found him, I was going to kill your father with this gun!" he bragged. Thankfully, his wife was more accommodating and the tense moments passed.

A few months later, David developed bronchial pneumonia. Doctor's fees and medication prices were exorbitant, and I had to stay home to take care of him. I now had no job and no money. I became extremely nervous and began suffering from severe pain in the intestines. The medical tests revealed a bad case of hepatitis, and I had to be hospitalized for three months. I was not allowed to leave my bed, and when I did so to wash my hair, I collapsed on the floor. A couple of friends contacted a Sufi lady to take care of David. He was to go to Bakhti, but her household was not suitable for a young child.

Through friends of friends, a lady who had a foster family was found. "Mamma May" welcomed David to her home in Long Island where she looked after four other small children in need. I was very relieved and grateful for this act of love and selflessness.

However, after several weeks, Mamma May called me to say that the authorities had visited her and had decided that David was one too many children for her space and facilities (David shared a single bed with another child, sleeping foot-to-foot).

Thank goodness May knew a couple who had no children of their own; so David now went to their care. "Mamma Kay's" husband played a lot of boy's games, and David loved that. He was there for over two months before I was well enough to take him home. A kind acquaintance with whom we occasionally stayed, actually a wealthy friend of Vilayat's, Mrs. Richard in New York City was kind enough to send her car and chauffeur to pick me up from hospital to take me to visit David at the home of Mamma Kay and her husband on Long Island.

When I knocked at their door, wearing a summer dress, happy to see David after three months and looking forward to being able to take care of him again, he remained in the arms of Mamma Kay, clutching his new foster mother even tighter as I approached. My heart fell and I knew I should never allow such a long separation again.

The more I spoke to him, the more David hung onto her. So I decided to leave and I told David that I would come again. The same procedure was repeated the next day. When I saw my little boy again, I said, "Hello David. Perhaps you would like to come home with me today." I sat on the couch and waited. David watched me, from the safe distance of Mamma Kay's arms. He then went to play with Kay's husband. I followed him and sang to him, hoping he would recognize my voice. David showed me his toys, and we were both very happy. I told him that Roy was the chauffeur. "Yes," exclaimed David, who remembered the man. He had remembered that Mrs. Richard had given him all those great presents from the foot of the Christmas tree. Something was now familiar. "Do you want to come with me?" I asked again. "Yes," came the reply. He accepted a kiss and it began to feel like old times again.

After my three months at the Presbyterian hospital, and now confronted by David's needs, I urgently needed a place for us to stay, a job and someone to take care of my toddler while I worked. However, an old and faithful companion, dizziness, returned to trouble me once again. I had no money and I wondered where the next meal would come from.

Mrs. Richard called and told me that Miss White would be picking us up and taking us to a new place, a cold-water apartment. I managed to find a waitressing job and put David in a day care center when, one evening, I felt I might be getting the mumps. My old acquaintances, Peter and Dagne Peterson, were kind enough to come and take David to their home in Long Island for a couple of weeks. I accompanied David there, and though he would be staying in a very pretty house and have a friend to play with (their girl Linda was about David's age), he cried pitifully when I left for the train station.

"Mamma Dagne," who was from Sweden, prepared wonderful meals and Peter, of royal Danish descent, was a very kind person; and I was sure David would be in good hands. My recovery was slow and the Petersons told me that David was no trouble at all and that he grew happier by the day. Meanwhile, I secured a good job at the Holland America Line shipping company, and I phoned David as often as I could but he never spoke, he only grunted his yes and no. I tried to visit him once a month, but he did not seem overjoyed to see me. I was relieved that he was with a family and going to kindergarten. His life was secure and he loved his "sister" Linda.

After each visit, I returned to New York happy but I missed my little dolly. This constant separation made my world feel empty. Two weeks slipped into two years before I realized that I would lose my boy forever if I did not make a drastic change. A gnawing desire grew ever stronger inside: I would take David home to France. But what would await us in Fazal Manzil?

COMING HOME

Claire Harper: The time of our departure for France was approaching. I gave David a calendar on which he checked off each day until the scheduled departure date. The night before our departure, Madeleine, an office colleague, kept David for the night. I bid my work colleagues farewell; we were to depart the next day.

David was five years old and looked very handsome in his new outfit as we mounted the steps onto the ship. Looking down, our friends waved us off. We were shown to a lovely cabin and waited for the ship to move. The ship's horn blasts warned us of the imminent departure as our excitement rose. The sun shone brightly on the deck as we sailed away to the Old World in the month of August, 1958. As we explored the ship, David was delighted to discover the dining rooms, the lounges, the cinema. We sat on deckchairs as I savored the thought of finally going home. On board, the meals were excellent, the cabin comfortable; the five-day journey was a real treat. My ever-dear Vilayat was there to meet us in his smart new Opel Capitaine. Hidayat was there to greet us as well, though his joy was somewhat overshadowed by the suffering resulting from a serious ear infection. We were all three so happy to be together, united again—save the great void left by Noor.

Upon arrival in Fazal Manzil, we were met by sweet Mary, looking lovely. But we were also welcomed by eagles in the hall: Vilayat's passion for falconry was clearly visible. Reaching our floor, it became apparent that little space was available: Doctor Guillaume was still occupying a large part of the floor for his practice. Some of the walls were painted different colors, others papered. All were shabby and neglected; the rooms lacked furniture. Two metal camp beds were brought over from the Mureed House. There was no kitchen to speak of.

During World War II our home had been misused, abused and pillaged. While we were in England, the German SD (Reichsicherheitsdienst) occupied Fazal Manzil. After the war, the French government and the Red Cross used our home to house the homeless and the wounded. Many soldiers died in the cellar. The roof leaked, and many of the rooms and halls were damp. The central heating had been ripped out, and most of the furniture had been taken by locals. Needless to say, the state of repair in the house was catastrophic following the war, and it is a pity that we were not told that repair and renovation costs would have been refunded by the French government.

Vilayat arranged for us to receive a monthly allowance from the Murshida Fazal Mai Stichting. Unfortunately, the foundation's assets had diminished catastrophically during the war years, so they could grant us only a small income. We needed paint, cleaning products and food foremost—the rest would have to wait. We made our pennies stretch. I found a man to whitewash the ceilings. The room with the best view was David's, with a panorama of Paris in the distance. I had workmen put three more windows in for additional light. Plumbers installed a bath, washbasin, a toilet and a kitchen sink. Funds from Holland for house repairs were at the budget's edge.

I noticed that I had not received any rent for the many years that the doctor used two rooms of my apartment. When I brought up this query with Vilayat, he said that Dr. Guillaume had promised to pay for repairs in lieu of rent. The roof was in sore need of repairs but none occurred. In an effort to modernize, the so-called "repairs" to our floor were the removal of eight marble fireplaces and the knocking down of a wall, both acts completed without asking permission.

Several years after the war, a member of Pir-o-Murshid's Sufi group in England bequeathed a house in the neighborhood of Fazal Manzil to Vilayat. In view of my return to Fazal Manzil, Mary suggested that Vilayat donate this house to Dr. Guillaume so that he would move out of Fazal Manzil. It appears, though, that his new villa was not large enough for a consultation room for his medical practice. For this reason, he kept the use of two rooms on my floor as, according to French law, he first needed to find an equivalent space with similar rental conditions.

At about this time, the town of Suresnes decided to use the area across the street from Fazal Manzil—including the spot where Murshid had wished to build the Temple of the Universel—to build an extensive apartment block complex for low-income families. As a result, Dr. Guillaume's newly acquired home and medical practice had to be demolished!

Nekbakht, out of the goodness of her heart, built a new home for Dr. Guillaume and his family. Now he had enough room for his practice. Dr. Guillaume did not tell me he was finally moving out, but I heard the noise of furniture being moved and was relieved to see the back of him and the daily foot traffic of patients up and down our stairs. I was so relieved that the front door could be locked early and not at eleven at night or later, as had often been the case.

At long last, sufficient funds were available to put in a proper kitchen and bathroom. Once the workers had finished the masonry and plumbing, brooms were brought out to clear away the mess. I admired these men: they spoke such beautiful old French—to my dismay I had no money to offer them a tip. I was very sorry and told them so. They left just as politely as when they had first come.

Once the new bathroom and kitchen were installed, I realized that I should have been advised differently. Everything was too cramped resulting in a tiny kitchen that had to be accessed through the bathroom! Years later, a wall had to be built elsewhere in order to accommodate the bathroom separately from what now became a decently sized kitchen with enough room for a round dining table.

However, the house was still cold. The hot water and central heating systems had broken down or been stolen during WWII, so we now had to buy small coal stoves for each room. Of course, long metal chimney pipes had to be installed, resulting in a rather unaesthetic appearance. The coal man would deliver his "black gold" in a 50-kilogram sack that he dumped into a coal box on the landing, accompanied by a cloud of dust. Needless to say, these frequent visits would have to be followed by a thorough cleaning of all the settled coal dust.

We owned no washing machine. Everything we needed to make life easy had to be purchased. My dizzy spells resumed—some of them required a doctor who gave me an injection of calcium. We had no medical insurance. Day after day I would carry on with the work of repairing and painting the house. After months of painting the walls on my own, summer announced its arrival.

When he was nearly seven, I put David in the public school in the lower part of Suresnes. As I had not enough funds for the tram, I would walk David to and from school at the bottom of Suresnes. Though David was English-speaking, he learned French fluently within a few months, and his first year class included classical poetry to learn by heart. His good memory was a great asset. The classes were not co-ed; this was a boy's school—the way of life was different then. The director soon referred to David as an interesting pupil.

Starting second grade, David changed to a school closer to Fazal Manzil. The first month in the second school, David was second best of his class. When I told Vilayat, he said to David, "Why were you not first of the class?" The following month he was first and, from then on, he and two other boys always claimed first, second or third best of the class of more than thirty students.

During summer vacation, French schoolchildren usually spent time in the country at their grandparents', or families would escape to the seaside. This meant that during the summer months, David had no friends to play with.

Perhaps for this reason, he looked forward to going back to school. Or was it because of his teacher? David's main teacher was a lovely young woman, Mlle Dufour, who loved her students. I once invited her to the house. She loved David. Her memory still impresses us. Her magnetism won our admiration.

Vilayat was extremely upset that the Sufi land was going to be requisitioned by the local authorities. He had an architectural blueprint drawn up to build a university on that spot, but his well-planned and ambitious project was rejected.

Vilayat and Mary were soon to leave for India for the winter. I was most upset. This was one of several journeys to India that my brother and sister-in-law undertook. The first one was in 1955, when they traveled with Mary's sister Barbara and their good friend Kathleen in a VW bus across inhospitable lands for months on end till reaching their destinations in northern India. They undertook a total of four overland trips to India, each wrought with enough adventure and interesting tales to fill volumes of storybooks.

During these four journeys, as well as on the occasion of many subsequent trips to India by plane, Vilayat would go on forty-day retreats in the Himalayas.

On the second overland journey in 1959, Vilayat came home much sooner than planned, flying back ahead of Mary as he was suffering from a severe eye infection. His eyes had been blinded while practicing a sun-viewing yoga exercise, and his vision was now extremely poor. First Vilayat consulted a specialist in Holland who had come highly recommended. As his conditioned worsened, he consulted a Paris specialist but nothing seemed to be able to help. I suggested to Vilayat that he consult the local eye doctor in Suresnes. "That would be useless and a waste of time," he commented. At my insistence, however, he accepted my offer to accompany him there. It just so happened that our "local eye doctor" was in fact a well-respected specialist who was sometimes called to Switzerland on special missions. Once treated with the right antibiotic drops, Vilayat soon recovered his vision. When Vilayat returned from India, he offered me a job doing office work for him.

From 1962 to 1966, Claire and David returned to the United States, choosing California this time rather than New York. For the first three years, David attended a spiritually focused school at the East West Cultural Center in Los Angeles, a place that embraced all spiritual walks. Here he learned yoga, breathing practices and the teachings of Buddha, alongside the standard academic curriculum. The fourth year, David went to public

Junior High School in Hollywood. He also attended dance school and, later, drama classes, which led to his landing a small part as a French boy in a Doris Day film entitled *Do Not Disturb*. Vilayat stayed with them occasionally, as he gave lectures in the Los Angeles area and even appeared on television.

Claire Harper: In the summer of 1966, David returned to Fazal Manzil, where he continued the rest of his school years in France. I moved to New York, where I often worked two jobs to support my son and myself. Finally I returned to Fazal Manzil in 1971, upon the birth of David's daughter Sura.

In the 1970s, Hidayat practically lived in his VW bus, traveling the roads of France and Germany to eke out a living. Accompanied by his dog Mickey, Hidayat sold the World Book Encyclopedia door-to-door at US military housing areas. A daunting and unrewarding job, to be sure, but Hidayat met the challenge with courage. Now and again he would return to Fazal Manzil. His apartment was empty after the departure of his wife, Iman, and his three children for the United States.

By this time, thanks to Vilayat's continuous efforts, Fazal Manzil was now again the Sufi Khankah it had been during the time of our father. At regular times of the year, he organized meetings of either French or international mureeds. Summer School was re-established, as well as regular Universal Worship ceremonies. A large-scale project was the construction of the Khankah, a greenhouse-style structure that could seat up to one hundred visitors while offering a nice view of the lower garden. Later Vilayat constructed twenty cells for mureeds at the lower end of the garden. Unfortunately, they burned down in 1961.

Bit by bit, Vilayat and Mary refurbished the reception rooms where dinners for spiritual leaders and notable public figures took place on a regular basis. Mary and I spent much time in each other's company. In a similar way to my mother before her, Mary often suffered the criticism and envy of some of Vilayat's mureeds. Throughout their marriage, Mary devoted her time to cooking healthy and delicious food for her husband and making sure his clothing was clean and in order. She not only kept the house spotlessly clean but constantly sought to improve the beauty of their home. She often spoke of it as "Murshid's house" and that it should be a place of beauty in homage to him. Mary often accompanied Vilayat on his journeys and conferences, as far as the limited budget allowed. The house felt very empty whenever they were both away, especially for the long months they often spent in India.

Just like his father before him, Vilayat's Sufi work came under suspicion of the authorities, and I remember that he and Mary were whisked off one day in a large black car. Sick with worry, I thought they must have been kidnapped but was grateful when they were returned safely in the evening. The French Ministry of the Interior had employed their security department to scrutinize Vilayat's activities just in case he was working undercover toward an uprising of the North African Muslim world (there was considerable trouble at that time regarding France's former colonies of Morocco, Tunisia and Algeria).

In the same spirit of universality as his father, Vilayat sought to introduce various aspects of Sufism in a way suited to the times. Every summer he led meditation camps in the Alps where music, dance and zikr were part of the schedule. Giving lectures in English, French, German and Dutch, Vilayat traveled extensively throughout Europe and the United States, only occasionally returning home to Fazal Manzil. Each year he organized and chaired an inter-religious congress in Paris where representatives of various faiths would attempt to find the similarities—not the differences—of each religion's viewpoints on a chosen theme. Vilayat published numerous books, as well as countless newsletters such as his classic *Keeping in Touch*. He was also fascinated by new developments in science and often spoke at conventions featuring dialogue between scientists and spiritual teachers. He strove to incorporate the latest scientific thought into his talks on esoteric and mystical themes. He not only brought this ancient school of wisdom into the twentieth century but applied it to the heralding in of the "New Age."

Claire Harper: When David was in his teen years, Vilayat indicated that he would later carry on the Sufi work as his successor. At the birth of Vilayat's sons, Seraphiel (later called Zia) and Kerubiel (later called Mirza), David was relieved to know that the charge and responsibility of carrying on Vilayat's legacy would now be in one of the son's hands. David's contribution was and remains that of music. He recorded the songs of our father and our uncles and also composed music to the poetry of our father.

Wanting to honor Fazal Manzil as the home of our father and of the Sufi Message, in the 1970s, with a power jet at the end of a hose, I used to wash down the outside walls of the house. There was always a lot of chimney soot and pollution from the cars on the street. It ran down like mud, revealing the original colors of the volcanic stone imported from Italy. Sometimes in hot weather, I would also scrub down the double steps in front of the façade using a brush and detergent. Moss and grime washed away so that the balustrade looked like new. It took rather a long time but it was worth it.

From the 1950s on, Hidayat has been most creative on the musical level, bringing Eastern and Western music together. His compositions include *La Monotonia*, the *Ghandi Symphony*, the *Zikar Symphony*, the *Message Symphony*, as well as numerous choral pieces such as "Chanson Exotique," "Awake for Morning," and a collection of Sufi hymns. In 1988 Hidayat assumed the role of Representative-General of the International Sufi Movement and Pir-o-Murshid of its Inner School.

One notable incident in the 1970s was the return of Tipu Sultan's royal seals to the family. An Englishman, Alex Bowlby, after reading Jean Fuller's book about Noor, contacted Vilayat and Mary. He had inherited several treasures from an ancestor who was among the victorious (and pillaging) British soldiers at the Battle of Seringapatam and felt that three of these heirlooms should symbolically be returned to descendants of the sultan. Apart from the seal of India and another seal, the *pièce de resistance* was Tipu's personal seal. An intricate layout of Arabic writing cleverly forms a stylized tiger, befitting of the Tiger of Mysore. Mr Bowlby promised to one day hand over the "tiger's head"—one of twelve gold tiger heads with emerald eyes that adorned Tipu's throne—but this never came to be.

In the 1990s, the temple was built in Fazal Manzil's lower garden. It is a place of universal worship dedicated to the memory and sacrifice of Noor, and it is here that Vilayat's funeral took place in June 2004.

Claire Harper: David founded a folk-rock band in the early 1970s and earned some recognition for his numerous compositions in the form of records, one of which hit the top-twenty charts. In 1976 David moved with his first wife, Celia, and daughter, Sura-un-nissa, to the Pyrenean foothills in the southwest of France, where he built a large stone house and founded a spiritual commune. Mary and Vilayat built a house there in the early 1980s as well. In 1986 David moved to the Bavarian Alps, where he began his vocation of educational tours and travel.

NEW HORIZONS FOR VILAYAT

A Tribute by Claire

Claire Harper: Sailing away on June 17th, 2004, on a torrential, stormy sea to emerge into the skies of tomorrow, has my dearly precious brother Vilayat gone. The absence of his life shall never be forgotten.

Vilayat wished very earnestly to survive his illness. He suffered excruciating pain, thus becoming a victim of medical limitations and old age which took him sooner than expected—never ever to be in his gentle presence again. When in this life, Vilayat planned to do much more work, more books, and see more of the world. Why has he gone, against his steel willpower? Where has he gone? Only the Great Lord knows.

Has the breeze of destiny lifted his soul on that steep icy slope leading to the summit of Paradise where creation blossoms endlessly, to join the great Masters whose language, beyond our understanding has sublimated into the music of the spheres? Or is Vilayat climbing the highest mountain in search of his favorite eagle, Shabaz, the "King's Bird"?

While on Earth, when Vilayat mounted a paraglider, he wanted to rise higher and higher. This experience must have led his imagination to step into the next rocket. He always wanted to see the beyond: quite a challenge for body, heart and soul.

Or, in the company of angels has his soul risen to alight on the stars above? When on Earth, he was fascinated by the role of the stars. Since we are made of the same material as a star, the idea made him appear as bright as they are. If our consciousness is immortalized, then there must be life in the unknown worlds—perhaps more spectacular than on Earth.

Or could Vilayat be standing at the jeweled gates of heaven's glistening temple, waiting to ask the Great Lord to bestow on us a peaceful and united world? Perhaps by now, he is in the presence of venerated Father, of lovely sweet Mother and heroic fairy Sister whom he adored, forging a plan to ban wars on earth, thus preventing an annihilation of the planet from the ozone disaster, from pollution, greed, famine and destruction. Or is Vilayat searching for them in the midnight mist of the unknown?

Vilayat would grieve very intensely about Noor's terrifying fate in action during the second, red-hot, angry world war, at the mercy of the wicked. She was one of the fifty million who perished from the brutality and suffering caused by that war. Noor, twenty-eight, with life in front of her, wrote stories for children, poems to console her sweet mother and she played on her beautiful golden harp. A fragment of her spirit of justice was heard in her last word, "Liberté," echoing throughout creation and thus encouraging the living to continue to free the world from oppression. From the hands of the Great Consoler, Vilayat would help Noor to forget the price of freedom.

Vilayat himself showed great tenacity, bravery and endurance during the war, learning to pilot a plane with the British Royal Air Force in hardly a few weeks. Later, as an officer in the British Royal Navy, at the onset of the D-Day landing, he would neutralize the mines to help his crew. This devotion to helping others was instrumental in preparing himself for the work of the Message. Throughout his life, Vilayat's courage never failed him.

His kindness, compassion and stamina were present in his everyday activities. His speaking voice was gentle; likewise, his singing voice, carrying the double tone of both East and West, resounded in the atmosphere.

At this moment, could Vilayat be holding high the golden cord of life, swiftly twirling in a huge bubble in outer space, exhilarated by the colors that do not appear in our rainbow?

On Earth, Vilayat's mission appeared challenging. His work has been a constant task of fortitude—what more sacred a vocation is there than that of helping the wellbeing of others? Vilayat has always been caring of others: helpful, generous and humble. His gait has always been majestic at every step of the way towards his goal. He has always been a delightful being of one's remembrance.

Vilayat cherished his cello, but had hardly time to play. But when he did, music reigned supreme. At those moments, he must have thought of his Father, who gave up music for the spreading of the Message.

Where has Vilayat gone? In a cave meditating, surrounded by hostile tigers watching over him? Or, in my imagination, could he be on the lawn of some faraway Eastern palace walking barefooted on the early morning dew?

When on this earth, Vilayat showed greatness of spirit and strength of willpower in whatever he was doing. He did not allow time to go by without using it towards a creative purpose.

Vilayat loved his home, Fazal Manzil, and his office on the roof, surrounded by books and affording a broad view of Paris and the Bois de Boulogne. He would mount and descend the stairs with, on his mind, a new flair for a new future. He hurried to write it on his computer. The demands that were put on him were countless. His family meant a great deal to Vilayat and he was constantly concerned about our wellbeing. He proved this not only in words but in deeds. Even though he has gone, one senses a helping hand of consolation. He has inherited the gift of Father, who wished to be the Great Consoler.

Then again, could Vilayat's soul be spreading out the golden wings of the Message of Love, Harmony and Beauty, to interpret it from high, dropping wisdom confetti to us on earth so as to feed our spirit. The wick on the candle of an exceptional life has waned, only to burn its light still brighter in the heavens.

Vilayat has proven to be the apex of his calling. The tremendous load of creative work to help humanity is the realization of Father's wish. One can feel the appreciation from Father, blessing Vilayat with the symbolic crown of accomplishment for helping humanity and his dear ones. He has earned, after Father, the patriarchal seat in Fazal Manzil. How could such a special person leave without knowing? Some thinkers are awaiting his rebirth. May it be so, if it is the Divine Will!

Vilayat knew the power and vitality that nature imparts; its beauty also offered him the great incentive to deliver his lectures in large tents in the Alps. Vilayat is worthy of esteem for taking time to devote to his responsibilities which he has left to posterity.

Thank you, Great Lord, for having given Vilayat the opportunity to live in this world. Looking for the treasure which is hidden in the depth of the Great Lord's Heart, little does Vilayat know that this treasure is he.

Homage to my ever-present Brother Vilayat who has done his utmost best to help humanity. One more ring has been fastened to the chain of the Chishti Sufi Order.

Please, Great Lord, bless Vilayat and hold him tight against Thy flaming heart with Thy abounding and unending Love Divine.

Watch over him and protect him by Thy Divine Grace.

May he never be alone in this mighty Universe.
May he always be delighted in the realm of hope, joy and peace.
Enfold him with Thy tender care.
Surround him with Thy celestial music.
Initiate him with the magic of Thy illuminated Divine Glance.
May he glow as a new star by the lights of the highest heavens.
Embrace my dearly precious Brother Vilayat with deep respect and eternal affection, sympathy and love.

A TRIBUTE

A Man for All Seasons

This was Vilayat—a man who dared—a man whose life played many parts.

He was a cellist, rapturing in Elgar's Cello Concerto—the vibrato he had learned from Pablo Casals, in the few lessons he had had with that great master.

He was the falconer flying high in the loftiness of space, throwing his eagle in the upward currents of air, often reciting the poem of Gerard Manley Hopkins, "High there, how he rung upon the rein of a wimpling wing in his ecstasy."

He was the ascetic, denying comforts of the self to realize the paradise within and the beauty without.

Infinitely patient, and yet paradoxically impatient, he strove for perfection. He pounced on the gates of heaven for divine oneness, for realization, quoting Dylan Thomas, "Rage, rage, against the dying of the light." But he knew that light can never be extinguished, it can only become brighter, and Pir spiralled even higher.

He brought his mureeds to unknown worlds in his blissful meditations.

He was a healer, but healed with humility.

He travelled without much aforethought, but arriving, he was excited and exhilarated because he always had great expectations.

In his mind, he voyaged into space and combed the galaxies. He was a believer, and yet at times agnostic. "There is no tangible proof in another world, and yet I am convinced in the visibility of the invisible. We are brushed by angel's wings conjuring up the celestial heavens, whilst our feet are often heavy in the mundane, terrestrial world. Let us dance together in the rays of sun," and throwing off his heavy white wool burnous, he would dance to Bach with his beloved disciples, turning and twisting like a pivot let loose from its moorings.

This was his delight, this was his world, this was Pir Vilayat.

by Begum Mary Inayat Khan

UNCLE EAGLE

Pir Vilayat was affectionately known to me as Uncle Eagle, a name that he chose for me to call him. Most people knew him as an inspiring teacher, an erudite lecturer, a master of meditation who led our awareness into cosmic realms. Above all, he was respected as the head of the Sufi Order in the West, an ancient school of Indian esoteric study. Upon moving to the family home, Fazal Manzil in Suresnes, at the age of five, my first recollections are those of my Uncle Eagle taking us on long expeditions in his yellow Ford Opel.

Some of these excursions, though I was unaware of it at the time, were to places in France where his sister Noor had been involved in her undercover work as an agent for British military intelligence. Further afield, our travels took us to Germany where my uncle sought to glean more information about Noor's terrifying months in south German prisons prior to her tragic end at Dachau's dreaded concentration camp.

My uncle loved to drive. The opposite of "calm and collected" when he took the wheel, he would plow and zigzag through the anarchic French traffic as fast as his three-ton camper van would go. He expected others to respect the urgency of his mission and the size of his vehicle—woe to those who didn't: they would hear some genuine French street dialect addressed to them by a far too aristocratic-looking and somewhat eccentric gentleman.

Uncle Eagle would often drive me into Paris where he had some errands to make, invariably stopping at the Bazar de l'Hotel de Ville, a department store with the largest hardware department in France. Here he was in paradise. His sense of innovation running wild, he would purchase bolts, brackets, hinges and anything that he felt would mutate a static object into something foldable, retractable, adjustable or collapsible, even, preferably, empowering an innate piece of plywood into a highly useful element that could serve several purposes. Throughout his life, Uncle Eagle—perhaps borrowing inspiration from the genial inventor Leonardo da Vinci—harbored a fondness for creating original contraptions made of chipboard, metal and Plexiglas. These ranged from the precarious and wobbly perches with which he surrounded himself in his rooftop office crowning Fazal Manzil (where he could work tête-à-tête with his eagles) to the monumental wooden bookcases lining the walls of his reception rooms or the complete furnishing of his numerous RVs. Tables, sideboards, tucked-away beds and even an eagle perch hidden inside a closet for smuggling a large bird of prey across a border (!) were designed and implemented by my ingenious uncle. Often honored with the task of cutting out plywood, drilling two zillion holes, assembling supports with bolts and screws and sometimes starting the whole project again from scratch when it didn't quite work out, I offered up many an hour of manual devotion in my teen years.

A highlight each year in July was the much anticipated departure for the meditation camp. My uncle had always loved the high mountains, having hiked and camped in the French and the Swiss Alps in his youth. Loading the truck with tons of large army tents, cooking-gas bottles and piles of camping equipment, we were off to the high mountain pastures of Switzerland. With Uncle Eagle at the wheel, I always found my perch high on the equipment. Carefree, I would ride just a wingspan's length from another traveling companion, an imperial eagle that, like me, perched high above coils of navy rope, wooden-headed sledgehammers and an array of esoteric books. My uncle would never part from his reading matter, mostly works of erudite philosophers and thinkers of old, as well as works on comparative religion or the mystical aspects of modern-day science. As a New Age pioneer, he blazed trails in bringing about a universal understanding of the unity of humankind. As a spiritual master, he taught meditation and self-exploration, creating an awareness of the cosmic nature of our own beings.

As a child, my uncle was impressed by *Temujin*, an old tale of the love between a young boy and a large eagle. Following his hero's example, Uncle Eagle developed a passion for the ancient art of falconry, traditionally a hunting sport in both Europe and the East; my uncle's interest was in the cultivation of a friendship between the bird and himself. Whenever Uncle Eagle launched a falcon or an eagle from his gloved fist into the freedom of the sky, I could feel his spirit soaring alongside the bird in flight. It was this very sensation of mastering gravity, of experiencing the weightless and exhilarating freedom of movement of our spirit that he sought to share with us in his meditation camps.

Each upcoming meditation camp in the Alps would require a lot of preparation work, both physical and organizational. Assisted by an eager team, Uncle Eagle could devote his time to the two activities he loved: preparing his lectures and flying his bird.

Over the years I knew Uncle Eagle to train a number of falcons and eagles but his favorites were the imperial eagle, Majesty, and his golden eagle, Shabaz (the King's Bird). In some cases he had personally rescued these birds from a life of misery: one of the eagles had been kept in a dark garage for six months, others he took in when they were close to death, caringly nurturing them back to perfect health. His last bird was taken from the nest; the forestry department knew of a nest where two eaglets had hatched. The law of nature allows only one eaglet to survive; the weaker is habitually killed or deprived of food by the stronger. Uncle Eagle, a mureed and I set out in the middle of the night to reach the birds' aerie by early dawn. A daring climb and dangerous leap to a ledge secured our prize. The young eaglet was caringly raised and trained by its new father, Uncle Eagle.

To Uncle Eagle, this passion for falconry was an intrinsic part of his genealogical background. His ancestors from Afghanistan and India were of a society where hunting with a bird of prey was a symbol of prestige and social standing. To my uncle, it was more of a love affair. The birds enjoyed the same privileges that most people bestow on their household pet: these huge eagles would have a place of honor, perched in the sumptuous living room in Fazal Manzil in winter and, in summer, atop the stone balustrade leading to the front door. What a welcome for visitors to the house!

The butchers in Suresnes knew my uncle by name: "Ah, Monsieur Khan! I have kept some fresh chicken necks for you!" The birds' diet allows for only healthy, fresh meat—preferably game—and my uncle saw to it that they were served only the best. Every now and then we drove to the nearby woods, the Bois de Boulogne, for special training. To begin with, a bird would grow accustomed to flying a short distance to the outstretched fist, containing a scrap of food. With time, the distance was increased and, finally, the eagle could be released into the sky to soar free to its heart's content.

After a given time, Uncle Eagle would swing a lure on a string or blow a whistle, depending on the level of training the bird had received, and coax it back with some meat on his heavily gloved hand. There was always that feeling of anxiety, of breathless anticipation as to whether or not the bird would want to return. Majesty had been so well trained that Uncle Eagle could allow him to follow the car. On the road, the bird would follow his master's vehicle as he drove toward the Alps and then return to him when called!

Every year in September, Uncle Eagle and his wife Mary would go on vacation. When in my early teens, I was privileged to be taken on a couple of these two-week journeys. Usually headed for the Alps as its destination, the RV would bounce along the rutted roads of France and Switzerland. Stopping in the most scenic wilderness locations, we would set up camp: a long iron rod, topped by a wooden block, was immediately pounded into the ground for the traveling eagle to claim as quarters for the night. Mary would set about making dinner on the camping stove, and Uncle Eagle would prepare a purchased quail or the chance road-kill hedgehog for the eagle's evening meal.

Always an early riser, Uncle Eagle made strong black tea first thing each day. He had developed an art of tea-making to which he strictly adhered; first boiling the water to preheat the teapot, then using loose tea he would count one spoonful for each person and, of course, "one for the pot." After porridge, his standard breakfast, we'd head out on some breathtaking hike high up into the mountains. Dressed in traditional climbing gear, my uncle would carry the eagle on his wrist until the large bird grew too heavy. During the hikes, we'd take turns lugging the majestic bird. A highlight, though, was letting the eagle glide high above us, to return some time later at the blow of a whistle.

Those early years were filled with a rich sense of purpose, as well as of carefree happiness. Without his knowing it, my uncle became a role model for my own life. As the years rolled by I became more involved in singing, and Uncle Eagle would teach me old French songs that he had loved when he was young. He showed great pleasure whenever I performed any of the French chansons of the Golden Years: "La Mer," "La Vie en Rose," "Plaisir d'Amour" or "Je Tire ma Révérence."

We never spoke of spiritual quests or of the benefits of meditation. He sometimes told me stories of his youth but never mentioned the heroic mission he volunteered for in WWII as officer in charge of a mine-sweeping division, clearing the waters for the D-Day landings.

My uncle probably never realized just how much I loved him—but he knew that I was always eager to do whatever he asked of me. Even though I rarely saw him during the last years of his life, Uncle Eagle continuously honored me by playing tapes of the Sufi songs that I had recorded. One of the last gestures he made for my benefit was to send me a tape of his own voice for me to learn a song: "Awake for Morning in the Bowl of the Night," a poem of Omar Khayyam, set to music by his father Pir-o-Murshid.

Mine is a privileged memory of one of the planet's greatest sons: not just that of Pir Vilayat but that of my beloved Uncle Eagle. May his heart forever dance to Bach's *Mass in B-Minor*. May his soul be crowned by the Almighty.

By David Ray Harper

Birthday Greeting written on June 19th, 1994

Dear Uncle Eagle,
A father figure to me you have been
In my childhood and still to this day.
Your love and the guidance you've given to me
Have helped me each step of the way.
Looking back at the years of frivolous youth,
I realize nothing was said
Of the purpose and strength you lent to my life
In times when I oft was misled.
A Master, a Guide, and Inspiring Soul—
Forgiving and caring are you.
So on this special day the words I must say:
"There's no better uncle than you!"

EPILOGUE

Claire Harper: I continued to live in Fazal Manzil until the late 1990s, when I moved to the Bavarian Alps to live with David and his second wife, Christine, as well as my two granddaughters Tara (born 1990) and Sashell (born 1993). Though this is not the house of my childhood, Fazal Manzil, I have made a new home here in the autumn of my life (I am ninety-one years of age at the time of this publication), surrounded by the majesty of spectacular mountains. My family cares for me with love and devotion and I feel blessed in countless ways.

As part of his professional activities, David delivers thoughtful, history-intense tours of sites related to World War II such as Dachau Memorial Site, where he also tells the tale of my dear sister Noor. At times his tours take him to the D-day landing beaches of Normandy where Vilayat had his part to play in the fight for freedom. Ironically, we live at the foot of Adolf Hitler's former headquarters in the Alps, whose frightening history David and Christine have made it their mission to relate to visitors, as a lasting reminder of the dangers of dictatorship and fanaticism. In this way, I see the circle of life completing its course from generation to generation.

My brother Hidayat and his wife Aziza live close by—in Munich—only ninety miles away. Near us both lie the ashes of the third of us Rubies Four, our sister Noor, in a makeshift pit at Dachau outside of Munich. I ponder the orchestration of God in leading three siblings permanently to Bavaria, the very home of the tyrant by whose hand our family learned the meaning of loss.

May these memories and my son's contribution in our family's research offer the reader a brief incursion into the lives of my parents and their family.

Claire, Berchtesgaden 2010

Thy Rosary of A Hundred Beads

as originally written by

Begum Pirani Ameena Inayat Khan

I pray all errors in this book
You will forgive and overlook,
For I most humbly do confess
I was not born a poetess.

But since this heart was crucified,
My hand, doth my Beloved guide,
That on His children is bedewed
Tear-drops of thoughts in solitude.

Ameena

THY ROSARY

Oh Beloved! Hast Thou not left for me
Just a little souvenir touched by Thee,
Mayhaps a cloth in which Thy feet were clad,
Yea, to console this wretched heart made sad?

Nay Beloved, this sacred treasure Thine!
N'er could I dare to even call it mine.
Lo, behold! A light round my neck I see,
Most Holy One, it is Thy Rosary!

JULY 5TH, 1927

O Beloved, cruel fate hath stayed me on,
Thy first abandoned birthday to receive,
Would that mine eyes were closed before the dawn,
Sparing these heavy hours that but aggrieve.

Thy blessed form unseen forevermore,
Thy perfect soul doth rest in peace beyond,
And this poor wretched me, bereft and sore,
In deepest thought that do not but despond.

Thy children four commemorate this day,
And represent The "Message" just begun,
The wheel of life hath turned in such a way,
God grant my prayer, ere this year be done.

MY BELOVED HAS GONE

The brilliant sun shines no more
And happy springtime runs away.
The warm summer hides under cover
And even the beauty of autumn is seen no more;

The sky is filled with dark clouds
And cold gloomy winter has come
To stay forever and forever since
My Beloved has gone.

A PROPHET'S WIFE

Ah yes! Many may blame or scorn,
And say 'tis but folly to mourn,
Chosen to be a Prophet's wife,
Unaware of the purpose of life.

My defence is simple but strong,
And it lasteth ever so long,
For it hath no beginning nor end,
O Love, thou alone doth amend.

As the flute calls out in despair,
From the tree cut hollow and bare,
Even so, this longing heart cries
'Till merged into Love's paradise.

THY PRECIOUS HEAD

Golden hair of sun rays,
Sparkling eyes of diamonds,
Eyebrows that all Sufis praise,
Of topaz that responds.

Lips so red with rubies glare,
Skin of pearls selected,
Crowned these with emeralds rare,
Thine own most sacred head.

KING OF KINGS

King of all Kings,
Saint of all Saints,
Sage of all Sages,
Murshid of all Murshids,
Prophet of all Prophets,
 - Even so was He.

HUMILITY

To kiss Thy feet, to kiss Thy feet,
What greater joy can be,
When lover and Beloved meet,
In all humility.

WEEPING FOR THEE

Oh, living form of bones
Where hast thou lost thy flesh?
Well done, weep on until
Thy bones become languish.

HE WAS ALL

He was all that was, is and
Ever will be, my Heart,
My Soul, my Life, my All.

HIGHER

Higher, Thou wert than the Mount Himalayas,
And deeper than the deepest seas,
More calm and peaceful than the stillest lake,
Purer than the river Ganges.

Thou gavest more fruits than blossoming trees,
Thy light was brighter than the sun,
Thy love, more fragrant than the choicest rose.
Thy voice, even the birds, hath won.

PRIDE MUST FALL

O child mine, so high and proud,
Yea, for all these years,
What doth befall thee that I see
Thee in such humble tears?

Mother dear, it was false pride,
O cans't thou not see,
Unveil thine eyes and behold,
"His" figure dazzles me.

Yes my child, thou sayeth true,
"His" Light covereth all,
Now I see with eyes unveiled,
Before "Him", pride must fall.

SURRENDER TO THEE

O Beloved, to kiss Thy Holy feet!
A blessing far too great for such as me,
Mayhaps some dust that Thou hast trodden on,
To ease my soul and bring me nearer Thee.

ONCE UPON A TIME

Once upon a time, the love for thee I bore,
True love of a mate, but now forevermore,
That love hath vanished, to higher love, I soar,
Love of a worshiper upon thee I pour.

A SUFI LULLABY

Pure as silver lilies
In the heavens the stars are shining,
Graceful as the Houries,
Sweet perfumed roses o'er thee entwining,

Fanned by nightfall's cooling breeze
Midsummer's day is at last declining,
Sleep beneath the darkened trees,
Heavenly guidance enshrining.

Mids't the jasmine bed lie
Peacefully of Abbah's love dreaming.
Brilliant as the fire-fly
Through eyelids drooping a light is gleaming.

Bulbuls sing sweet lullaby,
Innocent smiles are from thee beaming.
Bathi sleep 'till morn is nigh
With Allah's love ever streaming.

O! MIGHTY POWER

O! Mighty power, oft' hast thou tried in vain
To tear asunder or to put in twain
Our love, which naught but death can separate,
And yet even death fails, disconsolate.

GREATER THAN THE GREAT

Greater than the Great
More noble than the Noble,
Wiser than the Wise,
More gentle than the Gentle,

Braver than the Hero,
More loving than the Loving,
Purer than the Pure,
More spiritual than the Spiritual,
Kinder than the Kind,
More gracious than the Gracious,
Higher than the High,
More humble than the Humble,
Forgiveness itself –
So was my Beloved.

HEART OF MY HEART

Heart of my heart,
Soul of my soul,
Whither hast Thou gone,
To the eternal goal?

Didst Thou not know
My life was Thine,
Thy feet, I worshiped,
As great Allah's Shrine?

O DEATH

O Death, why do they from thee flee,
Why fear upon them be,
Whilst this poor soul doth welcome thee,
From prison walls set free.

O Beloved Thou gavest me Thy heart,
And no one lives more true than Thou,
How then can e'er my love for Thee depart,
Allah bear witness to my vow.

I WOULD SEEM BUT A DREAM

I would seem but a dream from whence I wake to the real,
Ay! To the pangs of my hearts unheeded appeal,
To the depths of despair where the strains of the lyre,
May'st n'er again reach me from that heavenly sphere.

AS THE DAYS OF OLD

As the days of old were the days of toil
So the days of toil are now,
And so hath it been, and so shall it be
Till God maketh all anew.

DAYA

Daya, once more to see Thy face so sweet,
No sacrifice, I spare,
Just once to throw myself down at Thy feet,
God of mercy grant my prayer.

WHAT CARE I FOR THESE THINGS

Beloved what care I for these things,
These gardens and palaces of kings?
Tis true it were a rare and pleasant dream
With Thou to share with me a life supreme!

Would, that in a humble hut
Thou wert with me singing Thy gamut,
And I to wash Thy feet in hopefulness
'Stead of a palace in my loneliness.

GARDEN OF SPLENDOUR

Garden of splendour, Love's design
Laden with flowers and fruits divine,
A vision of Allah's Holy Shrine.

Dewdrops of Love's own happy tears,
Freshen anew through endless years
Casting aside all cares and fears
Rejoicing in the highest spheres.

Message of love that waneth ne'r,
O Dove, Thou bringeth through the air
And thrilleth my soul with answered prayer.

Light of my Life spread forth Thy ray
Breaking the night into the day
Let not thy lovers go astray
But ever rejoice on love's pathway.

AT THY FEET

With unceasing peace for many an age,
O Holy one, Thou art blest.
Numberless souls to pay the homage,
And kneel at Thy feet to rest.

ALLAH'S MERCY

Then perchance Thou wilt "He" call
If Thou suffereth much,
Allah's mercy is with all,
If our belief is such.

SUFI COLOUR

May it shine from the far distance as the brilliant sun,
For he was and is the shining sun,
So let Him ever remain in His illumination.
Let no black decorate His Holy Tomb,
For He is living, ever living in the richness of His warm colour.
Let the cachet in which His Holy body lies be of pure white.

IF DREAMS WERE TRUE

If thoughts were manifest and dreams were true
I'd roam oe'r land and sea in search of you,
And in a hidden cave near waters blue
I'd kiss the garment of my pain anew.

(From Murshid to Begum)

The reward of my good deeds,
My soul, and my life;
The forgiveness of my sins,
My Sharda, my wife.

On her birthday in 1921

With a worldful of love,
And with a heartful of prayers.

ANSWER TO POEM OF 1921

The honour of my virtues,
My heart and my soul,
The tolerance of my faults,
My 'Daya', my Goal.

(From Murshid to Begum)

A heart full of love,
A soul full of life.
I dedicate to my Sharda,
My soul and my wife.

On her birthday 1922

(From Murshid to Begum)

At all my busy hours in life,
Everything I do,
You are only my consolation,
And I think of you.

My work keeps me away from home
But I leave my heart,
At home, to be ever with you,
Our souls can never part.

Happiness be with our little ones,
Right guidance from above,
I wish good luck in this house,
And my deepest love.

Prosperity and success,
Long life and good health,
May be yours always Sharda
My treasure, my wealth.

With a world of love
Mari Calleja on your birthday
from your own

1922

ANSWER TO POEM OF 1922

Day by day and night by night
Every thing I see,
I feel Thy presence in it
And I think of Thee.

In every thing I may do,
Thy love guideth me,
When Thy gentle voice I hear,
I'm in ecstasy.

While the Holy Deity
Watcheth over all,
Eagerly I wait to hear
Thy whispering call.

(From Murshid to Begum)

A most loving mother
And a wife so true.
Most dearly Beloved,
My Sharda are you.

It's only your pleasure,
Which I try to do.
If I have a treasure
My Sharda it's you.

All my success in life;
Who is credit due?
Who is my inspirer
My Sharda it's you.

Many friends I have known,
But faithful are few,
And my only best friend
My Sharda are you.

And when life is blue,
Who is always near me,
My Sharda, it's you.

Health, wealth and happiness,
To my Sharda give.
God always protect her
And may she long live.

May 1923

ANSWER TO POEM OF 1923

The highest inspiration,
Beloved so true,
The only consolation,
My 'Daya', are you.

If e'er there is a pleasure
Searched the world thro'
If e'er there is a treasure,
My 'Daya', 'tis you.

And now that life be over,
Naught care I to do,
But fly from earthly cover,
My 'Daya' to you.

(From Murshid to Begum)

To my Sharda,

As pure as the water,
Of a gentle stream,
As near and as dear,
As milk and cream,

As sweet as the honey comb,
As sacred as the church of Rome,
As pretty as the flower,
Of Lover's dream.

Written in bed
April 1925

ANSWER TO POEM OF 1925

As brilliant as the sun,
With its rays of gold,
As kind as Thy name.
Buddha hath foretold.

As sacred as the mosque
With incense Divine,
As beautiful as stars
In the heavens shine.

As holy as the Shrine
Given Thou in pride.
Pure as the chosen one,
Rassoul prophesied.

(From Murshid to Begum)

May 8th 1926

On your birthday

You will cherish my love
And long you will live,
My many shortcomings
You'll always forgive.

Have we not much suffered
And did we not play?
Let us then continue
Being happy and gay.

Stand with strength and courage
With me in my strife,
Be forever my Sharda,
My nice little wife.

Our little children
Always we shall love,
Raising our hands will ask
Blessings from above.

April

ANSWER TO POEM OF 1926

O, purest heart e'er born,
Selfless and blameless,
May Allah's crown adorn
Thy head, most gracious.

Yes, we have suffered much,
But with love's sweet joy,
And soon with Allah's clutch,
All grief we'll destroy.

Life's difficult pilgrimage
Was play, with Thou near,
But now, strength and courage,
From me, disappear.

NOOR'S POEMS

As originally written

The Song of the Night

(Dedicated in gratitude to my beloved Father and Mother)

Who has heard my painful cry
Who has heard my sigh?
Lo! In my enchantment deep
Nature is asleep,
Ah! The rosebud is bedewed
With my tears bestrewed
Nature's moved to ecstasy
In my mystery
Deep in my divine abode
Treasures are bestowed.
Softly doth the moon caress
The deep wilderness
Diamonds in the sky doth gleam
In eternal dream
Who has heard my painful cry
Who has heard my sigh!
Lo! In my enchantment deep
Nature is asleep.

Noor-un-nisa Inayat Khan

A Wish

A deeper wish, a wish more true
Then that I have in store for you
Indeed upon this earth is none
And n'er can be a sweeter one.
Little rays of dreams come true
Sunny skies forever blue
Happy hours of endless cheer
May be yours this coming year.

Noor-un-nisa Inayat Khan

The Song of the Ocean

Who has heard my eternal dreamy voice?
Who has understood my song?
And lo! I make my whole being rejoice!
Singing eternity long.

Of purest, finest emerald am I,
With fringe of sparkling silver,
Divine reflection of the speechless sky,
Flowing, flowing for ever.

Morning sprinkles on me dewdrops of gold,
Twinkling in the joy of morn,
Like stones of topaze in my immense fold,
At the symphony of dawn.

Midday's resplendent smile exalts my being,
And makes me a golden glow,
Seagulls are moved to ecstasy by seeing
Such a vast, glorious flow.

The fascinating fires of the evening,
Inflame my heart as fairies,
My soul arises, and with beauty blooming,
Falls in myriad rubies.

When the soft blue veils of night have fallen,
I become an enchantment.
In my vast bosom stars fall from heaven,
And glitter in charming scent.

In my peaceful depth are treasures bestrewed,
In sweetest serenity.
Precious stone, bright pearls and jewels bedewed,
In abodes of mystery.

When, from far, the call to arouse, I hear,
With passion overwhelming,
My power and fureur, e'er mightier
Through my soul is vibrating.

And when soft breezes lull me fast to sleep,
Ah! So gently do I flow,
Singing and dreaming in my slumber deep,
And sweetly does my flute blow.

The rocks are heartless and blind to my goal,
When I say for what I long,
They send, to vibrate at the depth of my soul,
My deep and appealing song.

My beauty, my splendor, my radiance,
With mystery always gleam,
Divine is my uplifting fragrance,
And mystical is my dream.

Who has heard my eternal dreamy voice?
Who has understood my song?
And Lo! I make my whole being rejoice
Singing eternity long.

Noor-un-nisa Inayat Khan

The Lamp of Joy

A mermaid once went in a ship
Upon the stormy sea,
And as she sailed along, the
Waves arose and sprung in glee,
For on the ship she hung a lamp
Which gave a light so sweet,
That anyone who saw its flow
With joy was sure to meet.

Noor-un-nisa Inayat Khan

The Butterflies

Little dancers of the air,
As gracious as can be,
With your colored wings so fair,
Dance, O dance to me.

When the sun is nicely smiling,
On the golden glowing hill,
When the dainty birds are singing,
Butterflies, then show your skill.

When the sun is going to bed,
In its nightgown red, so red,
When the tiny flowers close,
Butterflies, then take repose.

Noor-un-nisa Inayat Khan
(written about 1929)

The Night Fairies

When the moon is softly beaming,
And the birds are fast asleep,
When the children are all dreaming,
Then sweet fairies, come and creep.
Oh! Form your pretty chains, so fair,
From the twinkling stars so bright,
While dancing through the fragrant air,
To the flowers of the night.

When the red sun begins to shine,
And birds sing at dawn of day,
Hide in the hearts of flowers fine,
Till evenings last sunny ray.

Oh! Dainty fairies, come to me,
Take me gently by my arm,
When I'm in dreamland, o'er the sea
Take me to your land of charm.

Noor-un-nisa Inayat Khan

To Our Amma

! Ah! Beloved, Amma,
A treasure stored deep in our heart,
'Tis flowers of our gratitude,
A treasure that n'er will depart.

Behold! For their petals are carved
With Allah's own heavenly art,
Their beauty on his longed for day,
To you and Abba we impart.

I harken to their tender request,
Their voice is appealing and pure,
The hearts of the rocks may it melt,
May its echo ever endure.

Their fragrance is lasting and sweet,
And far o'er this world may it soar,
Exalting our souls with its charm,
In light may it live evermore.
Through life's struggle and through life's strife,
May we treasure as our life's gem
The seed in our heart, you have sown,
Ah! Quote in the sacred Nirtan,
And always remember this:
The path of the heart is thorny,
Which leads in the end to bliss.

Noor-un-nisa Inayat Khan
(written in 1929)

To Our Dear Amma

As flowers rich and flourishing
Unfold to greet the May,
The fruit of our awakening,
We offer you this day.

To you we owe our happiness,
To you our Dear Amma,
With blessings and tenderness,
Of our beloved Abba.

Our many faults and errors,
We ask you to forgive,
For pardon n'er a mother
Could so tenderly give.

If gratitude was manifest,
In flow'rs of charming hue,
A thousand of the loveliest,
We'd give straight to you.

The seed of our worthiness,
We ask you to help grow,
You planted it with tenderness,
That it may shine and glow.
This poem Abba has written
To console your heart,
His thoughts through his dear children,
To you he doth impart.

Noor–un-nisa Inayat Khan
(written in 1931)

To Our Dear Little Amma

Ah! See sweet nature flourishing
To greet the month of May
And all the flow'rs of love in spring
We offer you this day.

The world adorned with charms may be,
And filled the 'mazing hue,
But n'er an hour as sweet can be
As when we're all with you.

'Tis you who in your heart doth rear,
The plant of our success,
That it may grow and bear each year
The fruits of worthiness.

How oft throughout life's puzzling path,
Our feet have gone astray,
Ah! Dear Amma you will forgive,
Our endless faults, this day.

Abba's own hand is o'er our head
Though far away to seek,
And deep within our longing heart
His voice doth ever speak.

Ah! See the tiny sparks of light,
As diamonds from above,
They come to show us in their flight
The far off hand of love.

Noor-un-nisa Inayat Khan
(written in 1932)

To Our Dear Mama

Amidst the flowers of spring was found
Some years ago this day,
The little bud that nature crowned
The sweetest queen of May,

And from her heart with treasures sown,
In petals fair and bright,
Four little buds have gently grown,
And opened to the light.

And love along has nurtured them,
Throughout this world of strife
Whilst facing on her tender stem
The blowing winds of life.

Your little ones, O! dear Amma
You will forgive this day,
'Tis through your hand that our Abba
Doth ever guide our way.

The sun doth never hide his face,
If not to shine anew,
The rainbow pierceth through the space
To change the tears to dew.

He hath bestowed within your heart
The blessings from above
His thought from far He doth impart
In tiny sparks of love.

Noor-un-nisa Inayat Khan
(written in 1934)

To Our Beloved Amma

O! sweet and longed for month of May,
Amidst the flow'rs that thou didst spray,
A little gem came from above,
And brought on earth Allah's own love.
Her little heart thou didst adorn,
And deep within four buds were born
And love hath brought them to unfold.
To all the beauty life doth hold,
Although life gives us each our way,
And we grow older every day,
We will remain forevermore,
Your little children as before,
To whom is due our joy in life,
If not to your unswerving strife,
And through your love and at your side,
His little children He will guide.

Noor-un-nisa Inayat Khan
(written in 1935)

To Our Beloved Amma

A little lute each baby heart
Doth carry from above
And mother plays on baby's heart
The ten dearest notes of love.

And each brings forth a gift that grows
As baby grows each year,
The love of mother ever flows
Her little plant to rear.

And when it plays an instrument,
With talent and with art
'Tis always on the lute God sent
In every little heart.

And all the music that this day
To you we all impart
The same did Mamma always play
In baby's little heart.

Noor-un-nisa Inayat Khan
(written in 1936)

Ora Ray

A little fairy told me why the flowers wake in May
She said: "it's for the birthday of a little Ora Ray
The sun, they say, is jealous of her lovely golden hair
The flowers look their sweetest just to try and be as fair."

Oh! There is no other birthday half as sweet as this, you see,
The birdies give a concert on a branch of every tree
I met some little sparrows as I skipped along the way
"Her naughty little children are so proud!" I heard them say.

Of course it is quite natural for they know as well as we
There's not a sweeter mother over land or over sea
You come and see us dancing on our bonny eighth of May
You'll see the moon bend over just to watch us sing and play.

This secret little fairy came and whispered in my ear
And this is why the whole world wakes to greet our mother dear.

Noor-un-nisa Inayat Khan
(written in 1938)

To Amma Dear

The sweetest little mother
Is our little Mamma dear
And the day that brought her hither
Is the sweetest in the year.

When the big stork brought down dearest,
All the birds began to sing.
For indeed she is the fairest,
Of the blossoms of the spring.

With the gold of all the sunbeams,
Were her pretty tresses spun,
That when her radiant hair gleams
It should rival with the sun.

And the blue so pure and tender,
Of the clear resplendent skies,
Is reflected in the mirror,
Of her sparkling little eyes.

And the spring has whispered to her,
All the secret of its charms,
Therefore is its joy felt ever,
In the clasp within her arms.

Every drop of love's own ocean,
Love that brings forth nature's art,
All the love of earth and heaven,
Is within her little heart.

Noor-un-nisa Inayat Khan
(written in 1939)

To Mama Cute

I wonder why our mother dear
Is sweet and sweeter every year
Why she was born this month of May
And why her name is Ora Ray?

It was a lovely day of May
When all the rays come out to play
They slide along and come to peep
To wake the daisies from their sleep

And midst the rays from father sun,
Came down a naughty little one,
And that is why she is so fair
With shining eyes and golden hair.

And that is why she's born in May,
And why her name is Ora Ray
For midst the rays from father sun
Came down a tiny little one.

Noor-un-nisa Inayat Khan
(written in 1940)

The Birthday Man

I saw the little birthday man,
Skipping 'long the way,
I stopped awhile and listened,
To hear what he would say.

He put his little finger
Upon his little head.
He blew the dandelions, and
Danced around and said:

"Why, this is my best birthday,
For on this very day,
The storks brought down a girly
Whose name is Ora Ray."

"I must put on my sweetest,
And wear my golden crown.
I'll take my happy knapsack,
And wear my grand new gown."

"She has had cloudy hours,
And many cloudy years,
And many hard adventures,
And many many tears."

"Life has been very naughty,
But I shall right the wrong,
And make her whole life happy,
Just with my little song."

"I'll set the bluebells ringing,
And blow away the cold,
And all the bees a singing,
Shall chase away the old."

"There's loads of joy I've hidden
Within my tiny sack,
Although it weighs but little
Upon my tiny back."

"I've stored it all for ages
To give to her this day.
I've asked the sun to smile,
And all the flowers to say:

"The world's full of good tidings,
And all its happiness
We give you this birthday
With three cheers for success."

Noor-un-nisa Inayat Khan

Three Stories by Noor

Two Stories About Poland

I

Many queens have reigned in Poland, many a princess had lived in the palace of Krakow, but none as lovely as the Princess Wanda; for never had the people of the country beheld such beauty, nor the people in yonder lands heard of such charm.

Day after day, the city of Krakow was crowded with envoys from distant lands. They crossed the icy northern seas and the stormy seas of the south to ask her for her hand.

One day, the streets of Krakow echoed with the blast of foreign trumpets and steel of armoured troops. The people rushed to the windows. It was an envoy indeed, this time from a neighbouring land, a land they called Germany.

Oftimes had the Princess Wanda heard tales about the king of Germany. The men in his gloomy country were forever at war. The people who worked on the land died of hunger, for all they reaped was taken away from them. And he loved not his people, nor did they love him.

Such were the tales told about the king of Germany, and Wanda resolved that she would never marry a king who loved his people so little. Thus she called the envoy and said: "Return to your king and tell him I cannot love him, for he loves not his people; and as I can cannot love him, I shall not marry him."

The envoy returned to his country, the armoured troops and trumpeters following, and he delivered the message to the king.

The king rose from his throne, and the walls of his palace shook as he spoke.

"How many can we throw into the battle?" he shouted, "and how many has Poland?"

"Sir," replied the counselor, "ours are sevenfold."

And summoning the envoy, he said:

"Return this very day to Poland and tell Her Highness that if she accepts not my offer, we shall attack her country with forces sevenfold hers in number and weapons."

Such was the message delivered to Wanda.

The dusk was falling over Krakow, and the hour had come when all were gathered round the firesides. The city was happy indeed, and a great peace reigned over it. Wanda watched it as the thousands of little lights glimmered in the dark, she watched it as the moon bent over the city, and big tears rolled down her cheeks. Never, she thought, must Poland die.

Early the next day she called upon the royal gown makers. They came in haste and listened to her orders. "You shall make for me a wedding gown," she said, "of finest silk, embroidered with the flowers of Poland, the flowers I love."

But Wanda was sad as she spoke, and they knew not why; and the people of Krakow wondered and talked, and great was their impatience to know whether Wanda, whom they all loved, would marry the king they hated so.

Thus was Wanda clad in a gown of whitest silk, and the train bore real flowers in the folds.

She placed the crown upon her head and called her people.

They came in masses from the plains and valleys, and the trumpets blew so hard that they came from the hills and crowded on the banks of the Vistula.

And Wanda spoke to them all.

"My people" she said, "a mighty enemy is at our gates. You all know him, for long have tales been told about him. He threatens to attack Poland if your Princess Wanda will not marry him. Can a princess marry a prince she cannot love?

"My people, I know you will fight whatever the enemy be, for you are sons of a brave and mighty country, but the enemy's forces are sevenfold ours in number and weapons. Therefore, my people, I have resolved to leave you, for having left you, he shall have no cause to declare war. I am young, it is true, and happy I would be to live with you for years and years to come. The fields of Poland are growing the first corn, and Poland shall be lovely soon; I must leave you, though, for the prince I marry must be noble and great.

"My people, as long as you live, Poland shall not die. If the whole world crushed it to dust, it would rise again through you. I must leave you now, but remember Wanda sometimes, perhaps at dusk when the old tales of Poland are told."

With these words, she bent over the Vistula like a pure white swan and disappeared under the waters.

The people wept bitterly and mourned for her. They built a mound there where she stood, so that Wanda should never be forgotten. But the people of Poland know that Wanda can never be forgotten, for the Vistula still repeats her words as it flows. "Poland shall never die. If the whole world crushed it to dust, it would rise again through you. Poland can never die."

II

My children, there is a country far, far away called Poland. You have heard about it. It is a brave country, a country of warriors and knights.

Have you seen their flag flying in the wind? Have you seen the proud eagle on the red background? Why is the red flag like the setting sun, and why is the eagle white? Just listen, and I shall tell you all about it.

Long, long ago, Poland was a very happy country. The knights who defended the land were so mighty that no enemy dared approach the Polish soil.

Have you ever seen white eagles? They lived in Poland long, long years ago, high up in the cliffs, and they were kings of the rocks. Their piercing eyes watched over Poland, and their wings spread out as wings of steel to protect it.

One day, long, long years ago, the knights of Poland were travelling through the country with their king, Boleslaw the Brave. The hour was late, and they halted awhile as their horses' mouths were foaming. The vast country lay below. They laid their spears and lances on the hot sand and looked upwards. The sky till the horizon was red as blazing fire. All was silent, not a leaf stirred; then, in a gush of wind, two white wings spread out against the sky. It was the white eagle. In one mighty glance he viewed the cities below, and a great majesty surrounded him.

Then, slowly descending, he flew towards the open space where they stood, for there lay his nest at the summit of the oak. There he gently spread his wings, glanced once more at Poland and laid down to rest.

"Indeed, this shall be our sign," said King Boleslaw, "Forevermore the white eagle against the sky of Poland shall be our flag, and as long as it flies our country shall not fall. Hawks cannot beat the white eagle nor can they live in its nest. We shall erect a castle on this spot, great and massive. It shall be called the nest. The knights of Poland shall dwell in it and as long as they live, Poland shall live."

Such were the words of the king and there where the nest lay, a castle and city were built. It was called Gniezno, which means the nest. It still stands massive and unchallenged as the years pass by.

The flag is now torn down, and the Eagle of Poland wounded, but it can never die. White eagles never die. As soon as its wings are healed, it will return to the nest, and Gniezno shall be full of knights with lances and spears, and Poland shall live again forevermore.

Snowdrop

Great Sun had a little daughter with sun-ray hair and sky-blue eyes; and Great Sun loved her dearly, for when she played about in the clouds, the whole sky would ring with sweet laughter.

But one day, she peeped down from the white clouds, and three little tears rolled down her cheeks. The big world lay down there, so brown gloomy, and Oh! It looked very sad indeed. And while Great Sun was not looking, chut! chut!—very quietly she flew down from the sky.

She skipped along the big, big world, and as she went along, green blades of grass sprung up, hundreds of them, thousands of them, then daisies and golden cups. Even the ugly branches, the long, lanky branches of the elms and oaks, the branches of all the trees in the world were suddenly covered with tiny green leaves.

"How lovely!" thought Great Sun's little daughter, and so happy was she that she sang and sang till all the birds in the world started to sing, and all the big, big world was full of song and joy. And so happy was Little Daughter that she danced and danced till little white rabbits came bouncing out from every hole, from every side—brown spotted ones, little wooly ones, too.

Great Sun smiled from the sky as he had never smiled before, so happy was he to see how lovely his little daughter had made the world. And so happy was he, that he woke earlier every morning and went to sleep later every night so as to gaze longer at the lovely world where his daughter dwelt.

Everyone loved her dearly. Only one living being did not love Great Sun's little daughter. It was Queen Winter. For since Great Sun's daughter had come on earth, Queen Winter had no longer reigned over the world. She called her best guards, and … crack, crack, crack, along they came: Frost-Bite, Fog-Gloom, North Wind and all the others.

"Woo … oo …," said Winter, "mighty guards, the Kingdom of Winter is in danger. Great Sun's little daughter is loved by everyone, and I, your queen, am being forgotten. If you wish that the kingdom of cold abide, Great Sun's little daughter must die."

"Woo … oo …!" said Frost-Bite.

"Woo … oo …!" said Fog-Gloom.

"Woo … oo …!" said the blasty North Wind.

"When Great Sun is asleep, you shall seize her and hide her under the earth, so far away that no soul can find her again!"

And when Great Sun had gone and all the world was fast asleep, tiptoe, crack …. crack, they went into the woods.

The little girl was sleeping beneath the bough of a pine tree.

No one saw them come up to the tree. No one saw little daughter frozen stiff by Frost-Bite; made invisible by Fog-Gloom; and carried away by North Wind, so far away that no one could find her again. No one saw except two little robins who were sitting on the bough and they followed quietly behind. No one saw them put Great Sun's little daughter under the earth except the two little robins. They hid and watched.

The world became very sad as the days went by.

The little green blades lost their colour and faded away. No one knew where the daisies and buttercups had vanished nor why the birds had lost their voice. The tall trees wept so hard that all their lovely leaves fell to the ground. No more white backs came peeping out of holes. The air was full of sighs, and Great Sun awoke later every morning and went to sleep earlier every night, so sad was he to look upon the big, big world where little daughter was no more to be found. Sometimes he would hide his face for days behind the clouds, and Queen Winter reigned over the earth.

"Where is she?" muttered the trees as they swayed up and down.

"Where is she? Twii! Twii!" asked the birds as they shook the frost off their wings.

"Where is she?" whispered everything.

One day, two little redbreasts sitting on the bough of a pine tree fluttered their wings and flew away, far away to the spot where Great Sun's little daughter was hidden under the earth.

Too … too … with the tip of their beaks, they tapped on the ground.

"Are you there, little daughter?" they called, "Twii! twii! are you there?"

" Yes, robins," she whispered, "I am here."

"Do come back, Little Daughter," they pleaded, "the big, big world is so sad without you."

"I cannot, little robins," she whispered, "for if I did, Queen Winter and her guards would kill me."

"Do come back, Little Daughter," twittered the robins, "the tall trees have lost all their leaves, so hard have they wept. The birds sing no more. No one knows where the daisies have vanished, and the Great Sun is so sad that he rises later every morning and leaves us earlier every night. Sometimes he hides his face for days behind the clouds, and if you don't return, Little Daughter, he may never come again."

"Chut! I will come!" whispered little daughter, "but I will come as a flower as tiny as a drop and as white as the snow, so that Queen Winter cannot see me."

And Snowdrop grew out of the snow, but everyone knew it was Great Sun's little daughter. They whispered it to each other when Winter was not about. And new leaves grew on the branches again, and very shyly the birds sang again, and Great Sun smiled again as never before, and he woke earlier every morning and went to sleep later every night, for his little daughter was found and all the big, big world was happy once again.

Noor-un-Nisa Inayat Khan

Photographs and Illustrations

The Rubies Four Family Tree

DIRECT ASCENDANTS AND IMMEDIATE FAMILY

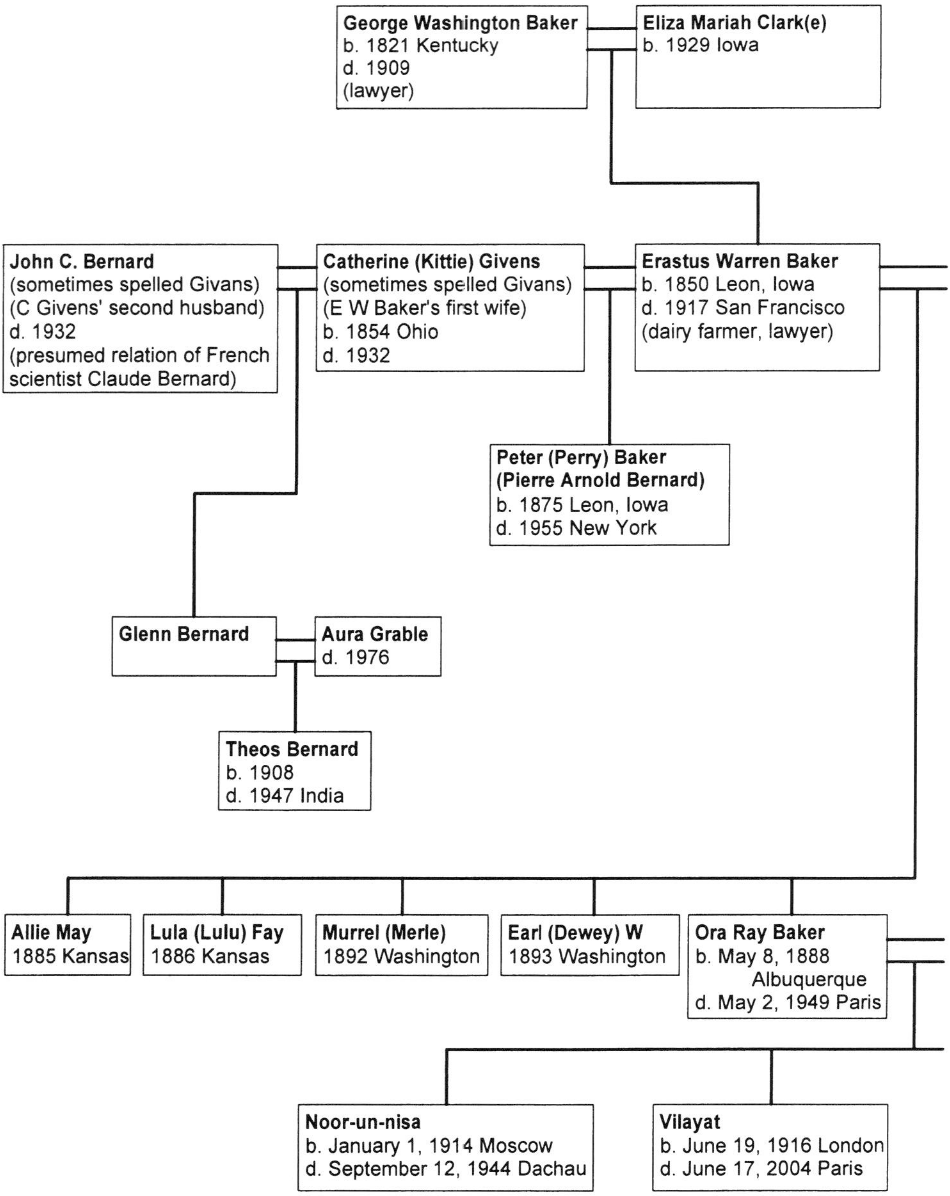

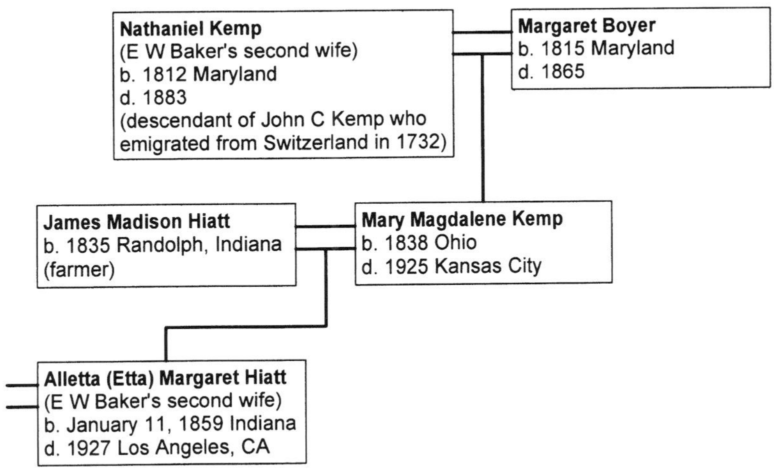
Nathaniel Kemp
(E W Baker's second wife)
b. 1812 Maryland
d. 1883
(descendant of John C Kemp who emigrated from Switzerland in 1732)
Margaret Boyer
b. 1815 Maryland
d. 1865
James Madison Hiatt
b. 1835 Randolph, Indiana
(farmer)
Mary Magdalene Kemp
b. 1838 Ohio
d. 1925 Kansas City
Alletta (Etta) Margaret Hiatt
(E W Baker's second wife)
b. January 11, 1859 Indiana
d. 1927 Los Angeles, CA

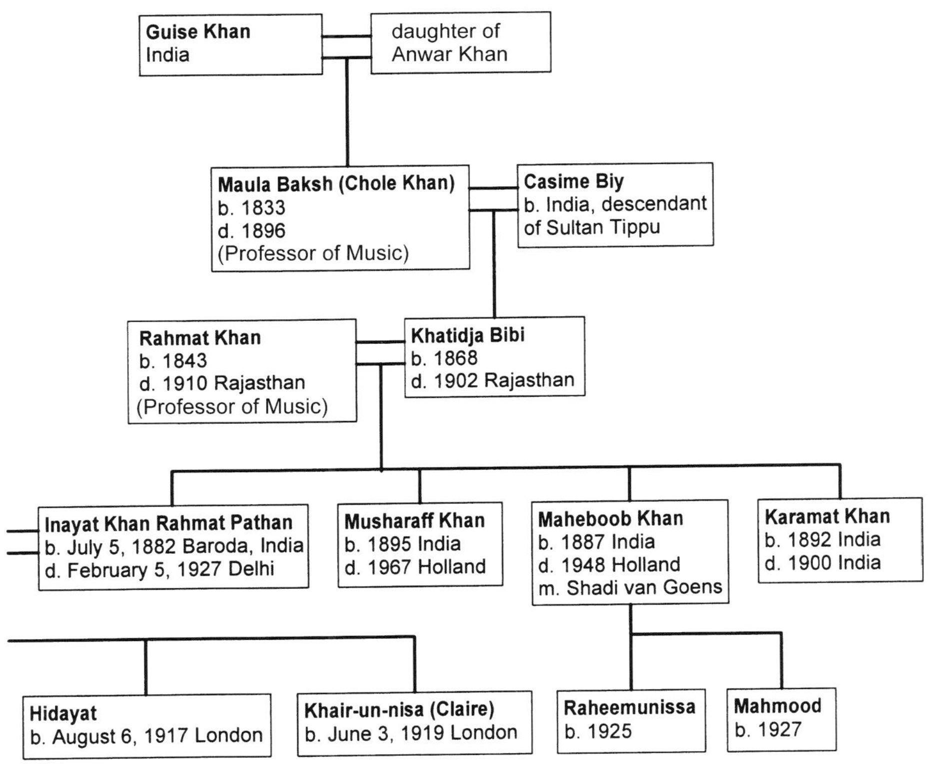
Guise Khan
India
daughter of
Anwar Khan
Maula Baksh (Chole Khan)
b. 1833
d. 1896
(Professor of Music)
Casime Biy
b. India, descendant of Sultan Tippu
Rahmat Khan
b. 1843
d. 1910 Rajasthan
(Professor of Music)
Khatidja Bibi
b. 1868
d. 1902 Rajasthan
Inayat Khan Rahmat Pathan
b. July 5, 1882 Baroda, India
d. February 5, 1927 Delhi
Musharaff Khan
b. 1895 India
d. 1967 Holland
Maheboob Khan
b. 1887 India
d. 1948 Holland
m. Shadi van Goens
Karamat Khan
b. 1892 India
d. 1900 India
Hidayat
b. August 6, 1917 London
Khair-un-nisa (Claire)
b. June 3, 1919 London
Raheemunissa
b. 1925
Mahmood
b. 1927

Kemp Family Crest

Erastus Warren Baker, Nyack, New York

Erastus Warren Baker, San Francisco

Home of Ora Ray's Grandparents

Ora Ray Baker's home

Ora Ray Baker.

Ora Ray Baker

Pierre Bernard

Pierre Bernard lying under elephant, Clarkstown Country Club, Nyack, New York

Pierre Bernard with elephant, Clarkstown Country Club, Nyack, New York

Pierre Bernard

Pierre Bernard bust

Theos Bernard in yogic posture

Theos Bernard, Tibet, 1937

Theos Bernard with Reting Rimpoche,
Regent of Tibet

Tipu, Sultan of Mysore, 1792

Tipu's Summer Palace, Sirangapatna, Karnataka, India

Tipu's seal

Tipu Sultan's tomb, Sirangapatna, Karnataka, India

Dargah (shrine) of Khwaja Moinuddin Chisti in Ajmer, India

Maula Bakhsh

Maula Bakhsh

The Late Prof. Mowlabux Founder of the Indian Musical Notation.

जन्म इ. स. १८३३
मृत्यु इ. स. १८९६ जुलई ता. १०

संगीत लेखन पद्धतीके उत्पादक प्रोफेसर मौलाबक्ष साहब.

अगर देश हितेशी हमेना जगाता, तो देशोन्नतीका किसे ध्यान आता.॥ १ ॥
अविद्याकि निंद्रामे सोताथा भारत, पर उपकारि फिरताथा घर घर जगाता. ॥ २ ॥
तपस्वी प्रतापी संगीत बिद्यान होती प्रगट केसे अंधेरा जाता. ॥ ३ ॥
विद्याकी दशादेख गायनका दुखडा, कहेताथा हादेव हा हा विधाता. ॥ ४ ॥
प्रतिष्ठित नहोती कभी गान विद्या,जो संगीतकी वोह रुचीना बढाता. ॥ ५ ॥
महांथा कठिन इस्को कागज पे लाना, अहो शारदाथी प्रसन वाक माता. ॥ ६ ॥
किसकी थि सामर्थ किसाकि थि शक्ती, जो ऐसे सभे साहिब मनाता. ॥ ७ ॥
अज्ञाथि विसकां सरब शक्तिमांकी, वोअत ऐव आयाथा विद्या रमाता. ॥ ८ ॥
आते न ऐसे जो भूमीपे विद्वान, हमे घरमे आकोन लेक्चर सुनाता. ॥ ९ ॥
इन्डीयाका प्रोफेसर मौलाबक्षदाता, पधाराहे परलोक डंके बजाता. ॥ १० ॥
इनायत नहोता कविश्वर कदाचिद, नसत्संग करता न हरगुणको गाता. ॥ ११ ॥

Professor Mowlabux (Maula Baksh) from musical notation book by Inayat Khan

Inayat Khan with medals

Gayanshala Music Academy in Baroda, India

The great 16th century singer Miyan Tansen

प्रोफेसर इनायतखां रेहमतखा पठान.

खुदाका शुक्र अहेसां हे जहां जिसने कियापयदा,
अजब कुदरत ये आलमको कियाहे नूर से शयदा. ॥ १ ॥
हवा आतिश आब ओर खाकका जलवाहे दिखलाया,
बशरेन जिसमे आला सबसे दरजा अक्कल हे पाया. ॥ २ ॥
किये हैवां परिंदे ओर चरिंदे इसहिके बसमे,
हुनर इल्मो इबादत हेभरी आदमाकि नसनसमे. ॥ ३ ॥
इलम कैहें अयां लेकिन इलम मुतकी बडाभारी,
के दरिया बेबहा जिसका जहांमें हे सदाजारी ॥ ४ ॥
अयशो अशरत शहेनशाहत को करते हें निसार इसपर,
इलम मुसकीका इनसांके जो दिलपे होवेपूरा असर. ॥ ५ ॥
न सिर्फ इनसान खुश आवाजसे दिल शाद करते हें,
मगर हेवां भिता कुरबान इसपर जान करतेहें. ॥ ६ ॥
नबत्तर खर से हे मरदूदजो मूसिक नजिस माने,
जमाले नूर नहिं जाने वो रबको केसे पेछाने. ॥ ७ ॥
हे दरिया बेबहा किशती मेरीको दे तिरा खालिक,
इनायत तेरि रहेमतकी हो मुजपर हे दोआ मालिक. ॥ ८ ॥

Musical notation book by Inayat Khan

Rustam-i-Dauran, the Nizam of Hyderabad

Inayat's Murshid, Syed Mohammed Abu Hashim Madani

The Royal Musicians of Hindustan. From left to right: Maheboob, Mohammed Ali, Inayat, Ramaswami, Musharaff

Ruth St. Denis.

Ora Ray, circa 1908

Ora Ray, New York, circa 1910

Ora Ray with fan, circa 1912

Hazrat Pir-o-Murshid Inayat Khan

Hazrat Pir-o-Murshid Inayat Khan in America

Ora Ray's ticket book

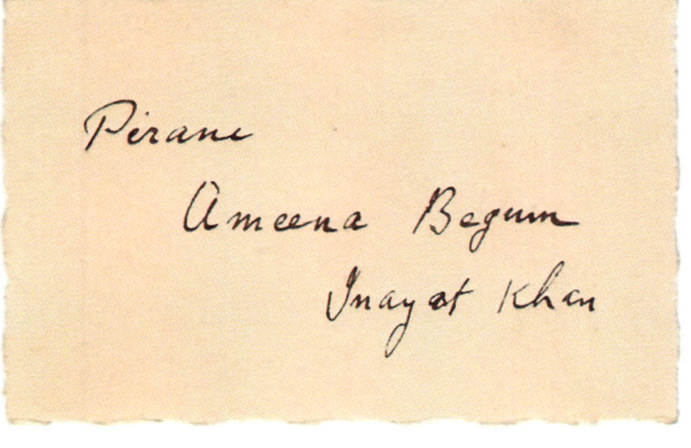

Ora Ray's new name in Inayat's handwriting

Pirani Ameena Begum Inayat Khan

Murshid with baby Noor in Russia, 1914

Murshid with vina

Khankah at Ladbroke Road, London

Maheboob (rear); Noor, baby Vilayat, Ameena Begum, Murshid (middle row); Mohammed Ali and Musharaff (front row) with mureeds. England, 1916

Vilayat and Noor in London, 1917

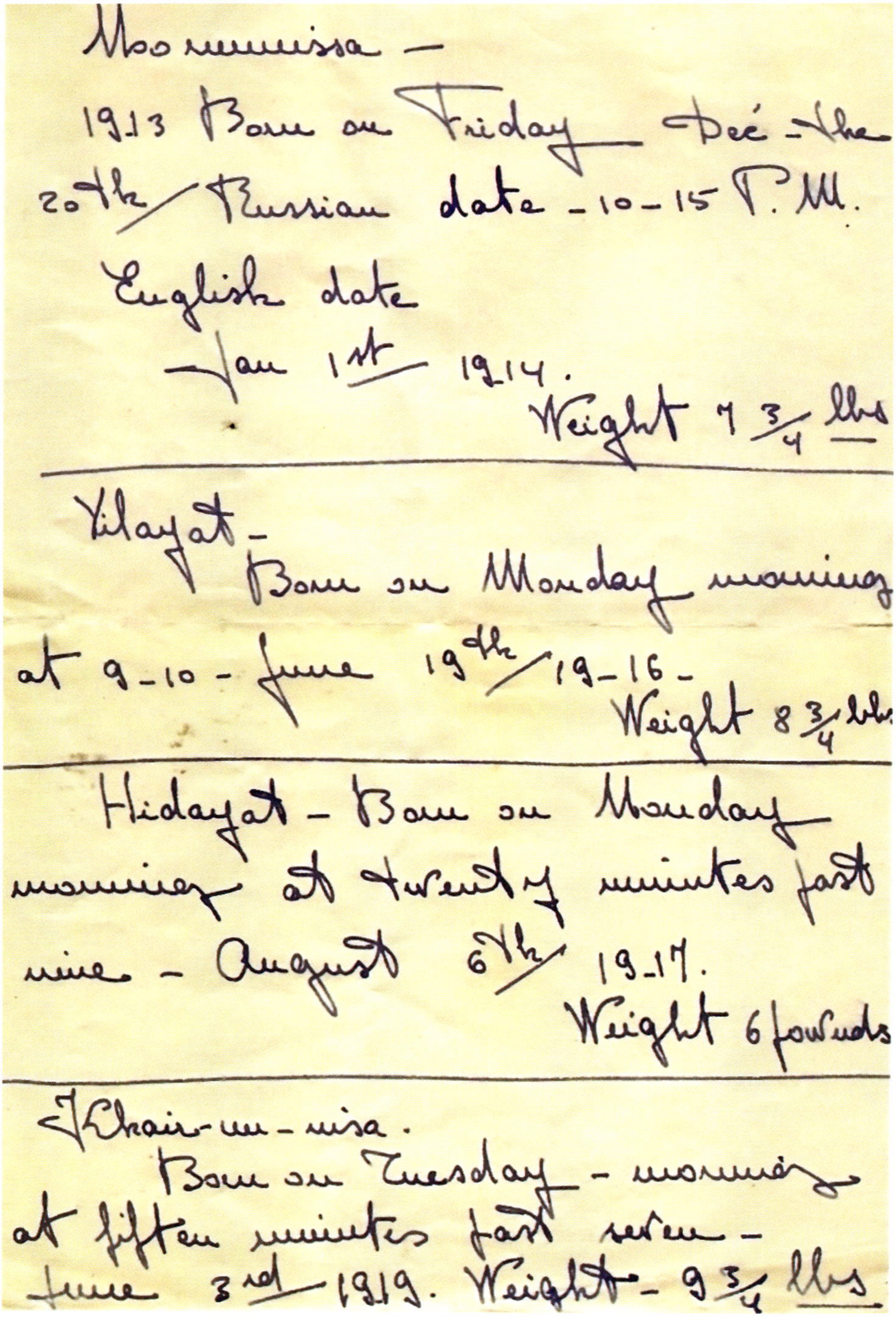

Moonunnissa —

1913 Born on Friday Dec. the 20th Russian date — 10 — 15 P.M.

English date

Jan 1st 1914.

Weight 7 3/4 lbs

Vilayat —

Born on Monday morning at 9 — 10 — June 19th 19 — 16 —

Weight 8 3/4 lbs

Hidayat — Born on Monday morning at twenty minutes past nine — August 6th 1917.

Weight 6 pounds

Khair-un-nisa.

Born on Tuesday — morning at fifteen minutes past seven — June 3rd 1919. Weight — 9 3/4 lbs

Ameena Begum's record of babies' births

Murshid and family with mureeds in England

Pirani Ameena Begum

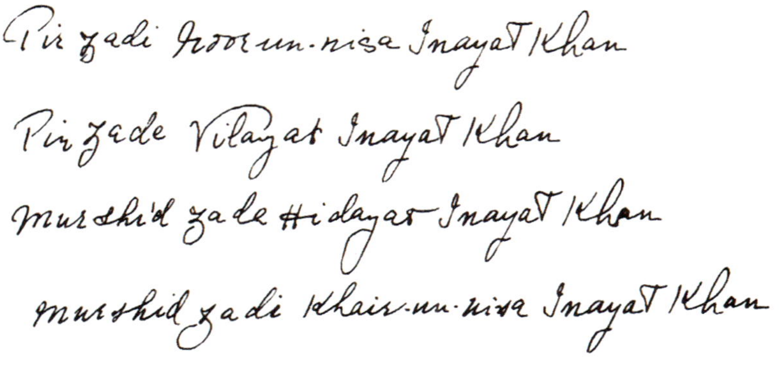
Pir zadi Noor-un-nisa Inayat Khan
Pir zade Vilayat Inayat Khan
Murshid zade Hidayat Inayat Khan
Murshid zadi Khair-un-nisa Inayat Khan

Children's Names in Murshid's handwriting

Murshid in turban

Fazal Manzil (House of Blessing) Suresnes, France

Hidayat and Claire, 1921

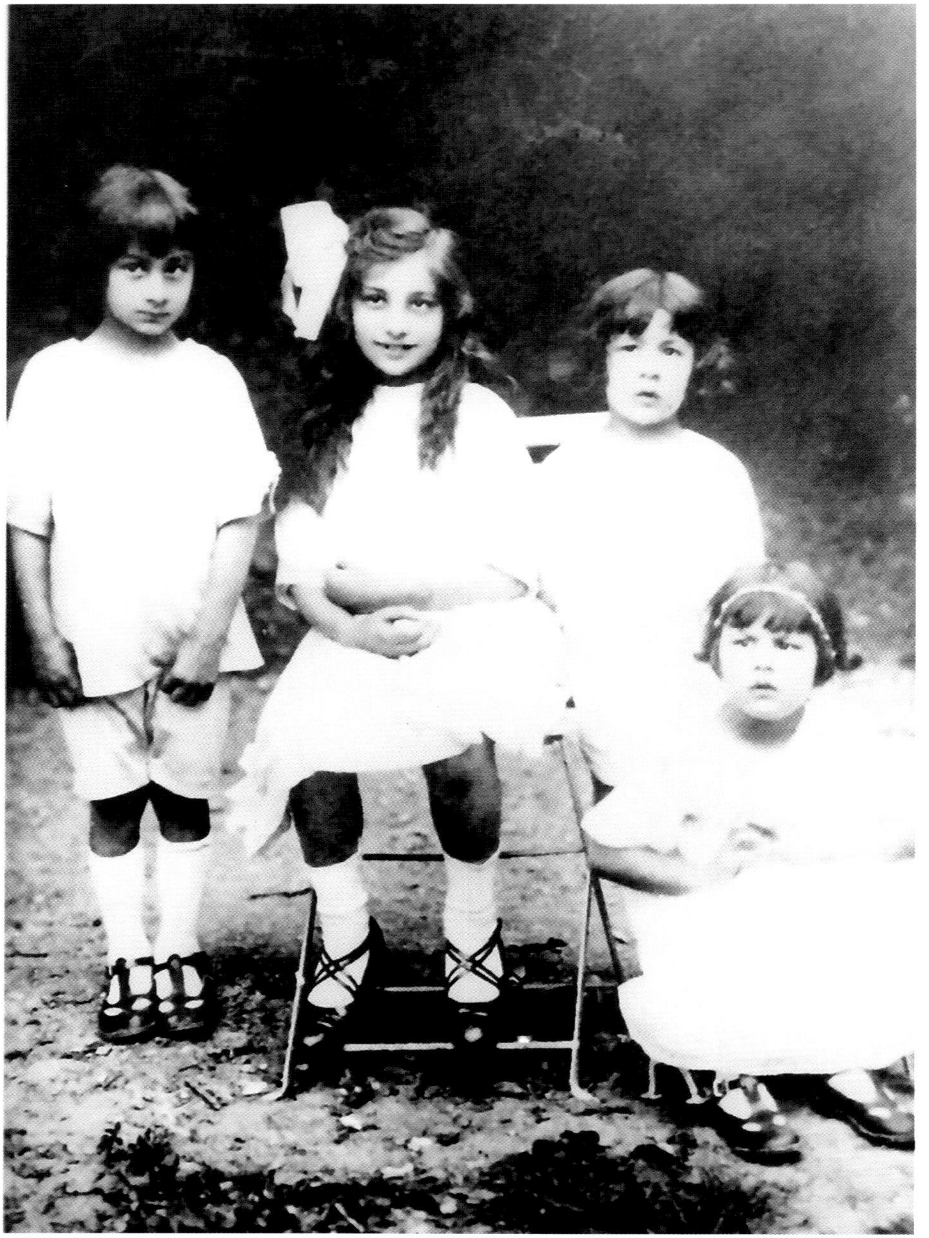

Rubies Four: Vilayat, Noor, Hidayat and Claire, 1921

Hidayat and Vilayat with Claire, 1921

Maheboob with Hidayat, Claire and Vilayat

Murshid and Claire in Suresnes, 1922

Murshid with his Rubies Four, 1922

Murshid with Noor, Hidayat and Claire, circa 1922

Rubies Four in the garden of Fazal Manzil:
Noor, Vilayat, Hidayat and Claire, circa 1922

Noor, Claire, Murshid, Hidayat, Ameena Begum, Vilayat (front row);
Maheboob and Musharaff (rear)

Inayat Khan family with mureeds in Suresnes, circa 1923

Zeb-un-nissa, Marquise Farinola

Sheikh Sirkar de Heer van Stolk and Sheikh Sirdar Baron Van Tuyll in Suresnes

Bhakti Van Stolk's painting of Ameena Begum

Artwork by Saida Van Tuyll (Willebeek Le Mair)

The field across from Fazal Manzil, site of the Summer School, with Mount Valerian in the distance

Mureed House behind Fazal Manzil

Mureed House

Quai near Sufi Movement Offices, Geneva, Switzerland

Murshid with family and mureeds, 1924

Rubies on the steps of Fazal Manzil: Hidayat, Claire, Vilayat and Noor

Vilayat playing the violin

Maheboob Khan

Mohammad Ali Khan, Suresnes

Murshid on the Sufi Land, Suresnes

Murshid in the garden, Fazal Manzil

Murshid and Ameena Begum, Summer School, 1926

Murshid and family with mureeds, Summer School, 1926

Murshid at Summer School, 1926

Murshid with mureeds at Summer School, 1926

Dedication of the Universel Temple Foundation Stone,
Summer School, Suresnes, 1926

Murshid at the gate, Suresnes

Murshid in India

Tilak Lodge, Delhi, India

Murshid's dargah today, Nizamuddin, India

Red Fort, Delhi, India

Thy Rosary of a Hundred Beads front cover

Thy Rosary of a Hundred Beads back cover

Thy Rosary of a Hundred Beads inside cover

Noor and Ameena Begum

Rubies Four as teens: Hidayat, Noor, Claire and Vilayat, Suresnes, circa 1929

Claire with Murshida Fazal Mai Egeling

Rubies Four on the Sufi Land: Vilayat, Claire, Hidayat and Noor

Hidayat, Claire, Noor, Vilayat with instruments

Noor, Hidayat, Fazal Mai, Vilayat and Claire

Claire, circa 1934

Noor, 1934

Noor's passport, 1934.

Noor with vina

Vilayat, 1935

Noor and Claire performing

Noor in sari with her vina

Noor in fur collar

Claire, circa 1935

Noor's painting of palm trees

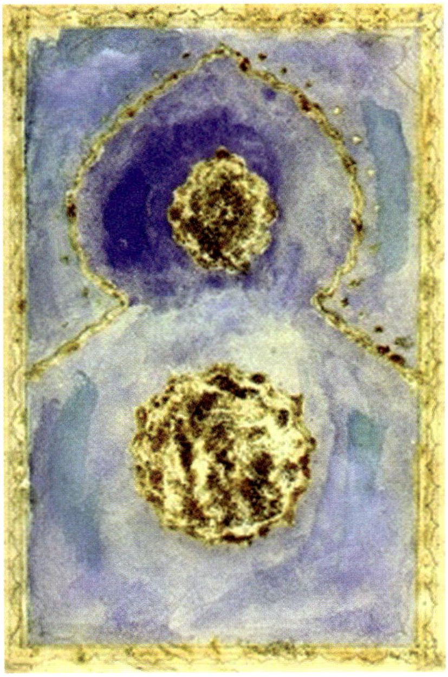

Noor's radiant painting

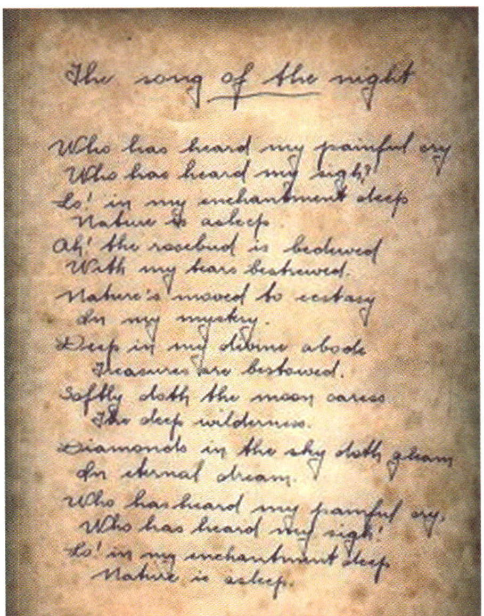

The song of the night

Who has heard my painful cry
Who has heard my sigh?
Lo! in my enchantment deep
Nature is asleep.
Ah! the rosebud is bedewed
With my tears bestowed.
Nature's moved to ecstasy
In my mystery.
Deep in my divine abode
Treasures are bestowed.
Softly doth the moon caress
The deep wilderness.
Diamonds in the sky doth gleam
In eternal dream.
Who has heard my painful cry,
Who has heard my sigh!
Lo! in my enchantment deep
Nature is asleep.

Noor's "Song of the Night"

Dedicated in gratitude
to my Beloved
Father and Mother.

Noor's writing sample

Musharaff with relatives and mureeds

Vilayat, 1936

Vilayat, 1937

Vilayat on horseback, 1936

Vilayat on Sufi Land, 1937

Vilayat

Claire, Holland, circa 1938

Claire, circa 1938

Noor dressed up

Noor on horseback, Holland

Noor and Azeem Goldenberg at Fazal Manzil

Cover art for Noor's "Jataka Tales" by Saida Van Tuyll (Willebeek le Mair)

Vilayat, Noor, and friend

Noor, Hidayat, Claire and "Sniffy" in Saida Van Tuyll's studio, 1938

Rubies Four, circa 1939

Vilayat in Royal Air Force gear

Vilayat in Royal Air Force

The type of plane that Vilayat would have piloted

Vilayat in the Royal Navy, 2nd row from front, 2nd from left

Vilayat's Royal Navy ship

Patron: HIS MAJESTY THE KING.
President: HER MAJESTY THE QUEEN.
Chairman of the Council: H.R.H. THE DUKE OF GLOUCESTER, K.G.
Chairman of the Executive Committee: The Hon. Sir ARTHUR STANLEY, G.B.E., C.B., M.V.O.

This is to Certify that

Mrs. Ora Ray Baker Inayat

County of London Detachment No. 312

has completed one year's **War Service** from 30.11.42 to 29.11.43 as duly certified, in accordance with the regulations under the auspices of the Society in connection with its humanitarian work.

First Certificate Awarded 11.5.1944.

Arthur Stanley. Chairman.

F. C. Davies Secretary.

No. W.S.3/ 35263

War Service Stripe for Ora Ray Baker Inayat

Ameena Begum

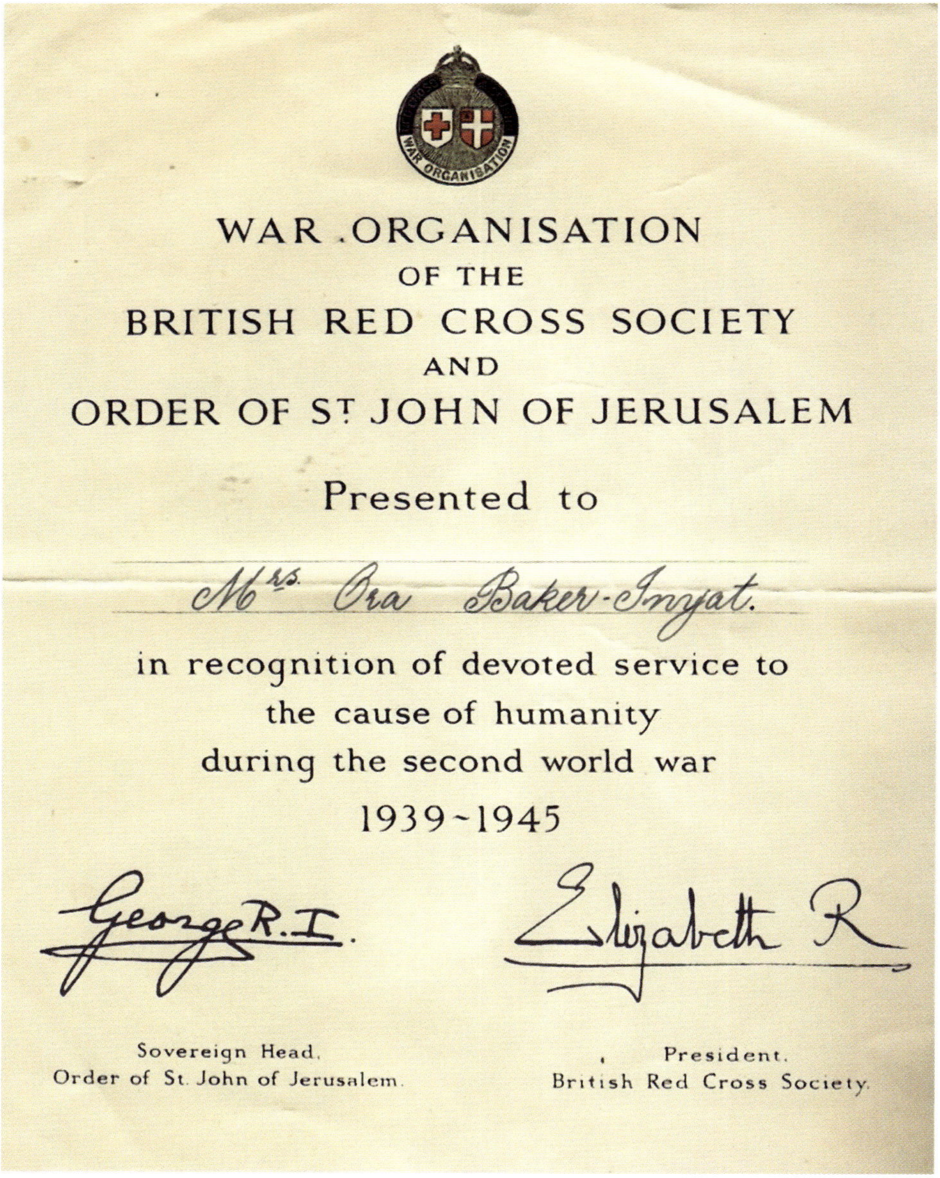

WAR ORGANISATION
OF THE
BRITISH RED CROSS SOCIETY
AND
ORDER OF ST JOHN OF JERUSALEM

Presented to

Mrs. Ora Baker-Inayat.

in recognition of devoted service to
the cause of humanity
during the second world war
1939~1945

George R.I.

Elizabeth R

Sovereign Head,
Order of St. John of Jerusalem.

President,
British Red Cross Society.

War Service Honor for Ora Ray Baker-Inayat

Noor in WAAF uniform, 1940

Noor's WAAF identity card

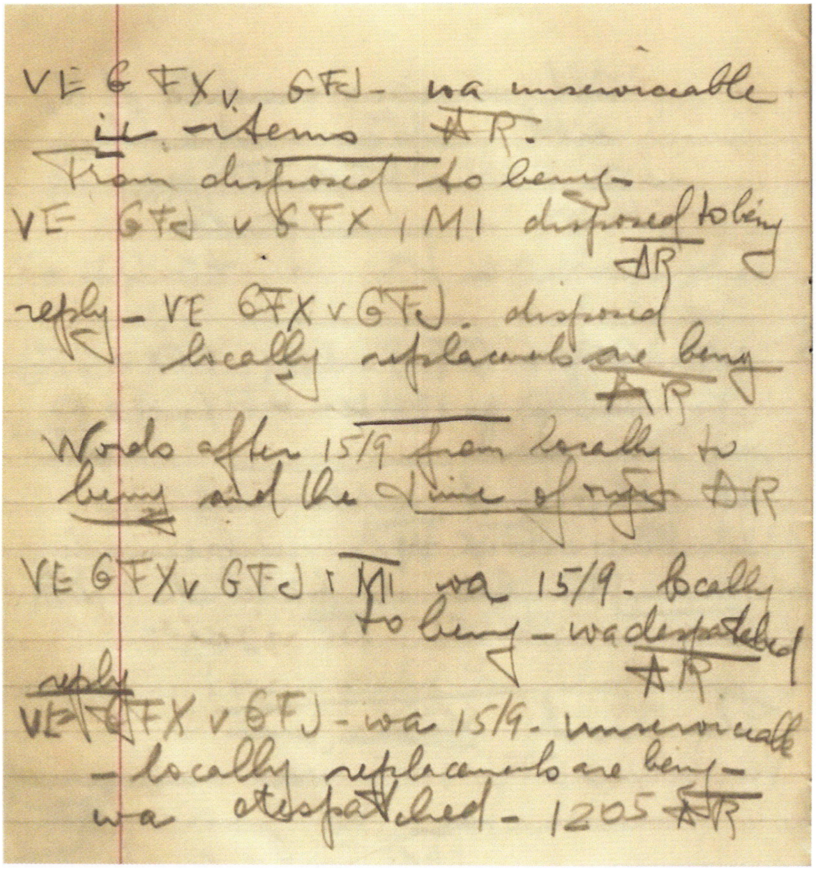

Noor's radio code training notes

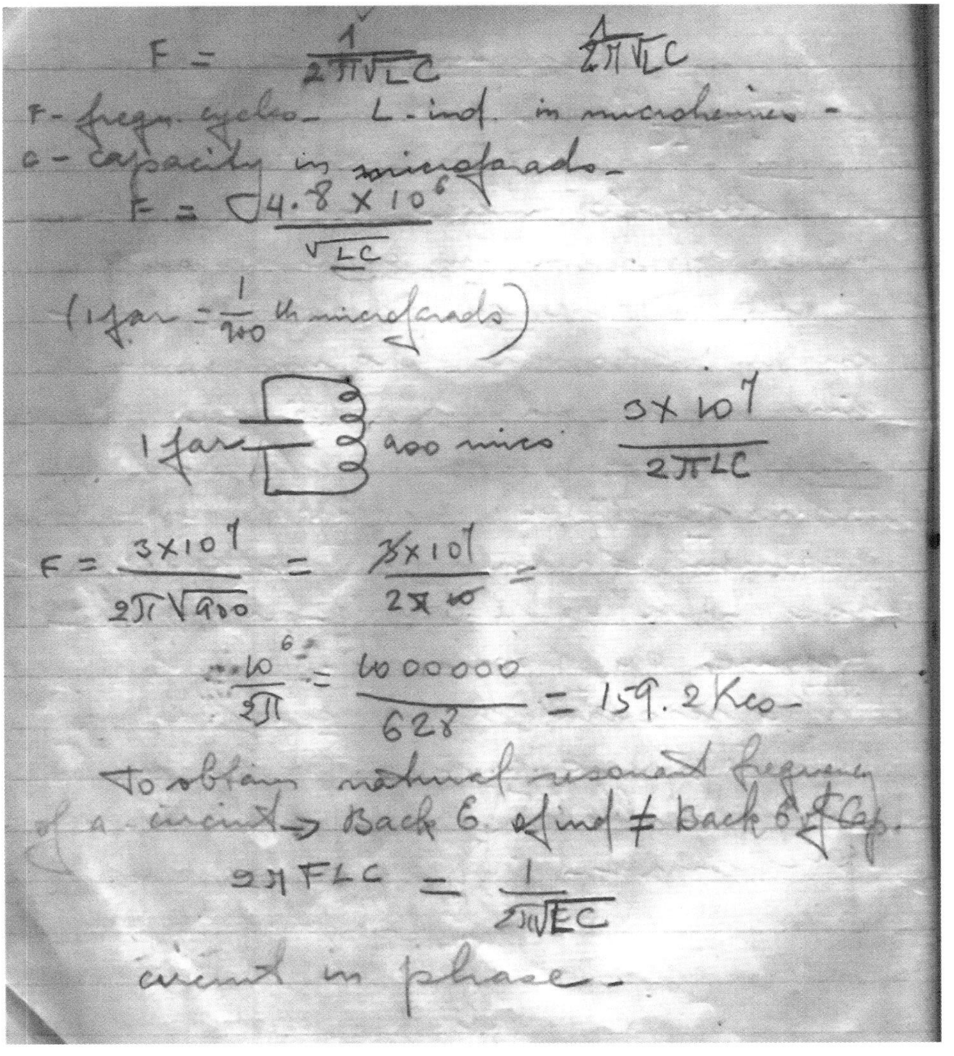

Noor's radio resonance formulas

Maurice Buckmaster, Head of SOE F Section

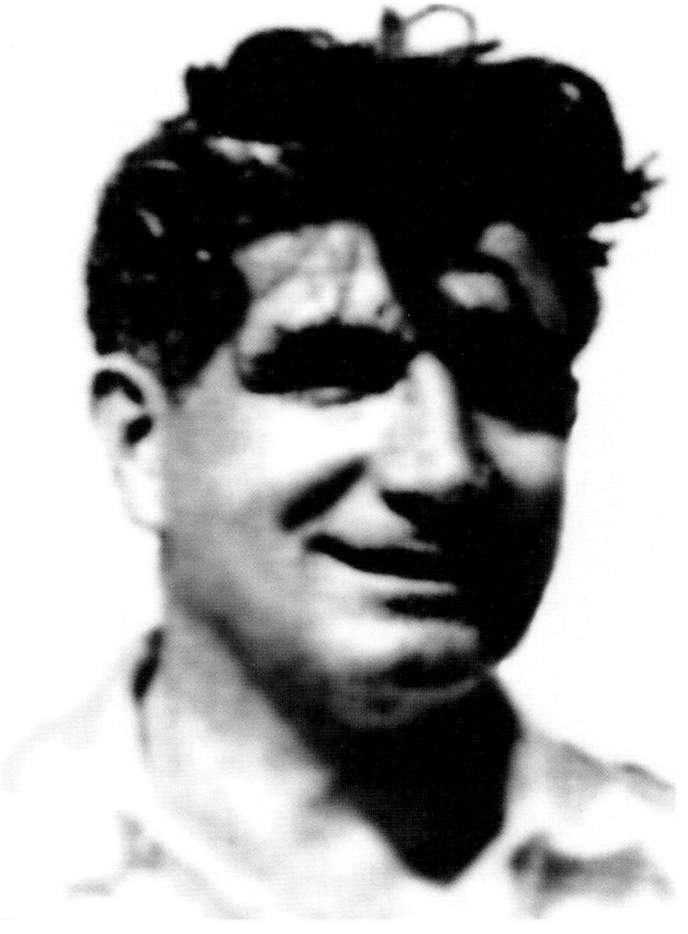

Double agent Henri Dericourt

SOE agent's radio transmitter

Prosper headquarters, Agricultural School in Grignon

Noor's radio station in Grignon greenhouse

Memorial to Eugene Vanderwynckt, Noor's protector at Grignon

Vanderwynckt home in Grignon

Dr. Jourdan's Home, Faubourg Poissonniere

David Ray Harper and ex-SOE agent Bob Maloubier in front of former Gestapo headquarters, Avenue Foch, Paris

Pforzheim Gerichtsgefängnis
(Angabe der Vollzugsanstalt)

Gefangenenbuch

1943/44

Angefangen am: 1. April 1943

Abgeschlossen am:

VollzO. A 1 Gefangenenbuch.
Arbeitsverwaltung des Zuchthauses Amberg.

Pforzheim prisoner record book for 1943/44

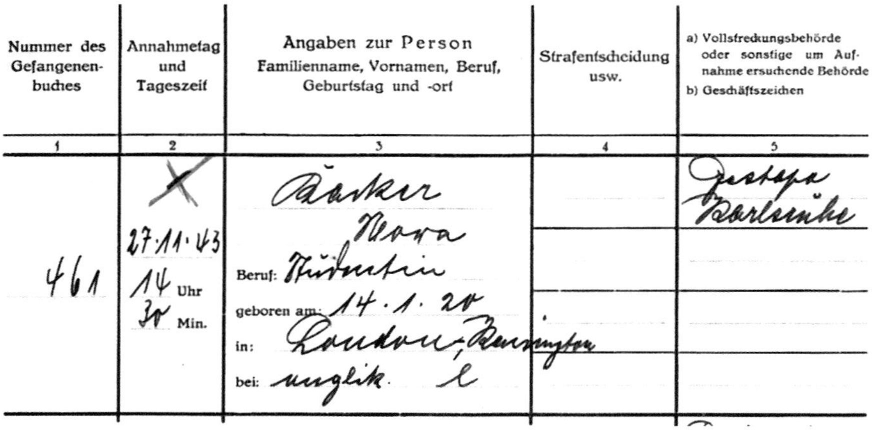

Nummer des Gefangenenbuches	Annahmetag und Tageszeit	Angaben zur Person Familienname, Vornamen, Beruf, Geburtstag und -ort	Strafentscheidung usw.	a) Vollstreckungsbehörde oder sonstige um Aufnahme ersuchende Behörde b) Geschäftszeichen
1	2	3	4	5
461	X 27.11.43 14 Uhr 30 Min.	Backer Nora Beruf: Studentin geboren am: 14.1.20 in: London, [illegible] bei: [illegible]		Gestapo Karlsruhe

Pforzheim prison record for Noor as Nora Backer
upon arrival from Karlsruhe on November 22, 1943

Wilhelm Ruppert, second in command of Dachau Concentration Camp
and Noor's torturer and executioner

David Ray Harper at entrance to Dachau Concentration Camp

Site of Noor's execution, Dachau

Marker at Noor's execution ground, Dachau

Crematorium at Dachau where Noor's body was burned

Memorial for SOE agents at Dachau crematorium.

Here in Dachau on the 12th of September 1944
four young Women Officers of the British Forces attached to the Special Operations Executive were brutally murdered and their bodies cremated. They died as gallantly as they had served the Resistance in France during the common struggle for freedom from tyranny.

Mrs. YOLANDE E M BEEKMAN...

Miss MADELEINE DAMERMENT...

Miss NOORUNISA INAYAT KHAN
George Cross
Member of the Most Excellent Order of the British Empire
Mentioned in Despatches
Croix de Guerre avec Etoile de Vermeil
Women's Auxiliary Air Forces
Seconded to Women's Transportation Service (F.A.N.Y)

Mrs. ELIANE PLEWMANN...

"But the souls of the righteous are in the hand of God, and there shall no torment touch them."

Noor's ashes rest in this Dachau grave among those of thousands of victims of human cruelty

Noor Inayat Khan

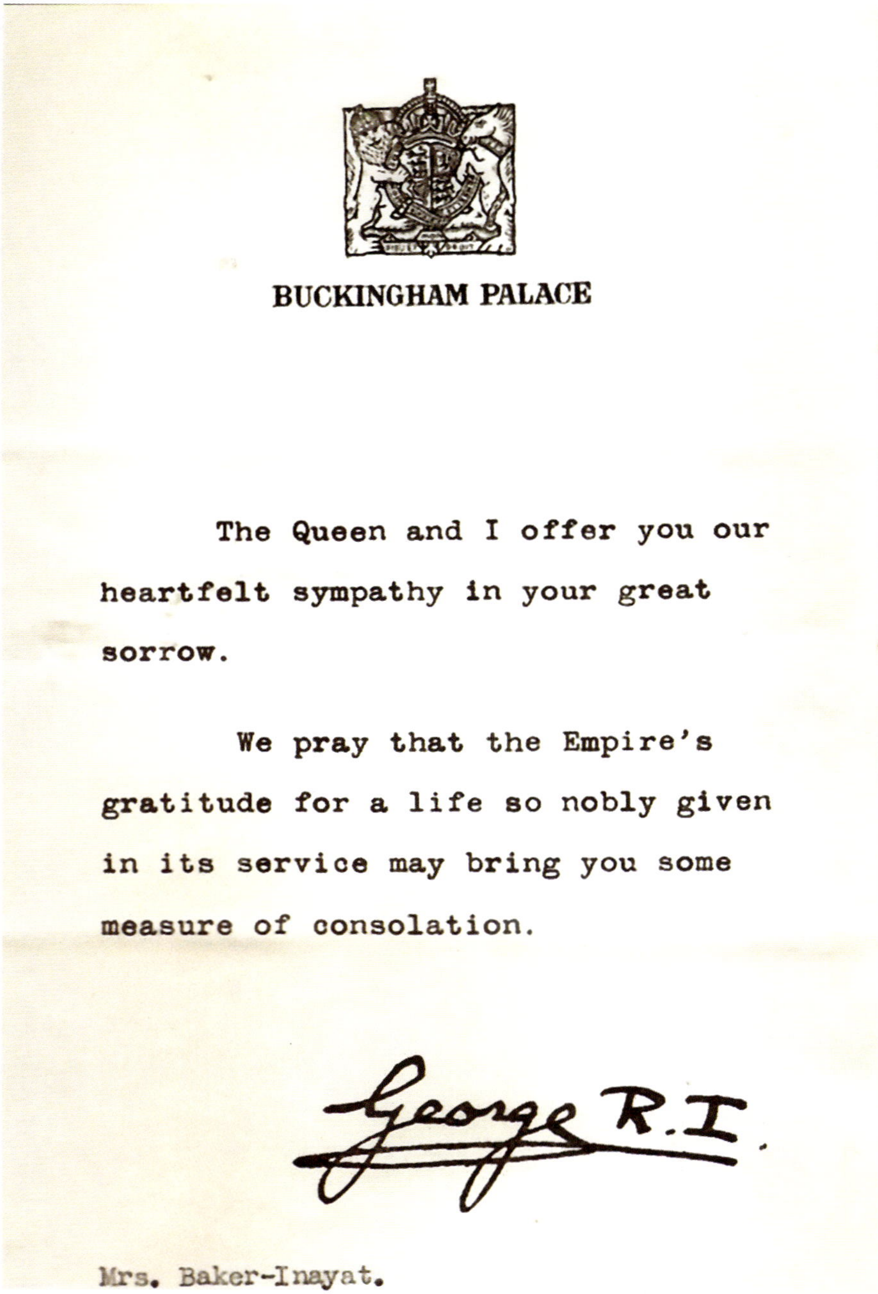

BUCKINGHAM PALACE

The Queen and I offer you our heartfelt sympathy in your great sorrow.

We pray that the Empire's gratitude for a life so nobly given in its service may bring you some measure of consolation.

George R.I.

Mrs. Baker-Inayat.

Condolence letter to "Mrs. Baker-Inayat" from the King and Queen of England

The George Cross awarded posthumously for Noor's courage

Memorial for FANY agents who died on active service,
St. Paul's, Knightsbridge, England

Noor's Croix de Guerre with Gold Star, France's highest civilian award

1953 memorial to members of FANY at Runymede

Noor's information panel at Dachau Memorial Site museum

Noor's memorial plaque at Dachau Memorial Site museum

Inauguration of Cours Madeleine named after Noor,
in Suresnes near the Seine River

England's Queen Mother at inauguration of monument to WWII heroes,
at which Noor was remembered, Blois, France

Vilayat, circa 1947

Vilayat, 1950

Vilayat, 1952, Paris

Mary Walls, 1952

Vilayat with mureeds on the Sufi field at Summer School, 1953

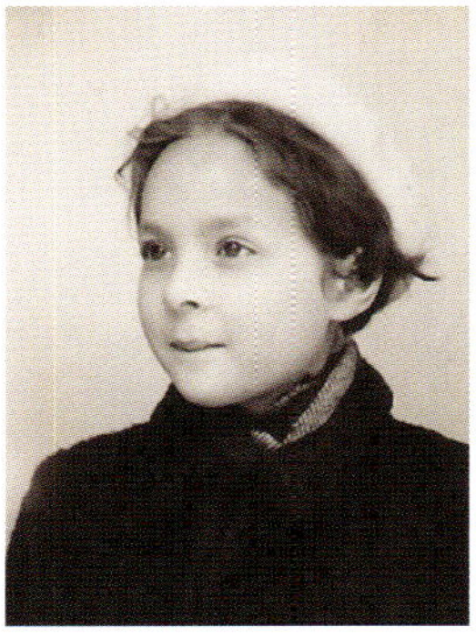

Hidayat's daughter Ina, age 7

Hidayat's son Fazl, age 4

Hidayat's son Gayan, age 3

Claire with baby David

Claire, David, and friend, New York, 1953

David and Linda Peterson at Christmas, 1956

Mary, Vilayat, Claire, Central Park, March 1957

Mary, Barbara, Vilayat en route to India, 1955

Barbara, Mary, Vilayat picnic en route to India, 1955

Vilayat, Mary, Kathleen
in Venice, 1955

Vilayat as entertainer
en route to India, 1955

Mary with Fakir, India

Pir Vilayat and Claire, circa 1960

David in Doris Day movie, 1965

Claire and David, 1967

Fazal Manzil Khankah with eagle on perch

Pir Vilayat with French mureeds, 1960s

Mary, Pir Vilayat and mureeds, 1963

Pir Vilayat with mureeds in Khankah, 1960s

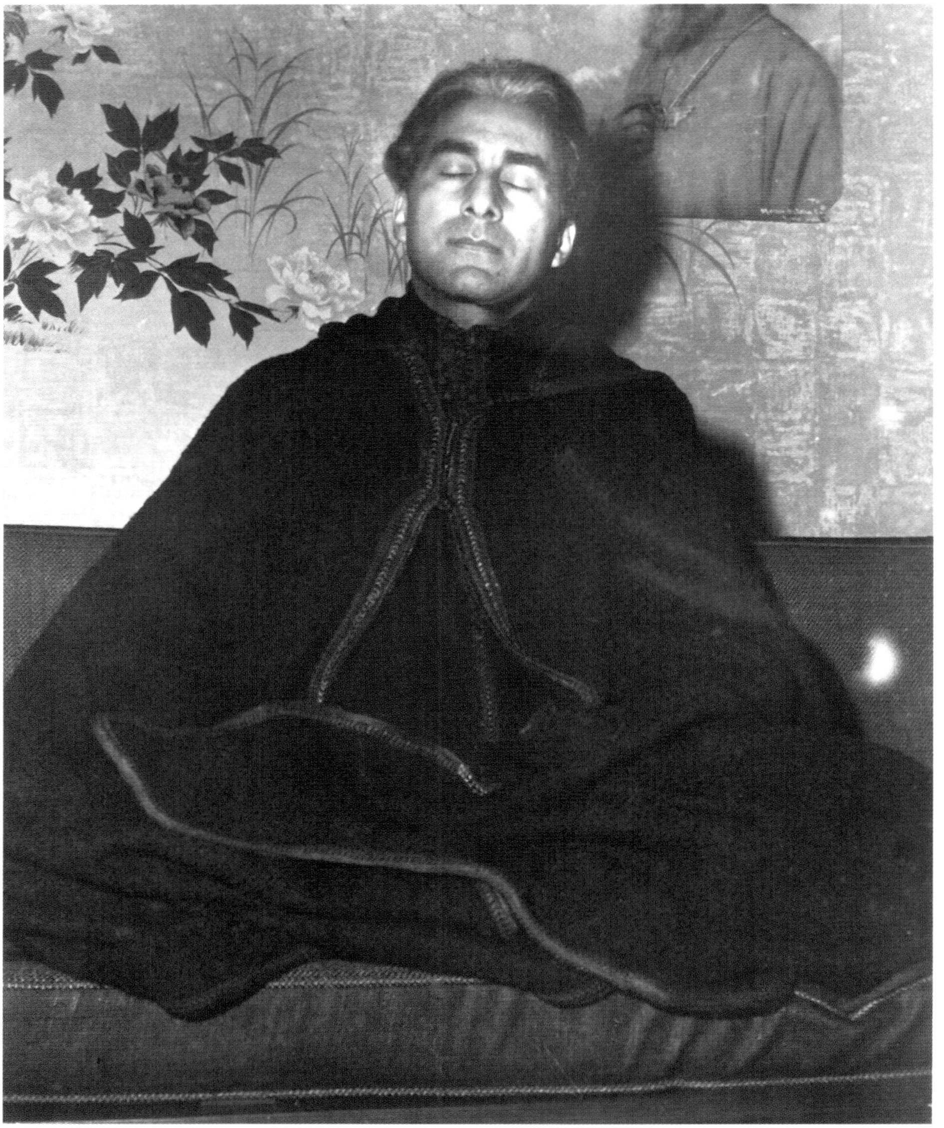

Pir Vilayat in meditation, circa 1965

Hidayat, 1965

Pir Vilayat with Mary at inter-religious conference in Italy, 1970

Pir Vilayat, 1970

Pir Vilayat and Shabaz

Kindred spirits: Pir Vilayat and eagle

Pope Paul VI, Pir Vilayat and Mary in Rome, circa 1974

Claire in 1973

Claire in 1978

Cover of one of David's recordings

Pir Vilayat with mureeds on retreat, Chamonix, France

Pir Vilayat at inter-religious conference, Italy

Pir Vilayat on elephant, India

Pir Vilayat with Taj Inayat, the mother of Pir's sons

Pir Vilayat initiating his son Zia, age 10, 1982

David singing at Zia's initiation event, 1982

Conference of the Birds: Pir Vilayat with eagle

Pir Vilayat playing his cello

Temple of the Universel at Fazal Manzil, dedicated to Noor Inayat Khan

Pir Vilayat with mureeds at the Temple of the Universel, 1990

Pir Zia with Taj Inayat, at Pir Zia's wedding at Maula Baksh House, Baroda, India

Pir Zia with wife Sartaj at their wedding in Baroda, India

Mayor of Suresnes and Pir Vilayat with WWII veterans
at the gates of Fazal Manzil, in the annual ceremony honoring Noor

Claire and Pir Vilayat at the Abode of the Message, New Lebanon, New York

Claire, Pir Vilayat and Mary in Pyrenees

Claire at Pir Vilayat's funeral in the Temple of the Universel, 2004

Pir Vilayat's dargah in Nizamuddin, India

Sartaj, Pir Zia, Ina, Gayan (rear row);
Zia's children, Hidayat, Aziza and Taj (front row), 2008

View from Claire's window, Bavarian Alps.

Claire's 90th birthday, Bavarian Alps, 2009

Claire's 90th birthday, Bavarian Alps, 2009

Claire, 2009, Bavarian Alps

NOTES

(1) Ora Ray's birth year and place: There are discrepancies regarding Ora Ray's birthplace and birth year. On her marriage certificate dated March 20th, 1913, she states she is 23 years old: in other words, born in 1890, in Albuquerque, New Mexico. Later, when working in England, she indicates to her physician and employers an age which would have her born in 1892. However, the Washington State census of 1900 shows that she was 12 years of age at the time of the census, in other words, born in 1888, and her place of birth is listed as Kansas.

(2) Ora Ray's siblings' names: Various documents show different names or spellings; for instance, Merle is sometimes spelled Murle or, in the 1900 census, Murrel. In the same census Ora Ray is written as one word, Oraray; and the youngest is listed as Dewy Washington Baker, not Earl.

(3) Ora Ray's mother: Ora Ray herself wrote that her mother's maiden name was Wyatt; later, she wrote Hiatt. Aletta (nicknamed Etta) Margaret Hiatt's father was born in Indiana, her mother came from Maryland, home of many of the Kemp family members. Aletta had a twin sister, Alice.

(4) Though it is often thought that the Kemp family came from Bavaria, further research has shown that this arose from a misunderstanding. Eight years before emigrating to Philadelphia, the family of Johann Conrad Kaempff (Kemp), born 1685 in St. Gallen, Switzerland (grandfather: Frederick von der Kaempe, born 1635 in St. Gallen; father: Christian Kaemp, born 1660 in St. Gallen; son Gilbert Kempf, born 1717 in St. Gallen), moved just over the border from St. Gallen to Untergimpern, in the German Kraichgau area between Sinsheim and Bad Wimpfen. Research of Ralph Kindred Kemp with the German Consulate states Untergimpern is now called Neckerar Bischofsheim in the state of Baden-Württemberg. In 1733 the family left for the United States on the Good Ship Samuel, and eventually went to New Holland in Lancaster.

Johann Conrad Kaempff made two voyages to America in 1733. It appears that on his first voyage he brought his son Frederick (Johann Friedrick Kemp) with him. Frederick would have been about 8 years old.

On his second voyage, he brought the rest of the family who were alive at that time (wife Anna Maria Sophia Feuerbach) and the rest of the children: Christian Kemp, Gilbert Kemp, Johann Petrus (aka Hans Peter) and Anna Catharina.

It is not strange that he would have brought one child with him on a voyage to a new land. His bringing one child, and then leaving him in America while he returned for the rest of the family, would have assured his wife that he would return. In those times, a man could sail to another country, desert his family, and never be heard from again.

Please note that immigration records for the two voyages in 1733 spelled the last name two different ways: Kempff and Kaempf. Also, note that the names were shortened to Kemp at this time. This was common for immigrants to America.

Throughout the several generations between Johann Conrad Kaempff (Kemp) and Mary May Kemp (Ora Ray's maternal grandmother), most of the Kemp males married recently immigrated German wives. We can deduce that Ora Ray's heritage featured a strong strain of German and Swiss heritage.

(5) Erastus Warren Baker: Ora Ray's father's records show him to have been born in Iowa in 1845; however, in the 1900 census he claims to have been born in 1850. His father was born in Kentucky, his mother in Iowa. Murshid mentions in his autobiography that Ora Ray's family came from Kentucky; in other words, this is what he was told by her. On her marriage certificate of 1913, Ora Ray states that her father is a lawyer, however in the 1900 census he stated his occupation as "dairyman"; perhaps he became a lawyer subsequent to that. It is a fact, however, that his father was a lawyer. Ora Ray writes her father's middle name as "Warner," when in reality—or officially—it was Warren. The confusion probably stems from the fact that Erastus Baker's father's second wife was Susan Warner. The reference to his being a journalist/editor is based on word of mouth.

(6) Huzurnawaz's full name was Floris Carsilius Anne Baron Van Pallandt De Vijk and his parents were Jan Anne Baron van Pallandt and Sarah Agnes Sophia Baroness van Pallandt. He went on to become the Dutch ambassador to Denmark. His son Frederick became a musical legend as part of the 1970s singing duo, Nina and Frederick, with hits such as "Puff, the Magic Dragon."

(7) It is said that the duke who commissioned the house went bankrupt and took his life in this room, formerly his bedroom.

(8) The circle of life: in 1732 Ora's ancestors, the Kemp Family, emigrated from Europe to the United States via Philadelphia. In 1913 Ora emigrated from the United States to Europe via Philadelphia.

NAMES

Names and titles of the family's members can be confusing. The following list may be found useful:

INAYAT KHAN: From adolescence until 1914 he used the full name Inayat Khan Rahmat Pathan (from about 1902 adding Professor as a professional title). Sufi titles: Murshid and Pir-o-Murshid. Known to his children as Abba. Called Daya by his wife (meaning "compassion" in Sanskrit) or Thea ("gift of God" in Greek). After his passing, the title Hazrat was conferred: it comes from the Arabic and may be used for any great man or woman, out of respect.

ORA RAY: Born Ora Ray (sometimes Oraray) Baker, later Ora Ray Bernard. Eastern title: Begum. Sufi name: Ameena. Called Sharda by Murshid (meaning "goddess"). He also called her Calleja Mari. Known to her children as Amma.

MAHEBOOB KHAN: Called Bouwa by the children, meaning "father" in the sense of closest uncle. Also known as Pyaromir. Sufi title: Shaikh-ul-Mashaikh in lieu of Pir-o-Murshid.

MOHAMMAD ALI KHAN: Called Taya by the children, signifying "adopted uncle." Sufi title: Murshid.

MUSHARAFF MOULAMIA KHAN: Called Chacha by the children, meaning "uncle." Sufi title: Murshid.

NOOR: Full name: Noor-un-nisa Inayat Khan. Also called: Babuli (father's daughter). This later became Babs, Babsy, Bably and other variants. During WWII she was known as Nora, Norah, and code-named Madeleine and Jeanne Renier; she was identified as "Nurse" in wireless recognition. Sufi title: Pir-zadi.

VILAYAT: Full name: Vilayat Inayat Khan. Also called Baijan (big brother). During WWII known as Victor, Vic, later Vicky. Sufi title: Pir-zade; later Pir.

HIDAYAT: Full name: Hidayat Inayat-Khan. Also called Baiyajan (little brother). Sufi title: Murshid-zade Khalif, later Pir-o-Murshid.

CLAIRE: Full name: Khair-un-nisa Inayat Khan. Also called Mamuli (mother's daughter). During the war years also known as Mams or Mamsi. Sufi title: Murshid-zadi. Later changed her name to Claire Baker, Claire Boulanger and finally became Claire Ray Harper.

GLOSSARY OF SUFI TERMS

cherag/cheraga: Title of Sufi ordained to perform the interfaith Universal Worship service

dargah: Shrine at the tomb of a revered Sufi

dervish: One who follows the path of Sufism

hazrat: Honorific title of a revered Sufi

Hejirat Day: September 13, the date of Hazrat Inayat Khan's departure from India for the West

khalif/khalifa: Title of designated representative of a Sufi teacher

khankah: Building that is dedicated to Sufi gatherings

khwaja: Master

madzub: Sufi who is more present and active in the unseen world than in this one

mureed: Initiated Sufi student

murshid/murshida: Sufi teacher

pir: Head of a Sufi order (literally "elder")

pirani: Wife of a pir

pir-o-murshid: Title of a Sufi who is both a pir and a murshid

pir-zade: Son of a pir

pir-zadi: Daughter of a pir

qawali: Devotional Sufi music

shaikh-ul-mashaikh: A Sufi sheikh of sheikhs

sheikh/sheikha: Sufi who is authorized to guide and initiate mureeds

silsila: Sufi chain of initiation

Universal Worship: Interfaith Sufi religious ceremony established by Hazrat Inayat Khan

urs: Date of the death of a revered Sufi, celebrated at a dargah or other place of pilgrimage

Viladat Day: July 5, the birth date of Hazrat Inayat Khan

Visalat Day: February 5, the date of Hazrat Inayat Khan's passing from the earthly plane

zikr: Sufi ceremony of remembrance of God, usually through chanting and music

SOURCES

Basu, Shrabani. *Spy Princess: The Life of Noor Inayat Khan.* United Kingdom: Sutton Publishing LTD, 2006. New York: Omega Publications, 2007. (D)

Bernard, Pierre. *Life at the Clarkstown Country Club.* New York: Clarkstown Country Club, 1935. (H)

Fuller, Jean Overton. *The German Penetration of SOE: France, 1941–1944.* United Kingdom: Longdunn Press, 1996. (G)

———. *Noor-un-nisa Inayat Khan (Madeleine): George Cross MBE Croix de Guerre with Gold Star.* London: East-West Publications, 1988. (E)

Harper, Claire Ray. *Memories.* Unpublished manuscript. (I)

Helm, Sarah. *A Life in Secrets: Vera Atkins and the Missing Agents of WWII.* United Kingdom: Doubleday, 2005. (F)

Inayat Khan. *Biography of Pir-o-Murshid Inayat Khan.* London: East-West Publications, 1979. (A)

de Jong-Keesing, Elisabeth. *Inayat Khan: A Biography.* London: East-West Publications, 1974. (C)

Van Beek, Will. *Hazrat Inayat Khan: Master of Life, Modern Sufi Mystic.* New York: Vantage Press, 1983. (B)

INDEX